COUNTERFEITED IN CHINA

KO-LIN CHIN

COUNTERFEITED IN CHINA

The Operations of Illicit Businesses

TEMPLE UNIVERSITY PRESS
Philadelphia • Rome • Tokyo

TEMPLE UNIVERSITY PRESS
Philadelphia, Pennsylvania 19122
tupress.temple.edu

Cataloging information is available from the Library of Congress.

ISBNs are 978-1-4399-2697-0 (cloth), 978-1-4399-2698-7 (paper),
978-1-4399-2699-4 (ebook).

The manufacturer's authorized representative in the EU for product safety is
Temple University Rome, Via di San Sebastianello, 16, 00187 Rome RM, Italy
(https://rome.temple.edu/).
tempress@temple.edu

9 8 7 6 5 4 3 2 1

To Catherine

Contents

LIST OF FIGURES AND TABLES

FIGURES

TABLES

ACKNOWLEDGMENTS

Many people have contributed to this research project, and I appreciate their assistance and support. First, I thank the business owners and workers who agreed to take part in my research and willingly shared their stories with me. I owe my greatest debt to these men and women, who are anonymous except for some pseudonyms here. I especially want to thank Laoban, Jane, Peter, Xiao Ma, and John. Second, I am grateful to the various facilitators in the counterfeit business (raw material suppliers, packagers, embroiderers, etc.) who not only let me talk to them but also let me enter their world and see how they conduct their businesses. Again, I can thank them only anonymously because their identities should not be revealed. Third, I am thankful to the key informants from all walks of life who have provided me with invaluable insights into the world of luxury goods counterfeiting.

Professor Fanquan Yang, a law school professor at Sun Yat-sen University, was my host in Guangzhou. Not only did his hospitality make my stay there a pleasant one but his knowledge about the legal system in China helped me understand how the system works. I owe him a debt that cannot be repaid. I also thank Jianhua Xu, a professor with the Department of Sociology, University of Macau, for helping me in so many ways while I was collecting data in China. I also thank his doctoral students, Anli Jiang and Qipu Hu, for collecting Chinese media reports on the topic and showing me around Guangzhou and Shenzhen.

Todd Clear, the former dean of the School of Criminal Justice at Rutgers, has always been very supportive of my research. He provided me with a generous travel stipend to go to China to explore the feasibility of conducting this project in China. Without the initial contact with potential research subjects on that first trip, none of the following trips to collect data would have been possible. I cannot thank him enough for jump-starting this study.

I am also grateful to two anonymous reviewers and my colleague James O. Finckenauer for their careful reading of early versions of this manuscript and their detailed suggestions as to how it could be improved.

I wish to thank Ryan Mulligan, the editor at Temple University Press, for helping me in shortening and improving the manuscript and coming up with the title for this book. I am also indebted to William Forrest, the editorial assistant at Temple University Press, for transforming my manuscript into a book. I also thank Michael Siegel, the staff cartographer with Rutgers' Geography Department, for preparing the maps included in the text.

This manuscript was carefully edited by Caroline Herrick, and I thank her very much for not only spending so many painstaking hours editing the manuscript but also providing me with many good suggestions on how to make the manuscript better. I also thank Cheryl Uppling for her excellent work in copyediting the manuscript.

Last, but not least, I thank my wife, Catherine, for her support and understanding while I was away in China for so many months. When she visited me in China, she accompanied me to some of the meetings with my research participants, and her presence helped me enormously in establishing a closer relationship with them. This book is dedicated to her.

It is hardly necessary to absolve others from responsibility for the views set forth, but I do so anyway, to resolve any doubt that those acknowledged necessarily share my assessments of the problems. Partial support for this research was provided by the School of Criminal Justice at Rutgers and a Distinguished Visiting Scholar Award from the University of Macau. The opinions are those of the author and do not necessarily reflect the policies or views of these two institutions.

LIST OF ABBREVIATIONS

AIC	Administration for Industry and Commerce (China)
AQSIQ	General Administration of Quality Supervision, Inspection, and Quarantine (China)
CBP	Customs and Border Protection (U.S.)
CCP	Chinese Communist Party
DFI	Direct Foreign Investment
DHS	Department of Homeland Security (U.S.)
EUIPO	European Union Intellectual Property Office
IACC	International Anti-counterfeiting Coalition
IP	intellectual property
IPEC	Intellectual Property Enforcement Coordinator (U.S.)
IPR	intellectual property rights
KMT	Kuomintang Party
MNC	multinational company
MPS	Ministry of Public Security (China)
OECD	Organization for Economic Cooperation and Development (Europe)
PRC	People's Republic of China
PRD	Pearl River Delta (China)
PVC	polyvinyl chloride
RMB	Renminbi (Chinese yuan)
SAIC	State Administration for Industry and Commerce (China)
SAMR	State Administration for Market Regulation (China)

SQTSB	State Quality Technical Supervision Bureau (China)
TRACIT	Transnational Alliance to Combat Illicit Trade
UNODC	United Nations Office on Drugs and Crime
USTR	United States Trade Representative
WTO	World Trade Organization

Counterfeited in China

1

Introduction

According to various sources, the trade in counterfeit goods is now the number one organized crime problem in the world, surpassing drug trafficking, human smuggling, and human trafficking (OECD/ EUIPO 2021; U.S. DHS 2020). A report by the United Nations Office on Drugs and Crime (UNODC 2013) estimated that transnational organized crime activities in East Asia and the Pacific generated nearly $90 billion annually for the perpetrators. Among these activities, the flow of counterfeit goods out of this region was worth $24.4 billion, much more than the smuggling of heroin ($16.3 billion), methamphetamines ($15 billion), or human beings ($1.7 billion) or the trafficking of human beings ($214 million). A report by the Organization for Economic Cooperation and Development (OECD) and the European Union Intellectual Property Office (EUIPO) concluded that trade in counterfeit and pirated goods amounted to as much as $464 billion, or 2.5 percent of world trade in 2019.[1] When considering only imports into the European Union, fake goods totaled as much as $134 billion, or up to 5.8 percent of imports (OECD/EUIPO 2021). Regardless of how reliable these estimates are, the consensus is that counterfeiting is proliferating, the amount of money involved is enormous, and almost every country in the world is affected by it (Federal Research Division 2020).

The Commission on the Theft of American Intellectual Property (2013) has alleged that the mass production of counterfeit goods damages consumers (by financially defrauding them and compromising their safety), brand owners (by causing them loss of revenue), state authorities (by causing loss of tax revenue), workers (by causing job loss), innovation, and economic growth. It has also fueled the advancement of organized crime groups (Albanese 2012; Anderson 1981; Chow 2003; UNODC 2013); enabled offenders to expand their activities to other types of transnational crime, such as human smuggling, human trafficking, drug trafficking, and money laundering (Albanese 2012; UNODC 2014, 2019); and corrupted the criminal justice systems of many countries (Chow 2003; Thomas 2007). Moreover, counterfeiters are accused of engaging in violence to achieve their goals and using their profits to support terrorism (Wall and Large 2010).

Of the many major producing, transiting, or consuming countries for counterfeits, China is the most significant because the country allegedly produces at least two-thirds of the world's counterfeits (IACC 2013; OECD/EUIPO 2021; UNODC 2013, 2014, 2019). The U.S. Customs and Border Protection (CBP) has revealed that China accounted for 87 percent of the value of the counterfeits it seized between 2008 and 2010 (Commission on the Theft of American Intellectual Property 2013). A report by the United States Trade Representative (USTR 2021) reiterated how China has continued to play a prominent role in the global counterfeiting business. Seizures of Chinese-made counterfeits also dominate statistics in Europe, Australia, and New Zealand and other parts of the world (IACC 2013; UNODC 2013). China is also reported to be the world's most important market for fake luxury goods (Thomas 2007). (See Figure 1.1.)

The problems associated with counterfeiting are multifaceted, significant, and growing. Yet, there is little in the way of a grounded systematic study of counterfeiters. Nor has there been in-depth research into how these offenders exploit international commerce or communication systems to conduct their illegal activities. For policymakers and criminal justice practitioners to become more effective in combating counterfeiting, there is a critical need for more and better information about the counterfeiters, their organizations, and their methods of operation. In this study, I attempt to provide this information by interviewing counterfeiters and their associates in China.

Questions about Counterfeiting

In this study, I explore several questions that are pertinent to the examination of the supply side of counterfeiting, namely: (1) What is counterfeiting? (2) What is the size of the counterfeiting industry? (3) What kinds of merchandise are counterfeited? (4) Where are the hubs of counterfeiting? (5) What is the relationship between counterfeiters and organized crime? And

Figure 1.1 China. (*Map by Rutgers Cartography*)

(6) What is the impact of counterfeiting? I do not examine questions related to consumers' perceptions of, attitudes toward, and purchase intentions regarding counterfeit goods because there are many studies on these issues (Carpenter and Lear 2011; Hieke 2010; Jiang and Cova 2012; Jiang and Shan 2016, 2018; Pratt and Zeng 2020; Radon 2012; M. Ting, Goh, and Isa 2016; Varela, Lopes, and Mendes 2021).

What Is Counterfeiting?

According to Martin Dimitrov, the author of *Piracy and the State: The Politics of Intellectual Property Rights in China* (2009, 15), "IRP [intellectual property rights] laws cover three broad subcategories of rights: copyrights, patents, and trademarks. Copyrights protect literary, artistic, and creative works, including books, music, motion pictures, and computer software. Patents protect new, nonobvious, useful inventions, such as the molecule of sildenafil citrate, the active ingredient in Viagra. Trademarks (e.g., Coca-Cola) protect the brand names of goods, ranging from clothing to food to electronics." A trademark is a word, design, symbol, device, or combination of those elements that is used by a manufacturer to label its goods and set them apart from goods made by others (Orscheln 2015).

The World Trade Organization (WTO 2024) defines product counterfeiting as "unauthorized representation of a registered trademark carried on goods identical or similar to goods for which the trademark is registered, with a view to deceiving the purchaser into believing that he/she is buying the original goods." According to Professor John Spink and his colleagues (2013, 2), "The key elements of this basic definition are if the product is similar and if there is deception of the consumer." However, Joseph Forgione (2016–2017, 198), a trademark enforcement lawyer, argues that "trademark counterfeiting is defined as the act of manufacturing or distributing a product or service bearing a mark that is identical to or substantially indistinguishable from a registered trademark." Whether the intent is to deceive buyers of counterfeit goods is not important.

We need to find out whether deceptive or nondeceptive counterfeiting is the norm in the counterfeiting industry. According to Anita Radon (2012, 75), a Swedish business professor, some observers have suggested that "deceptive counterfeiting can be observed mainly in markets for automotive parts, consumer electronic products such as computers and stereo equipment, pharmaceuticals and medical devices. The luxury-brand market, however, often shows the other side, where consumers are involved in non-deceptive counterfeiting."

What Is the Size of the Counterfeiting Industry?

A 1981 *New York Times Magazine* report by Susan Heller Anderson alleged that counterfeiting generated $450 million in profits for counterfeiters in 1980. Estimates of the total value of counterfeiting have increased exponentially in the new millennium. Instead of hundreds of millions of dollars, the estimates have shot up to hundreds of billions of dollars. According to Wall and Large (2010), Havoscope's Global Black Market Index assessed that the global counterfeit goods and piracy market is worth approximately $750 billion. The OECD and EUIPO (2019, 11) appraised that the volume of international trade in counterfeit and pirated products [in 2016] could amount to as much as $509 billion. By the late 2010s, many sources asserted that counterfeiting had become the number one transnational crime, involving up to trillions of dollars and surpassing other cross-border crimes. One source estimated that worldwide $1.8 trillion in knockoffs are sold yearly (Zuccaro 2016, 145–146). According to a report by the Federal Research Division of the U.S. Library of Congress (2020, i): "As of 2018, counterfeiting is the largest criminal enterprise in the world, with domestic and international sales of counterfeit and pirated goods totaling between an estimated 1.7 trillion and 4.5 trillion a year—a higher amount than either drugs or human trafficking."

Why did counterfeiting expand so rapidly? Dana Thomas (2007, 274), the author of the book *Deluxe: How Luxury Lost Its Luster*, explained why counterfeiting transformed from a small business into a big industry at the turn of the twenty-first century:

> Two things changed the game: the democratization of luxury and the rise of China. When luxury brands went democratic, they thought they could satisfy the middle market with lower-priced handbags and perfume. What executives didn't count on was middle-market consumers satisfying their craving for higher-end items by buying fake versions that they could pass off as real. At the same time China evolved into a capitalist market economy and the world's manufacturing center, with a new class of entrepreneurs who saw counterfeiting as a viable business. The convergence of the two—big demand and big supply—was cataclysmic. And it took luxury executives—and executives in most other industries—by surprise.

In their book *The Economics of Counterfeit Trade*, Peggy Chaudhry and Alan Zimmerman (2009, 19) provided several additional reasons for the growth of counterfeit goods: "low cost high technology which results in low investment and high profits; globalization and lower trade barriers; consumer complicity; expansion of channels and markets; powerful worldwide brands; weak international and national enforcement and finally high traffic and taxes."

Sally Engle Merry suggested that "quantification is seductive" because "it offers concrete, numerical information that allows for easy comparison of countries, schools, job applicants, teachers, and much else. It organizes and simplifies knowledge, facilitating decision making in the absence of more detailed contextual information" (Merry 2016, 1). She also said that "numerical knowledge is essential, yet if it is not closely connected to more qualitative forms of knowledge, it leads to oversimplification, homogenization, and the neglect of surrounding social structure" (Merry 2016, 1). This book attempts to provide an ethnographic account to supplement the many global indicators or estimates of counterfeiting.

What Kinds of Merchandise Are Counterfeited?

According to Chaudhry and Zimmerman (2009, 125), any product with a well-known brand has probably been a victim of counterfeiting in China, including Budweiser beer, Gillette razor blades, Marlboro cigarettes, Yamaha motorcycles, and Skippy peanut butter. The IACC, a global nonprofit association dedicated to fighting fake and pirated goods, has stated: "Counterfeiting in China continues to affect virtually all sectors in which our members operate, including apparel, footwear and fashion accessories (including leather goods, eyewear, watches and jewelry), portable phones and smartphones, pharmaceuticals, wine, liquor, golf and other sports equipment, food, beverages, agricultural chemicals, electronic components (including those used for military equipment), computers, printer ink cartridges, musical instruments, networking equipment, entertainment and business software, batteries, cigarettes, cosmetics, condoms, home appliances, ball bearings, and auto parts" (2013, 12–13). A report by OECD/EUIPO (2017, 23) revealed that some of the most counterfeited goods, based on their estimated value of global trade for 2013, were as follows: foodstuffs ($11.9 billion), pharmaceuticals ($16.2 billion), perfumes and cosmetics ($5.25 billion), articles of leather, including handbags ($8.54 billion), clothing and textiles ($27.7 billion), footwear ($13.3 billion), jewelry ($40.9 billion), electronics and electrical equipment ($121 billion), optical, photographic, and medical equipment ($29.2 billion), and toys and games ($9.72 billion).

According to Thomas (2007, 275), "While everything from Ferrari to mineral water is counterfeited today, fashion is one of the most popular sectors, because it's easy and cheap to copy and easier to sell." Forgione (2016–2017, 197) concluded that "as of 2016, apparel and accessories accounted for 20% of total seizures conducted by Customs." A report by OECD/EUIPO (2021, 20) also suggested that the most frequently seized products were footwear, clothing, leather goods, electrical machinery, and electronic equipment.

A recent report by the U.S. DHS (2020, 16) explained in detail what counterfeit goods were most frequently seized by the CBP in 2018:

> Apparel and other types of accessories, along with footwear, top the list at 18 percent and 14 percent of seizures, respectively. Commonly counterfeited items in these categories include brand name shoes such as Nike and Adidas, as well as NFL jerseys. Watches and jewelry follow at 13 percent of total seizures. During the Mega Flex operation on August 21, 2019, for example, CBP officers seized counterfeit Rolex

watches valued at over $1.4 million. Handbags and wallets represented nearly 11 percent of all seizures, including counterfeits of luxury brands such as Louis Vuitton, Michael Kors, and Gucci.

In sum, almost everything is counterfeited or copied nowadays in China, including famous Western-style architectural structures (Bosker 2013), aircraft carriers (Zhen Liu 2016), and fighter jets (Griffith 2023). Since it is not possible to include the counterfeiting of all types of items in this study, my focus is on three categories of luxury items: clothing, handbags, and shoes.

Where Are the Hubs of Counterfeiting?

By all accounts, China is currently the counterfeiting capital of the world, although other countries, such as India, Thailand, Turkey, Malaysia, Pakistan, and Vietnam, also play a role in this illicit trade (OECD/EUIPO 2017). Estimates of the extent of China's involvement in counterfeiting and IPR infringement vary, but most place it at around 80 percent to 86 percent of the world total in monetary value (Chow 2010, 753; Federal Research Division 2020; Hall 2018; Raustiala and Sprigman 2015, 263). We do not know how reliable these estimates are. However, customs statistics have consistently indicated that for the past two decades, most of the counterfeit goods seized by U.S. customs agents originate from China, including Hong Kong (Chong 2008, 1153; IACC 2013, 16; IPEC 2019, 32). OECD/EUIPO (2021, 34) reported that as far as fake leather articles and handbags are concerned, China was the origin of 59 percent of the total seized value worldwide in this product category between 2017 and 2019, followed by Hong Kong (China; 33 percent) and Turkey (5 percent).

Before the past three decades, when China became the counterfeiting capital of the world, other countries were active in the production and distribution of counterfeit or pirated goods (Alford 1995; Burns 1986; Freemantle 1986). For example, Anderson (1981) of the *New York Times* reported that Italy, Taiwan, South Korea, Japan, and Brazil were primary manufacturing centers for counterfeits in the late 1970s and early 1980s. As many legitimate businesses began to move their operations to China in the 1990s, many counterfeit business operators also followed in their footsteps.

What Is the Relationship between Counterfeiters
and Organized Crime?

One of the purposes of this study is to examine whether there is a connection between counterfeiting and organized crime in China. Academics, as well as law enforcement practitioners, have noted that transnational criminal activities are becoming more prominent because of globalization (Albanese 2012; Allum and Gilmour 2021; Beare 2003; Bullock, Clarke, and Tilley 2010; Fijnaut and Paoli 2004; Naim 2005; Siegel and van de Bunt 2012; Varese 2011; U.S. DOJ 2008). Cross-border crimes such as human smuggling (K. Chin 1999; Kyle and Koslowski 2011; S. Zhang 2007, 2008), human trafficking (K. Chin and Finckenauer 2012; Lee 2007; Mahdavi 2011; Parennas 2011; Picarelli 2007; Shelley 2010), drug trafficking (Arias 2006; Bunck and Fowler 2012; K. Chin 2009; Lintner and Black 2009; Paoli, Greenfield, and Reuter 2009; Tuckman 2012; Zaitch 2002), money laundering (Naylor 2003), trafficking in illegal wood products (UNODC 2013), and cigarette smuggling (von Lampe et al. 2012), among others (Albanese 2012), are nowadays affecting almost every country in the world and becoming a primary concern for international bodies, state authorities, and nongovernmental organizations.

Even though there is a consensus that transnational criminal activities are becoming increasingly prevalent, there is little agreement on how these criminal activities are related to traditional organized crime groups such as the Italian Mafia, Chinese triads, and Japanese yakuza. Some observers have suggested that these long-established organized crime groups, in addition to engaging in local crimes such as extortion, protection, gambling, prostitution, and loan-sharking, play a crucial role in almost all cross-border crimes, including sex trafficking (Farr 2005; Hughes 2000; Malarek 2003; Morawska 2010; Richard 1999; Shelley 2010), drug trafficking (Longmire 2011; Martin 1996; Saviano 2008), and human smuggling (Keefe 2009).

Other observers have argued that traditional organized crime groups do not play a key role in transnational criminal activities, even though some members of these groups may engage in a limited role as individuals, independent of their criminal organizations (Adler 1985; Campbell 2009; Decker and Chapman 2008; Keo et al. 2014; Zaitch 2002; S. Zhang 2008; S. Zhang and Chin 2003). For example, Finckenauer and Waring (1998) have suggested that Russian organized crime groups were not active in human smuggling or trafficking. Kyle and Dale (2011) have pointed out that the state agents in Ecuador and Burma were more likely than organized crime members to engage in human smuggling. Spener (2011) and Sanchez (2015) found that members of drug cartels do not play a vital role in the smuggling of Mexicans into the United States, and Parrenas (2011) found that Japanese organized crime groups were not engaged in the movement of women from the Philippines to Japan for commercial sex.

There is little empirical research on product counterfeiters. Antonopoulos and his colleagues (2018) conducted a study on the U.K. counterfeiting business and interviewed nine criminal entrepreneurs who were engaged in counterfeiting, among other illegal activities. Sara Liao (2020) interviewed eighteen women designers in China for her book *Fashioning China*. However, her research subjects were mainly involved in imitating name-brand products and not one-to-one counterfeiting. Therefore, we need to find out who the Chinese counterfeiters are and whether they are members of organized crime groups. Even if they are members of criminal organizations, we need to know whether they engage in counterfeiting as individuals or as part of a group.

Another issue discussed in the literature on transnational organized crime involves the overlapping of transnational criminal activities. Do transnational crime networks specialize in one type of crime, or do they engage in a variety of transnational crimes simultaneously? There is little agreement among academics and law enforcement practitioners on this issue. Some observers have suggested that there is overlapping in transnational criminal activities because the participants are interested in making money and will do whatever it takes to achieve that goal (Albanese 2012; UNODC 2010). Others, however, argue that transnational crime networks are highly specialized, and, for example, it is unlikely that a human-smuggling ring would be involved in drug trafficking (Gundur 2022; Sanchez 2015) or that a drug cartel would participate in the trafficking of women for commercial sex (Finckenauer and Chin 2006). In this study, I explore whether the counterfeiters I interviewed were involved in additional illegal activities, such as human smuggling, sex trafficking, and drug trafficking.

What Is the Impact of Counterfeiting?

Many observers are convinced that the counterfeiting industry negatively impacts people and society. The Transnational Alliance to Combat Illicit Trade (TRACIT), a private sector initiative to mitigate the economic and social damages of illicit trade, has proposed that counterfeiting and piracy undermine sustainable development growth worldwide in the following wide variety of ways (2020, 48–49):

- Stifles economic growth, prevents legal job growth, and drains over $700 billion from the global economy.
- Consumers are exposed to harmful ingredients and faulty products that pose clear health and safety risks.
- Pirating copyrighted works erodes investment and production of cultural and educational materials.
- Irresponsible disposal of hazardous and toxic substances into air and water jeopardizes groundwater and watercourse.
- Drains GDP, displaces legitimate jobs and economic activity, creates opportunities for labor exploitation and unsafe working conditions.

- IP [intellectual property] theft deters and discourages innovation, reducing incentives for companies to invest in R&D and inhibits creative industries from realizing their full potential.
- Drives production under unethical, unregulated and poor working conditions, utilizing child labor in its production and coerced migrants smuggled into a country selling counterfeit goods.
- Generates environmental hazards to soil and land from unregulated manufacturing and improper waste disposal.
- Helps fund other criminal activities, fosters corruption, and undermines the rule of law.

Some have examined the impact of counterfeiting on the United States as a nation. The Commission on the Theft of American Intellectual Property (2017, 16) has provided a comprehensive evaluation of how counterfeiting might have impacted the American economy:

The scourge of IP theft and cyberespionage likely continues to cost the U.S. economy hundreds of billions of dollars a year despite improved laws and regulations. The theft of American IP is not just the "greatest transfer of wealth in human history," as General Keith Alexander once put it; IP theft undercuts the primary competitive advantage of American business—the capacity for innovation. IP-intensive companies generate more jobs both directly and indirectly than firms in other sectors. The growth of the U.S. economy and the strength of the U.S. labor market depend on the ability of Americans to innovate and increase productivity. The scale and persistence of IP theft, often committed by advanced state-backed groups, erode the competitiveness of U.S. firms and threaten the U.S. economy.

According to OECD/EUIPO (2019, 32), the merchandise of American firms is the most likely to be counterfeited. After examining the data on seized counterfeit goods worldwide, they found that in 2019 "almost 24% of the total value of seized products refers to IP rights holders registered in the United States, followed by France (16.6%), Italy (15.1%), Switzerland (11.2%), and Germany (9.3%)." Two years later, in 2021, another OECD/EUIPO (2021, 29) report estimated that "almost 39% of customs seizures refer to products that infringe the IP rights of US rights holders. The United States is followed by France (18%), Germany (16%), Italy (9.8%), and Switzerland (4%)."

In sum, for some observers, counterfeiting is a serious crime that could lead to, or be linked with, a variety of other serious crimes. According to Jeremy Wilson (2015, 1): "Few crime problems are as wicked as product counterfeiting. Far from a victimless crime, virtually everyone is touched by it in some way. It affects consumer health and safety, reduces brand-owner profit and innovativeness, diminishes tax revenue while increasing prevention and enforcement costs, fuels organized crime and terrorism, undermines national security, and results in loss of jobs."

This Study

As mentioned earlier, counterfeiting is a problem for almost all business sectors (Chaudhry and Zimmerman 2009; IACC 2013; OECD/EUIPO 2017). Because luxury-brand goods are the products most often counterfeited (Thomas 2007; UNODC 2014) and because of limited time and resources, I focus on the design, production, and distribution of counterfeit luxury goods such as apparel, handbags, and footwear. I also examine the individual and group characteristics of the people who are involved in these activities. Trademarks can be counterfeited (the actual mark is simply duplicated) or infringed (a very similar mark is used to confuse the customer) (Mertha 2005). This study includes both types of trademark violations. Other IPR violations such as patent and copyright infringements are excluded.

Purpose

Most of the existing studies on counterfeiting are concerned with the following issues: consumer attitudes regarding nondeceptive counterfeit brands (Bian and Veloutsou 2007), the history and politics of protecting IPR (Dimitrov 2009; Mertha 2005; Phillips 2005), the impact of counterfeiting on brand owners and the economies of certain countries (Chow 2011; Hieke 2010), the wholesale marketing of counterfeit products (Lin 2011), brand- and product-protection strategies (Brauer 2012; Chong 2008; Staake and Fleisch 2008), or the threat assessment of counterfeiting (UNODC 2013). Empirical research on the social organization and modus operandi of counterfeiters based on face-to-face interviews with them is almost nonexistent (Chermak 2015). Thus, this study attempts to examine counterfeiting through the lens of counterfeiters by interviewing them in their natural surroundings. The specific goals and objectives of this study are:

1. *To examine the individual and group characteristics of counterfeiters and their relationships with organized crime*
   No comprehensive understanding exists of counterfeiters' individual and group characteristics and how they are related to one another. This study examines who these individuals are, how they enter and leave this business, how they learn about the business, and whether they are career criminals. It also explores whether

these offenders belong to a group, an organization, or a network; how these various entities interact and function; and the norms that regulate these entities. There are many organized crime groups in China. This study investigates the role these organized crime groups play in counterfeiting.

2. *To investigate the modus operandi of the counterfeiters*
   Other than anecdotal reports, little is known about the modus operandi of counterfeiters. This study takes a comprehensive and in-depth look at the methods of operation in counterfeiting by examining the following issues: (1) the different roles in counterfeiting and the likelihood of role switching and role overlapping in the counterfeit industry, (2) the supply chain of information, funds, and products among the participants, (3) the specialization, if any, in products or brands in counterfeiting, and (4) risk management or avoidance tactics.

3. *To analyze the economic aspects of counterfeiting*
   It is reported that the counterfeiting industry is highly lucrative. However, we need to find out how much money is made and how the profits are distributed among the participants. This study examines all economic aspects of counterfeiting by seeking answers to the following questions: (1) What is the amount of start-up money required and how is it raised? (2) How are payments and collections made? (3) What are the expenses? (4) What is the profit margin? (5) How are profits invested or concealed? and (6) What are the financial risks in counterfeiting?

4. *To assess the relationships between counterfeiting, violence, and corruption*
   It is alleged that the counterfeiting industry in China is controlled by individuals who are not only tied to organized crime but also as ruthless and violent as drug traffickers (Chow 2011). It is also reported that counterfeiting in China could not be so rampant without official complicity (Chaudhry and Zimmerman 2009; Mertha 2005). This study examines (1) how violence, if any, is often used by various participants in various stages of the supply chain, against whom, and why; (2) how vulnerable participants are to violence inflicted upon them by other participants, consumers, or law enforcers; (3) how corruption is adopted by various participants in various stages of the supply chain; and (4) the many forms of corruption.

5. *To understand the counterfeit goods' demand side*
   We have a lot to learn about how the counterfeit products manufactured in Guangzhou are distributed throughout China and the

world by individuals or groups for resale. This study helps clarify: (1) the individual and group characteristics of local and foreign buyers in Guangzhou, (2) how deals are made between sellers and buyers, (3) the power dynamics between sellers and buyers, (4) buying patterns, (5) how payments are made, (6) how transportation of goods is arranged, (7) the loopholes and weaknesses in interstate and international commerce, (8) the distribution of counterfeit goods in the buyers' hometown or base of operations, and (9) the reasons for and types of business disputes between sellers and buyers.

Research Approach and Rationale

Research Sites

This study was conducted in Guangzhou, China. Known as Canton in the past, Guangzhou, with a population of about seventeen million, is the capital of Guangdong Province, the most populous and prosperous province in China (Harney 2009; van Kemenade 1997; K. Zhang 2006) (see Figure 1.2). Located seventy-five miles north of Hong Kong, Guangzhou is China's historical and

Figure 1.2 The Guangdong Province. (*Map by Rutgers Cartography*)

Figure 1.3 The Pearl River Delta (PRD). (*Map by Rutgers Cartography*)

contemporary trade center (Bercht 2013). Jianfa Shen and Gordon Kee (2017, 31) have pointed out that "Guangzhou's long-standing establishment as a mercantile city helped it to remain the most important commercial and industrial city in south China." The city is situated in the middle of the Pearl River Delta (PRD), a manufacturing center of global importance that has been driving much of China's economic development (Enright, Scott, and Chang 2005; Midler 2011; Q. Sun, Qiu, and Li 2006) (see Figure 1.3). Guangzhou's GDP jumped from less than a billion U.S. dollars in 1978 to $428 billion in 2022.

Guangzhou is alleged to be the center of China's counterfeiting business (Cocks 2006; Mathews, Lin, and Yang 2017; IACC 2013; Thomas 2007). The city has eleven districts, Yuexiu, Liwan, Tianhe, Haizhu, Panyu, Baiyun, Huangpu, Nansha, Conghua, Zengcheng, and Huadu. Most of the counterfeit businesses are located in the districts of Baiyun, Zengcheng, and Huadu (see Figure 1.4). According to Alibaba (2016), a Chinese multinational technology conglomerate, there were 3,518 counterfeiting groups active in China in 2015. Of these, 1,385 were from Guangdong Province, followed by 454 from Fujian Province. The two provinces with the next-largest number of counterfeiting groups were Zhejiang (326) and Jiangsu (323).

Guangzhou is dotted with the largest wholesale markets in China. There are wholesale markets for antiques, cosmetics, Chinese herbs, clothing, computers, electronic appliances, fabrics, lighting, hardware, shoes, toys, tea, and

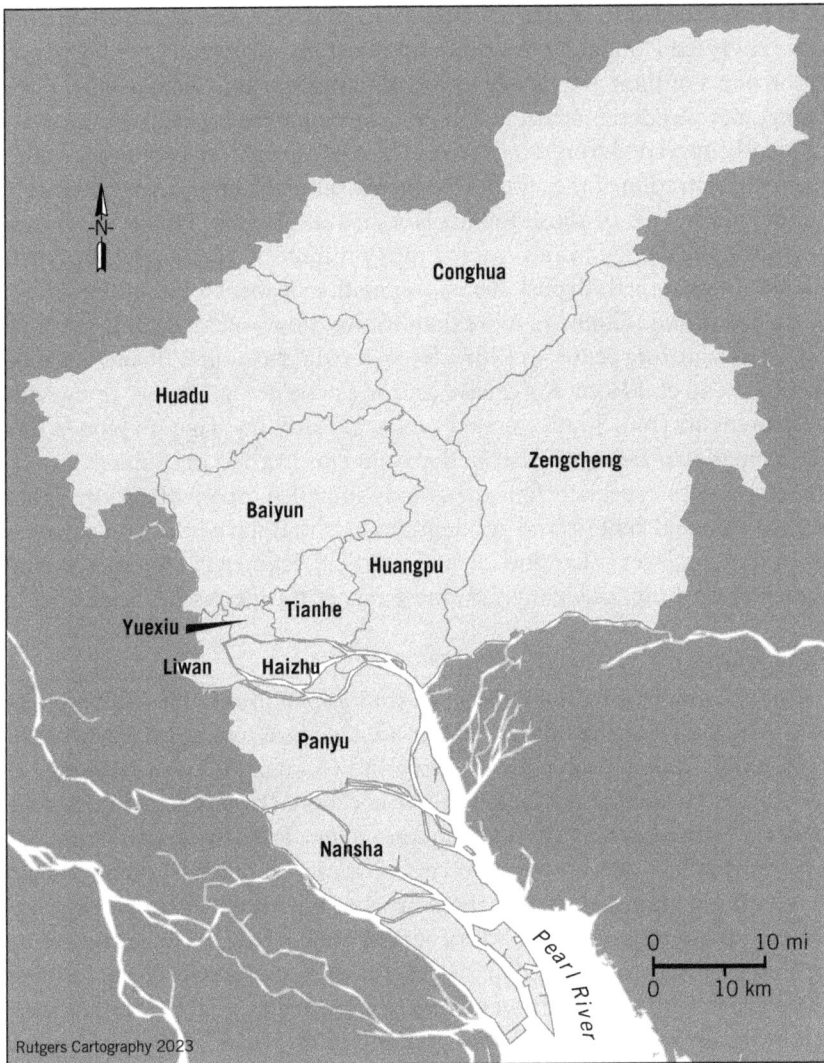

Figure 1.4 The districts of Guangzhou City. (*Map by Rutgers Cartography*)

stationery, among other products. Most finished goods have more than one market; for example, there are dozens of leather goods markets. Each market is either a large commercial building or a complex occupied by hundreds of so-called *dangkou*, or smaller wholesale and retail outlets. Besides enjoying the food, one of the appealing things to do in Guangzhou is shopping for cheap but high-quality clothing, leather goods, and electrical appliances in countless wholesale markets. In these markets, counterfeit goods are often traded alongside the goods that are not counterfeit.

I also traveled to nearby Dongguan to interview research participants there. I visited Dongguan five times for my study. Dongguan, with a population of 6.4 million, is located between Guangzhou and Shenzhen. In 1985, Dongguan was designated an economic development zone, and it was subsequently upgraded from a town to a city. There are thirty-two towns under the administration of the city of Dongguan, but most of my interviews were conducted in two of those towns, Houjie and Humen. Houjie is located southwest of Dongguan and is only a thirty-minute drive from the Shenzhen Bao'an International Airport. It has a population of about four hundred ninety thousand and is home to more than twelve thousand firms. It is the largest manufacturing center in China for shoes and furniture. Businesspeople from Taiwan and Hong Kong have a strong presence in Houjie, along with entrepreneurs from South Korea. Liaoxia, an "urban village" in Houjie, has the reputation of being the distribution center for a variety of counterfeit fashion accessories, especially footwear. Many so-called urban villages in China are commercial centers and residential areas that have been transformed from small villages (Zhanguo Liu and Lo 2020). Humen is a manufacturing center for clothing, and many Taiwanese-owned businesses are located there.

Data Sources

Primary Data: During the summer of 2018, I spent three and a half months in Guangzhou. During this period, I conducted face-to-face interviews with forty-three research subjects. I returned to Guangzhou in the summer of 2019 for three months and conducted an additional twenty-four face-to-face interviews. Besides the fifty-seven counterfeiters, I also interviewed thirteen key informants who were law enforcers, government officials, and investigators working for private firms. These firms provide a variety of services, including assisting foreign brand owners in conducting anti-counterfeiting investigations. I also engaged in informal conversations with a large number of people in China and Taiwan who were knowledgeable about the counterfeit business. I have quoted several of them in this book, although they are not counted as one of the seventy research subjects.

I used the chain-referral method to generate a convenience sample. The sampling chains started with a college professor in Guangzhou and a former footwear factory manager in Dongguan referring counterfeiters to me. Also, I came to know a leather supplier called Xiao Ma while I was eating breakfast at the hotel where I was staying.[2] He was there with one of his assistants to meet a leather exporter from Bangladesh who was a guest at my hotel. I learned a lot about counterfeiting from Xiao Ma because he was a well-established leather supplier with many clients who were involved in the counterfeiting business.

My second trip to Guangzhou, during the summer of 2019, was much more successful than the first, even though I interviewed fewer subjects this time. The reasons are manifold. First, my second trip coincided with a short visit to Guangzhou by Laoban (G2), a Taiwanese entrepreneur who operated a clothing business there for about twenty years before returning to Taiwan in 2015.[3] I was introduced to him by one of his peers, Jane (G1), a Taiwanese fashion business owner married to a Guangzhou man. In the summer of 2018, I took a side trip from Guangzhou to Taipei and interviewed Laoban there multiple times. When I learned that Laoban would go back to Guangzhou the following year to meet his former employees, who were now running their apparel businesses, I decided to join him there. Laoban introduced me to his former employees at dinner parties. After all the wining and dining, Laoban urged them to help me with my research project. After Laoban left Guangzhou and returned to Taipei, I interviewed eleven of his former employees or associates. They were not only much more cooperative and forthcoming than the subjects I found through other channels but also allowed me to visit their business premises and interview them more than once. Second, when I visited Guangzhou again in 2019, Xiao Ma (H4) not only spent more time telling me about the leather handbag business in Guangzhou but also introduced research subjects to me. The subjects he referred to me were, like Laoban's subjects, candid about their engagements in counterfeiting and the encounters they had with the Chinese authorities.

Thirteen key informants were also interviewed for this research. They were all from Guangzhou and included two anti-counterfeiting private investigators, two government officials, four law enforcers (one prosecutor who specialized in counterfeiting cases, one anti-counterfeiting officer from the Administration for Industry and Commerce [AIC], one crime-prevention police officer, and one economic crime police officer), and five who were legitimate business owners, college professors, or lawyers.

In sum, I conducted seventy interviews in Guangzhou and Dongguan, including fifty-seven counterfeiters and thirteen key informants. The counterfeiters I interviewed can be categorized into nineteen designers/organizers, twelve manufacturers, eleven distributors (wholesale or retail or both), and fifteen facilitators (suppliers or workers). As I address later, categorizing counterfeiters into these four different groups is problematic because there is often an overlapping of these various roles in the counterfeiting business. Of the fifty-seven counterfeiters, twenty-four were involved in the apparel business, seventeen in the leather handbag trade, and sixteen in the footwear industry (see Table 1.1).

I developed a questionnaire with both closed and open-ended questions to help me with the interviews. The questionnaire included the following

TABLE 1.1. INTERVIEWEES				
	Garment	Handbag	Footwear	Total
Counterfeiters				
Organizers/designers	13	4	2	19
Manufacturers	1	4	7	12
Distributors	4	5	2	11
Facilitators	6	4	5	15
Subtotal	24	17	16	57
Key informants				
Law enforcement officials				4
Government officials				2
Private investigators				2
Other				5
Subtotal				13
Total				70

domains of information: (1) background characteristics such as age, ethnicity, marital status, education, etc.; (2) reasons for, and processes in, entering the counterfeiting industry; (3) current role(s) in the counterfeiting industry; (4) modus operandi of the business; (5) dealing with others in the counterfeit business; (6) risk management; (7) money management; and (8) leisure, lifestyle, and self-perception. Because I interviewed a variety of participants in the counterfeit trade (designers, manufacturers, distributors, suppliers, workers), the domains listed here are just approximate and may apply to only some of the research subjects in my study.

Fieldwork: To supplement the interview data, I conducted extensive fieldwork in Guangzhou and Dongguan. First, I spent a substantial amount of time with my research subjects. I often had lunch or dinner with my subjects before or after the interview. I used this opportunity to learn more about them and their businesses. In China, when people get together to eat, they drink, often excessively. These occasions helped me establish rapport with my research subjects and set up a second interview.

Second, I visited my research subjects' business premises whenever there was an opportunity to do so. I always asked a research participant to meet at his or her business premises. If a subject was reluctant to see me in his or her business venue at our initial meeting, I tried to arrange a second or third meeting to find out whether we could meet at his or her place of business. Most subjects were willing to see me in their outlet stores or offices but not at their factories or warehouses.

Third, I got together with my subjects in their homes after we came to know each other well. I also met their family members. This allowed me to gain an understanding of their family relationships, lifestyle, financial situation, and other aspects of their lives.

Fourth, whenever I was free, I strolled the wholesale markets and shopping malls in Guangzhou. Most business stores in Guangzhou are open seven days a week from 9:00 A.M. to 9:00 P.M. I stayed at a hotel not far from most of the wholesale markets. With the help of a cheap, clean, and efficient public transportation system, I was able to roam the city at minimal cost (thirty cents for a bus ride within the city, less than a dollar for a subway ride, and two dollars for a taxi from my hotel to the wholesale markets). When I visited the markets, I had lengthy conversations with the saleswomen or the store owners.

I recorded my daily activities, observations, thoughts, and conversations with people I met in the field, including saleswomen, store owners, taxi drivers, and shoppers. I have successfully conducted similar fieldwork research in China on other topics, including human smuggling (K. Chin 1999; S. Zhang and Chin 2002; S. Zhang, Chin, and Miller 2007), organized crime (K. Chin 2003; K. Chin and Godson 2006), human trafficking (K. Chin 2014; K. Chin and Finckenauer 2011, 2012), and drug trafficking (K. Chin 2007, 2009; K. Chin and Zhang 2015).

I also took a short trip to Jinjiang City and Putian City in Fujian Province, which is adjacent to Guangdong. Fujian and Guangdong were the first two provinces designated by Deng Xiaoping for economic reform. Unlike on my trips to Dongguan and Shenzhen, on my trips to Jinjiang and Putian, I did not interview any research subjects; I just visited several hot spots for the production and distribution of counterfeit footwear and talked to as many people as possible about their cities and the counterfeit trade.

Jinjiang is one of the top ten fourth-tier cities in GDP because it is not only a leading center for the production of shoes but also a manufacturing hub for umbrellas, jackets, underwear, and other goods. Many enterprise towns with worldwide reputations are within the jurisdiction of Jinjiang. Before Putian became the so-called capital of fake shoes, this distinction belonged to Jinjiang. Gradually, the city transformed itself into a legitimate manufacturing center for shoes. Local name-brand sportswear and shoe enterprises such as Anta, 361, and Li Ning set up their headquarters in Jinjiang (C. Zhou 2021). Regardless, there is a market in Jinjiang with hundreds of wholesale and retail stores that sell only counterfeit shoes, and it caters to both local and foreign buyers. One can buy a pair of counterfeit shoes with names such as Skechers, Timberland, Columbia, North Face, and Balenciaga for less than $10.

With a population of 2.9 million, Putian is a third-tier city. There have been widespread reports in the local and international media about the city's booming footwear counterfeiting industry (Pierson 2017; Schmidle 2010). Many contract manufacturers for Nike, Adidas, Puma, Reebok, and other shoe firms are located in Putian. The media report that almost everyone in the city, including rank-and-file local authorities, the mayor, and the city party secretary, is complicit in counterfeiting. It is estimated that at least two hundred thousand individuals in Putian are involved in this trade. These entrepreneurs proudly claim that they want the entire world to wear name-brand shoes. In addition to producing the largest number of counterfeit shoes in China, Putian has perfected a far-reaching distribution system for local and international markets (Pierson, 2017).

Data Collection

I conducted all the interviews and the fieldwork. The interviews were conducted face-to-face in Chinese, with a structured questionnaire that is a mixture of closed- and open-ended questions. Each interview lasted between one and two hours. Ten subjects were interviewed more than once, and five were interviewed three or more times. None of the interviews were audio recorded or videotaped. The subjects were not paid for their participation. All the field notes were prepared in Chinese to ensure that nothing would be lost in translation during the initial documentation stage.

I have conducted several research projects with hard-to-reach subjects in the United States and Asia, including gang members, extortion victims, human smugglers, human traffickers, sex workers, and drug traffickers. However, I was surprised to learn that counterfeiters were as hard to reach as those subjects that I had studied before. The following is a list of challenges I encountered while collecting data. First, many Chinese are nationalistic. Not long after I arrived in Guangzhou, someone I was asking for help told me bluntly: "I want to help you, but I am patriotic. Helping you would be like betraying my country because I would be telling a person from the U.S. about the dark side of China. As you know, the U.S. and China are not getting along very well lately. I am sure my friends [in the counterfeiting business] will also feel the same if you ask them for an interview."

Second, some subjects were reluctant to admit that they were engaged in counterfeiting. They agreed to meet me and be interviewed simply because they were referred to me by someone they knew and respected. Even so, they would not acknowledge that they were counterfeiters and claimed to be only "someone knowledgeable." Danny (H3), a handbag manufacturer, told me this after he agreed to meet me: "Nobody will admit that he or she is a counterfeiter, even if you promise that the interview will be anonymous and that the interview will not be recorded or videotaped. All I can say is that I will help you, because I know something about this business, and many people I know are involved."

Third, it was challenging to arrange one-on-one interviews with some level of privacy in public places in Guangzhou. The city is packed with people everywhere and at all times, especially in the wholesale markets, the restaurants, and the subway. Once, I was meeting a group of shoe counterfeiters in an outdoor seating area of a coffee shop. A man in his forties showed up acting like he was mentally ill, murmuring to us something we did not understand. He pulled up a chair and joined us, ignoring that we were asking him to leave. We did not know what to do with him; he sat there for about twenty minutes listening to our conversation about the counterfeiting business and then got up and left. We were hoping he was not a government spy.

I was astonished when I realized how difficult it was to locate research participants for this study. When I asked Sonny (H10), a thirty-six-year-old handbag business owner, why it was so challenging to find a counterfeiter for an interview, he explained:

This is an illegal industry operating in a gray area, naturally, many people are not willing to tell you their stories. Drug traffickers and counterfeiters are not the same. The formers are involved in the kind of business that, if arrested, they may lose their heads [be sentenced to death], so they are all desperadoes. That is why they do not care. When you interview drug traffickers, they talk. Counterfeiters are different; they are scheming, intelligent, and cautious. Besides, many counterfeiters are trying very hard to whitewash their illegal activities by engaging in various legitimate businesses, like restaurants, construction, or the wine trade. They are doing this to find some legitimate businesses to justify their wealth; otherwise, if people ask you where you earn so much money, how will you respond?

It is not hard to understand why these people are guarded. In China, if a counterfeiter is investigated, fined, arrested, and imprisoned, you can say the person "has returned to the pre-liberation condition [a destitute period before the Communist takeover in 1949] overnight after working very hard for many decades." It is a serious incident because all his merchandise will be confiscated, all his assets and belongings will be forfeited, and he will be heavily fined and imprisoned. That is why when we [people in the counterfeiting business] are together, we wine and dine, get to know each other very well, and talk about everything. However, when it comes to our businesses, nobody asks another person any questions; otherwise, people will say, "Why the hell are you asking this?"

Jane (G1), a clothing business owner in her late forties, echoed Sonny's point:

Why are people not willing to be interviewed? That is because everyone in this business is connected. If there is a problem in a particular link, people in the other links will begin to worry about whether it will implicate them. If a factory is investigated, raw material suppliers, distributors, designers, or organizers who do business with this factory could also be scrutinized by the authorities. That is why everyone is very cautious. They want to protect not only themselves but also their business associates. Very often, their business networks are made up of people who are family members or relatives. This prompts them to be extremely careful when talking to an outsider.

Protection of Research Subjects

I was sensitive about protecting those who were willing to participate in this research. To protect the identities of the subjects, the interviews were conducted anonymously. The subjects were not asked to sign an informed consent form; they were offered an informed consent statement. The informed consent statement stressed that (1) participation was entirely voluntary, (2) refusal to participate would involve no penalty or loss of benefit, (3) the subject could refuse to answer any question he or she wished to, and (4) the subject could terminate the interview at any time. They were asked to give their oral consent to participate in the study. All interviews were conducted with the subject's full consent and understanding of the process. In all my interview records and field notes, I used pseudonyms in addressing my subjects and referring to the individuals mentioned by the subjects. The Institutional Review Board of Rutgers University reviewed and approved the procedures for the protection of the subjects for this research.

As mentioned earlier, people who engaged in counterfeiting were reluctant to talk about their businesses, and they were nervous about being interviewed even after I assured them of protecting their identities. However, because of my background as a college professor from the United States with roots in Taiwan, they were certain that I was not going to report them to the Chinese authorities or endanger them. I felt safe all the time when I was doing fieldwork or hanging out with my research subjects because most of them were referred to me by someone I knew.

Validity and Reliability

A study of this nature poses many challenges regarding validity and reliability. People from the counterfeiting industry risk being investigated, fined, and imprisoned if their identities and activities are revealed to the authorities. These concerns may affect their willingness to participate in the study and the level of their truthfulness. I employed the following strategies to increase the validity and reliability of the data collection.

First, I interviewed only subjects who were referred to me. Because potential subjects had been told in advance by the intermediaries about the nature of the study, they would not have agreed to meet me if they did not want to talk about their involvement in counterfeiting. Some potential subjects did just that when the go-betweens approached them. Some of the people I interviewed agreed to talk to me only after multiple attempts had been made by a middleman. Thus, those whom I interviewed were at least willing to assist me to a certain extent when they sat down with me for an interview.

Second, the interviews were conducted in a language or dialect the subjects preferred. I speak fluent Mandarin and Cantonese (a dialect spoken by the local people in Guangzhou and by people in Hong Kong). I conducted most of the interviews in Mandarin, as the majority of the people in the counterfeiting business in Guangzhou are not Cantonese-speaking locals.

Third, most of the interviews were conducted face-to-face, one-on-one, and without the presence of a third party. Fourth, I employed conversational interview techniques to gain the trust and confidence of the interviewees and only jotted down prompting points; I also set aside ample time for writing up detailed information right after the interview. Fifth, the interviews were anonymous; no identifiable information on the interviewed subjects was asked or kept, and this point was made very clear to the subjects. Moreover, to alleviate the subjects' fears, the interviews were not recorded or videotaped.

Limitations of This Study

This study has several limitations. First, only the counterfeiting of luxury goods is studied. Other counterfeit goods with a clear public health impact, such as medicine and food, are not included. And I only include three highly counterfeited types of luxury goods in my study: apparel, handbags, and shoes. As a result, my findings may be generalizable only to some of the luxury goods counterfeiting businesses. There is a need to study the counterfeiting of goods that affect our health and safety.

Second, my research does not include deceptive counterfeiting. All my research subjects were involved in nondeceptive counterfeiting. There is a good chance that there are differences between these two types of counterfeiting in terms of the participants, the modus operandi, and the profit level. I cannot generalize my findings to the business of deceptive counterfeiting.

Third, my sample is small and nonrepresentative. I interviewed only a small number of subjects from each category of participants in the counterfeit industry (fifty-seven), i.e., designers or organizers, manufacturers, distributors, and facilitators. I included only a limited number of key informants (thirteen) in my research. I relied on only five people to locate most of my research subjects. Findings based on a small and nonrepresentative sample will likely be skewed.

Fourth, my research site was primarily in Guangzhou. Even though I interviewed some subjects in Dongguan and conducted fieldwork in Jinjiang and Putian, my findings might not be replicated in other counterfeiting hubs in China. For example, counterfeiting activities in Wenzhou City, the capital of Zhejiang Province, are reported to be different from those in Guangzhou. I also did not include Yiwu City in Zhenjiang Province in my study, a city whose many nicknames include "World's Capital of Small Commodities," "Wall Street of Counterfeiting," and "Counterfeit Capital" (Lin 2011).[4]

Fifth, I do not study how counterfeit goods produced in China are transported overseas and distributed in urban centers around the world. For example, there is a booming retail market for counterfeit luxury goods in New York City's Chinatown. On any given day, peddlers can be found selling cheap counterfeit handbags, sunglasses, scarves, and other fashion accessories on street corners. It is apparent that they are well organized and have a division of labor. Everyone in the group plays a particular role: the solicitors approach passersby to see whether they are interested in buying counterfeit goods; the sellers conduct the sales, usually with the aid of a catalog, and negotiate prices; the runners retrieve goods from nearby warehouses and hand them over to the sellers; and the lookouts watch the streets and alert members of the network if there are signs of trouble. To fully understand how counterfeit goods from China end up in the hands of individual buyers outside of China, a different group of subjects must be interviewed. None of those subjects are included in my sample.

Sixth, the interviews were not recorded or videotaped. I had previously conducted interviews with different groups of research subjects in China, including illegal migrants, human smugglers, gangsters, drug traffickers, drug users, sex-ring operators, and sex workers. None of them were willing to talk if the interviews were to be recorded or videotaped. The same is true of the counterfeiters in Guangzhou. Thus, when I quote my research subjects in this study, I am not quoting them word for word but merely paraphrasing them.

Discussion Road Map

In the next chapter, I examine the development of product counterfeiting in China after the country adopted the reform and open-door policy in the late 1970s. I explore how the fostering of the three-plus-one trading mix and the explosion of contract manufacturing played a crucial role in introducing brand-name luxury goods into China and how the strong demand for these goods by Chinese consumers incentivized entrepreneurs to find ways to meet the demand, including counterfeiting. I also explore the various forms of IP violations in China and compare and contrast them.

In Chapter 3, I examine where and how counterfeit goods are produced. The production of these goods involves mainly four categories of actors: the designers or organizers, the manufacturers, the raw material suppliers, and the other business associates. For the designers or organizers, I examine the differences between counterfeiters, who engage in point-by-point counterfeiting, and infringers, who copy the style and elements of name-brand products but not the label or the logo. For the manufacturers, I explore the two primary forms of production facilities: factories and workshops. Raw material suppliers are rarely discussed in the literature on counterfeiting even though they play a crucial role in the trade. In this chapter, I examine suppliers of materials such as fabrics, leather, and metal fittings. At the end of the chapter, I investigate businesses that provide other essential services to the counterfeiters, such as packaging.

In Chapter 4, I focus on the marketing of counterfeit goods. First, I explore Guangzhou's major wholesale markets for leather goods, apparel, and shoes. They are popular places to shop for both counterfeit and authentic products. Second, I examine the four operating entities for distribution: *dian* (stand-alone retail-only shops), *dangkou* (stores for retail and wholesale merchandise), *xiezilou* (literally "office building," but for counterfeiters in Guangzhou, it is an office in which wholesale business is conducted), and *gongsi* (companies). Third, I probe how counterfeits produced in China are exported overseas. Finally, I investigate how the emergence of e-commerce has revolutionized the marketing of counterfeits in China and around the world.

I turn my attention to the counterfeiters in Chapter 5. I examine their demographic background, such as age, gender, education, marital status, place of origin, and nationality. I also investigate the pathways to becoming a counterfeiter and the self-perception and lifestyle of those who are engaged in counterfeiting. To bring the human element to the discussion of the characteristics of counterfeiters, I conclude Chapter 5 with the profiles of several individuals who participated in my study. These profiles are constructed from my interviews with them and my field notes after socializing with them and their family or friends over meals or other social events.

In Chapter 6, I explore the group characteristics of counterfeiters, focusing on the size of their business, its scope, its structure, and their business network. I examine how people and business entities in the counterfeiting sector cooperate or compete with one another and whether these activities lead to monopolies or violence. At the end of the chapter, I discuss the connection between counterfeiting and Chinese organized crime and the differences between the traditional Chinese organized crime subculture and the illicit enterprise subculture. I also examine *shanzhai* (literally, mountain fortress), or copying, as part of the illicit entrepreneurial subculture. This approach may help us understand why counterfeiting is not simply an illegal activity but also a mentality or an attitude embraced by the underprivileged who produce or consume counterfeit goods.

I explore the modus operandi of counterfeiters in Chapter 7. I focus on how they conduct their businesses to avoid being targeted by the authorities. Their risk management tactics involve two broad categories: (1) how to prevent their employees, competitors, private anti-counterfeiting investigators, clients, and other reward-motivated individuals from reporting them to the authorities for their engagement in counterfeiting, and (2) how to implement a variety of risk-avoidance business practices to minimize the chances of being caught. Finally, I examine how counterfeiters, like many legitimate business owners, must deal with routine business risks, including bad product design, inefficient distribution systems, fierce competition, demand volatility, and poor inventory management.

In Chapter 8, I examine the war against counterfeiting in China. I begin the chapter with an introduction to the various government and police agencies in China responsible for preventing and controlling counterfeiting and punishing those who engage in it. Private anti-counterfeiting agencies play an essential role in conducting preliminary investigative work on counterfeiting. I explore how private investigators conduct business in a counterfeiting center like Guangzhou. I also examine the various anti-counterfeiting measures adopted by the Chinese government. I conclude the chapter by examining the role of corruption in the various government and police agencies that are supposed to be preventing counterfeiting in China.

In the concluding Chapter 9, I examine what it was like to conduct a counterfeiting business during the "golden period of counterfeiting." I also explore the prospects for this industry by comparing and contrasting the viewpoints of those who are either pessimistic or optimistic about the future of their trade.

2

DEVELOPMENT

Not long after the end of the Cultural Revolution (1966–1976), China reestablished ties with the West and adopted its reform and opening up policy (Dikotter 2022; Gewirtz 2022; Muhlhahn 2019; Spence 1991; Vogel 2013; T. Wang 2023). China also began moving from a centrally planned to a market-oriented economy (Ang 2016; Gittings 2005). Government-owned enterprises crumbled quickly in the face of the rising private ventures (Yasheng Huang 2008). Foreign investors were lured to China to open factories in the many newly established special economic zones in the coastal areas (Harney 2009; K. Zhang 2006). Chinese leaders, especially then paramount leader Deng Xiaoping, encouraged the Chinese people to work hard, get rich, brush aside ideology, and focus on practicality (Vogel 2013). Gradually, China began to embark on a reform movement that helped usher it into the new millennium with impressive economic achievements (Ang 2016; S. Li 2022; Magnus 2018).

In this chapter, I discuss two main issues. First, I examine the emergence and evolution of the counterfeiting industry in China after it adopted the reform and opening up policy in the late 1970s. I focus on how both the implementation of *sanlaiyibu* (three-plus-one trading mix) attracted manufacturers from Hong Kong and Taiwan to move their factories to China and these factories became contract manufacturers for American and Western European multinational corporations. I also explore how contract manufacturing led to the development of a black market for unauthorized luxury goods produced in China (*yuandanhuo*, literally original order goods, including factory overrun goods and goods that are produced without authorization), how a market for copies evolved when the demand for yuandanhuo outweighed the supply, and, finally, how the counterfeit trade transformed from crude imitation (*fangmao*) to high-quality imitation (*gaofang*). Second, I explain the many forms of copying in China, including *yibiyi* (one-to-one counterfeiting), *cabianqiu* (edge-ball infringement), shanzhai (knockoff), and *fayang-guangda* (supplemental copying).

China's Reform and Opening Up Policy

After over two decades of fighting, Mao Tse-tung's Chinese Communist Party (CCP) defeated Chiang Kai-shek's Kuomintang Party (KMT) (Coble 2023). Mao proclaimed the founding of the People's Republic of China (PRC) on October 1, 1949, in Beijing's Tiananmen Square. The KMT retreated to Taiwan, an island across the Taiwan Strait, and continued to claim that the KMT-controlled Republic of China was the sole legitimate government of the whole of China. After the CCP came to power, it initiated massive movements, such as the antirightist campaign (1957–1959), to wipe out anti-revolutionary rightists hidden inside the party; the Great Leap Forward (1958–1962), to enable China to catch up with the economies of the United Kingdom and the United States; and the Cultural Revolution (1966–1976), to eliminate political rivals and to ensure Mao's absolute power (Marquis and Qiao 2022). These movements had devastating effects on all facets of Chinese society (Branigan 2023). By the time Mao died, on September 9, 1976, China was in disarray, and it was one of the poorest countries in the world (Spence 1991).

Mao's successor, Hua Guofeng, ended the Cultural Revolution and radical Maoism by arresting Mao's wife, Jiang Qing, and her three accomplices, dubbed the Gang of Four, on October 6, 1976. Hua also brought Deng Xiaoping back to Beijing from exile to resume work (Shirk 2022). Deng's return signified practicality over ideology in decision-making for the CCP leadership. Deng also dramatically improved China's relationships with the United States, Japan, and many other countries. The United States and China established full diplomatic relations on January 1, 1979, and Washington severed its ties with Taiwan at the same time (Vogel 2013).

Deng Xiaoping, who had studied in France as a young man, was determined to transform China from a rural backwater into an advanced industrialized nation like Japan or the United States. However, he had to convince the ultraleftists in the CCP of this, as they were against his policy of reform and opening up. Deng's many famous sayings paved the way for the whole of China to follow his path, as Ezra Vogel (2013, 391), commented:

The "cat theory"—"it doesn't matter if the cat is black or white as long as it catches the mouse"—was a creative way of winning further support for diminishing the importance of Mao's ideology; it suggested that doing what worked was more important than following a particular ideology. If Deng had simply said "ideology is unimportant," he would have provoked enormous controversy.... Another saying, "some people get rich first," helped lower the expectations of many who hoped to get rich quickly after the reforms, and helped disarm those who might feel envious of those who prospered before the benefits of reform had reached everyone.... "Groping for stones while crossing the river" was a creative way of encouraging experimentation and acknowledging that in a new situation they should not expect that all policies will work well.

Inspired and encouraged by Deng's many famous axioms, millions of Chinese "plunged into the sea of business" (xiahai), so that "everyone is [was] becoming a merchant" (quanmin jieshang) (Gittings 2005). "Groping for stones while crossing the river" not only asked people not to be afraid of experimentation and failure but also sent a message to the authorities to keep a blind eye to many shady business activities. As a result, many people in China obtained their first bucket of gold through business activities that were only partially legal.

Deng Xiaoping jump-started his economic reform by establishing four special economic zones in 1980, in the provinces of Guangdong and Fujian: Shenzhen, Zhuhai, Shantou, and Xiamen (Vogel 1989; T. Wang 2023). As explained by Vogel (2013, 399), export-processing zones in these special economic zones "had been designed to get around complex import and export rules by establishing zones where materials needed for production would come in, where local low-cost labor would produce goods that would then be exported without going through any of the usual formal import-export procedures." In 1984, affirming the success of his experiment, Deng announced the extension of the opening up policy to fourteen coastal cities (Vogel 2013). The 1989 Tiananmen Square incident temporarily slowed Deng's momentum due to the embargo of China by Western firms (Gewirtz 2022). However, with the help of Taiwanese investors, China came up with the so-called Guangdong Model (also known as sanlaiyibu), which enabled China to link to the global supply chain (Wu 2019). When Deng, then ninety and in bad health, embarked on a trip (called nanxun, or southern inspection tour) to Shenzhen in January 1992, he reaffirmed to his fellow citizens that China was on the right path to establish a strong and modern economy and urged them to continue with reform and opening up. He stated that China should dash forward and never look back (Friedberg 2022; Jin 2023; S. Li 2022). After China acceded to the WTO in 2001, according to Alexandra Harney (2009, 2–3), the author of *The China Price: The True Cost of Chinese Competitive Advantage*, "China has come to dominate global manufacturing in a way almost inconceivable before its rise. The prices it offers have been so low that starting around 2003, they have become known simply as the China price. . . . The only way for manufacturers elsewhere to compete was to move to China themselves."

In his book *Deng Xiaoping and the Transformation of China*, Vogel (2013, 406) summed up the impressive economic development in China as follows:

> Within three decades after Guangdong and Fujian were granted special status, Chinese exports had multiplied over one hundred times, from less than US$10 billion per year in 1978 to more than US$1 trillion, with more than one-third from Guangdong. In 1978 there were virtually no factories in Guangdong with modern assembly lines. Within three decades, a visitor to southern Guangdong would see skyscrapers, large industrial sites, apartment buildings, world-class hotels, superhighways, and traffic jams.

Sanlaiyibu (Three-Plus-One Trading Mix)

To improve the Chinese economy, Beijing sought a way to attract foreign capital and technology. According to various reports, Xi Zhongxun, then party secretary of Guangdong Province and the father of Xi Jinping, played a critical role in persuading the central authority in Beijing to allow Guangdong to embark on something unprecedented (Gewirtz 2022; Lu 2018). The elder Xi suggested to Beijing that, since there were few resources the central authority could offer to Guangdong, why did it not at least offer more power to local authorities in Guangdong to grant them the autonomy to engage in economic activities? In other words, to let them establish special economic zones where local enterprises would be given the privilege to manufacture for foreign firms. According to Vogel (2013, 398): "Xi [Zhongxun] and his colleagues, drawing on advice from Gu Mu [then vice premier], proposed that the entire province be allowed to implement a special policy that would give Guangdong the flexibility to adopt measures to attract foreign capital, technology, and management practices necessary to produce goods for export. China would supply the land, transport facilities, electricity, and labor needed by the factories, as well as the hotels, restaurants, housing, and other facilities needed by foreigners." Eventually, as mentioned in the previous section, four special economic zones were established: Shenzhen, Zhuhai, and Shantou in Guangdong Province, and Xiamen in Fujian Province (J. Cheng 2018; Vogel 2013; Wu 1997).

The first wave of the foreign entrepreneurs to arrive in those special economic zones, in the late 1970s and early 1980s, was predominantly from Hong Kong (Chang 2009; J. Cheng 2018; Enright, Scott, and Chang 2005; Sun, Qui, and Li 2006; Wu 1997). There was a close relationship between Hong Kong and mainland China because after the Chinese Communists took over in 1949, there were four massive waves of mainland Chinese (1957, 1962, 1972, 1979), who fled to Hong Kong, most from neighboring Guangdong Province. Many of the Hong Kong entrepreneurs who showed up in China in the late 1970s and early 1980s were originally from the PRD area, especially the city of Dongguan (Johnson 1994; Lu 2018). These migrants played a crucial role in developing Hong Kong into a world-class manufacturing and trading center. According to the sociologist Graham Johnson (1994, 59): "In the 1980s, the entrepreneurial skills and capital of these emigres were actively sought by their Guangdong kinsmen and fellow countrymen. Kinship connections and local loyalties have become a central part of local development initiatives. In the process, the delta region has become firmly linked to the global economy through its Hong Kong connections." Joseph Cheng (2018), a political scientist, has noted that the geographic proximity and cultural similarity between Hong Kong and China greatly assisted in establishing labor-intensive industries, with Hong Kong serving as the shop front and the PRD as the workshop.

Of the many stories depicting the transformation of China from a backward country to an economic powerhouse within a period of forty years (1978–2018), the establishment of the Daiping Handbag Factory is the most frequently told in the Chinese media and government reports. According to the *Southern Metropolis Daily* (2018b) newspaper in Guangzhou, the Daiping Handbag Factory, which produced copies of European handbags, was the first-ever sanlaiyibu factory. Sanlaiyibu is translated as the three-plus-one trading mix in English. Sanlai (literally, three provisions) means three types of contract manufacturing based on the supply of raw materials (for manufacturing), parts (for assembling), or samples (for reproducing) by foreign firms to manufacturers in China. The outside source may also provide equipment and technical know-how. Chinese entrepreneurs, supported by local authorities, provide land and labor to foreign firms. The finished products all belong to the outside source, and they export them out of China. The Chinese side collects a manufacturing fee from an outside source. Yibu is bushangmaoyi, a type of compensation trade. It means a foreign firm provides a Chinese firm with materials, equipment, machines, and technology to engage in the production of a commodity in China, and the Chinese firm repays the foreign firm with a certain amount of finished goods.

The experience of a handbag factory owner from Hong Kong explains how the first type of sanlaiyibu (contract manufacturing based on materials provided) worked. According to the storyline of the Daiping Handbag Factory, Mr. Zhang, a Hong Kong businessman, was struggling because of increased wages and manufacturing costs in Hong Kong. When he discovered he could produce his handbags in China for a lot less, he jumped on the opportunity and moved his factory to a town in Dongguan called Daiping (now Humen). Mr. Zhang, originally from China, provided the machines, the materials, and the technology, and the local authorities contributed the land, the facilities, and the labor. The finished goods belonged to Mr. Zhang, who exported them out of China. The workers received a salary that was low by international standards but more than triple the amount they could earn from government work units. Mr. Zhang paid his workers in Chinese yuan. However, he had to buy the yuan from the local government using American dollars he transmitted from Hong Kong and at an official exchange rate higher than the market rate. The local government made money from the differences in the exchange rate (Lu 2018).

Sanlaiyibu is also called the Dongguan Model or the Guangdong Model. According to J. Cheng (2018, 5), that is because sanlaiyibu was first developed and implemented in Guangdong Province, especially in Dongguan:

> The Dongguan model was basically the sanlaiyibu mode of operation. Dongguan offered land for the processing industries, while external investors provided capital, equipment, technology and management. Cheap labor came from the interior provinces. The development model relied on a new international division of labor with Hong Kong and Taiwan relocating their labor-intensive manufacturing industries to Dongguan, thus absorbing the latter into the international economy and production chains, allowing Dongguan to develop into the "workshop of the world."

Not long after the massive influx to China, especially the PRD, of entrepreneurs from Hong Kong, large numbers of businesspeople from Taiwan also began to arrive there (Gittings 2005; Hamilton and Kao 2018; Rigger 2021; Wu 1997). According to the sociologist Victor Nee (1994, 11):

> Driving Taiwan investment activities to the mainland were the exhaustion of surplus labor in Taiwan by the end of the 1970s, the escalating cost of domestic labor, and rapid currency appreciation. In order to remain competitive and retain their market share in the global economy, Taiwan exporters were compelled to seek lower-priced labor elsewhere. A seemingly limitless supply of cheap labor and low relative rents on land and buildings, coupled with the continued relaxation of political tensions between Beijing and Taipei, rendered the move to the mainland irresistible for Taiwan entrepreneurs.

The first group of Taiwanese investors were shoe manufacturers, and they built a booming shoe industry in Houjie (a township in Dongguan) from scratch (Lu 2018). As reported by Chung Chin (1994, 217), a fellow at a research institute in Taipei, based on official statistics from mainland China, "Taiwan's cumulative DFI [Direct Foreign Investment] ranked fourth, behind Hong Kong, the U.S., and Japan at the end of 1991. In terms of manufacturing investment, however, Taiwan may be second only to Hong Kong, since U.S. and Japanese investments are more often tilted toward resource- and service-related activities in terms of manufacturing investment."

Contract Manufacturing, Yuandanhuo, and Counterfeiting

Before China became the world's factory in the late twentieth and early twenty-first centuries, many factories in Hong Kong and Taiwan worked as contract manufacturers for fashion-brand owners in the United States and Europe (Hamilton and Kao 2018; Rigger 2021; Thomas 2007; van Kemenade 1997; K. Zhang 2006). As reported by business professors Benito Arruñada and Xosé H. Vázquez (2006, 2), there are many advantages to outsourcing manufacturing for original equipment manufacturers (OEMs):

> Outsourcing the entire manufacturing of a product allows original equipment manufacturers (OEMs) to reduce labor costs, free up capital, and improve worker productivity. OEMs can then concentrate on the things that most enhance a product's value—R&D, design, and marketing, for instance. . . . Contract manufacturing involves outsourcing an entire manufacturing process to the point where, in many instances, none of an OEM's employees will have physically touched the product they are marketing and selling. The practice began in 1981, with the manufacture of the first IBM PCs, but a decade passed before it reached such everyday products as toys, clothing, footwear, beer, and pharmaceuticals.

Taiwan, especially the city of Taichung, was the home base of major contract manufacturers working for American shoe companies (Wu 2019). However, when contract manufacturers in Hong Kong and Taiwan became alarmed by the increased production costs in their territories, they decided that moving their factories to China was the best option (Hamilton and Kao 2018).

Before the development of contract manufacturing in China, if local consumers wanted foreign products, their only option was to find them on the black market after the goods were smuggled into China. Many seaports along the southern coast became major centers for all kinds of goods smug-gled into China (Gewirtz 2022; Muscolino 2013). The appearance in China of many contract manufacturers owned by businesspeople from Taiwan and Hong Kong had a major impact on the development of the counterfeiting industry. According to Chinese regulations, all the goods produced by the contract manufacturers in China hired by Western brand owners had to be exported out of China without going through formal export-import proce-dures (Vogel 2013). Due to the strong demand for foreign products, yuan-danhuo (factory overruns) began to appear in the local markets. Yuandan-huo, literally "original order goods," applies to any branded product produced by workers from a contract manufacturer using authentic materials and accessories. Xiao Peng (G8), a Wenzhounese clothing business owner, ex-plained how this happened:

> The counterfeiting of ready-to-wear apparel started in China more than fifteen years ago. At that time, many foreign luxury fashion houses came to China because it was much cheaper to produce their garments here. They found out that there were many contract man-ufacturers and fabric suppliers in Guangzhou and Dongguan, so they outsourced their production to China. Contract manufacturers normally produce a different amount of garments than stipulated by the contract; they will produce more. For example, if the order is for 5,000 pieces, the manufacturer will make 6,000 pieces, simply be-cause there will be pieces rejected by inspectors working for the brand owners. After the required 5,000 pieces are delivered, the pro-ducer will sell the remaining garments, including the rejects, for a low price; this is just to recover the production cost because they have already made money from the deal with the brand owners. Before they sell the leftover merchandise, they will cut out the neck labels.

Chen Jian (H5), a leather handbag counterfeiter, explained why there was at one point such a strong demand for yuandanhuo in China:

> At that time, the smuggling of foreign goods was rampant, and that was how many goods entered China from abroad. Local people came into contact with foreign goods for the first time and thought prod-ucts from abroad were of good quality. Later, name-brand owners from abroad began outsourcing their production to China. The con-tract manufacturers here often produce more than the order simply because they have extra raw materials. Why not, right? As a result,

these surplus goods began to appear on the market, and Chinese consumers were particularly fond of these so-called yuandanhuo.

This same point was also made by John (F3), a former manager of a Taiwanese contract manufacturer in Houjie, Dongguan:

> As a contract manufacturer, it is impossible for us to make 10,000 pairs of shoes simply because the contract between us and a brand owner calls for producing this number of shoes. What if two pairs out of the 10,000 are damaged? You cannot ask the brand owner to just take the 9,998 pairs that passed inspection. It is also not possible to restart the assembly line. That is why we always produce more, like 10,200 pairs. Of course, the extra shoes might end up in the local markets. Most well-established brands will buy the extras from their contract manufacturers after the season, and then they will destroy them or sell them at a discount to outlet stores in the United States. Small brands, on the other hand, do not care much about the extra goods. They let the contract manufacturers do whatever they want with the extras.

In addition to the nondefective extras, defective goods might also circulate in the local markets. In fact, according to Xiao Yuen (G12), a forty-nine-year-old apparel entrepreneur from Yunnan Province, "At the very beginning, the branded goods available in the local markets were mostly defective originals. Take Calvin Klein, for example. Their inspectors were stringent; they would not accept any garments with minor defects. As a result, many of the garments rejected by them ended up in the local markets."

When local consumers discovered that yuandanhuo, regardless of whether they were extras or rejects, were affordable and of good quality, the demand for them exploded. When the demand far exceeded the supply, some contract manufacturers began to produce more than the order to satisfy the local demand. At the same time, people who were not contract manufacturers also began to enter the counterfeiting business. According to Xiao Peng (G8):

> After Chinese consumers bought these leftover garments and wore them, they were impressed. Ralph Lauren clothing was one of the brands. Consumers who bought these leftover garments thought they were gorgeous, comfortable, and superb. That was how Chinese people came to appreciate the value of foreign brand apparel. Because of the high demand, some contract manufacturers began to overproduce just to sell the merchandise in the local markets later on. In the meantime, some garment distributors also began to enter the coun-

terfeiting business. They bought fabrics from suppliers and asked manufacturers to make counterfeit garments.

John (F3) said quality-control workers were responsible for the initial flow of extras from contract manufacturers to the local markets, especially in the sneaker industry, and explained how that resulted in the development of the counterfeiting industry later on:

> Initially, QC [Quality Control] guys asked contract manufacturers to give them a few pairs of free shoes. They then turned around and sold those shoes to retailers. When the people here bought the shoes and found out they were of high quality, the demand for yuandanhuo increased dramatically. Soon, more than the shoes generated by the QC guys were needed to meet the increasing demand for yuandan sneakers, and that's how counterfeiting of name-brand shoes started.

Ah Ting (G22), a thirty-five-year-old garment distributor, provided another explanation for how the switch from extras to copies took place. Unlike Xiao Peng (G8), who said businesspeople who were not in contract manufacturing—such as distributors—seized the opportunity to produce fakes, Ah Ting argued that workers for the contract manufacturers were the ones who were producing counterfeits without the knowledge of their employers. These workers later became key players in expanding the counterfeiting industry:

> It all started with the outflow of defective goods from the contract manufacturers. Initially, the contract manufacturers put the faulty goods in their warehouses. Only later did they sell these goods on the market for a cheap price because they thought throwing them away would be a waste. People who bought these goods did not know anything about name brands; they bought them because they were cheap. However, they later discovered that these goods were of high quality, and thus a strong demand emerged. That was why some workers began to produce these goods in secret. They worked for the contract manufacturers during the daytime, but at night, these same workers would be producing the same items in the same factory using the same raw materials. They did that until name-brand owners stopped their outsourcing in China. When that happened, those who used to work in the contract manufacturing factories set up their own factories.

In sum, people in China went through about four decades of economic hardship after the Communists came to power in 1949. During that period, they were accustomed to wearing Soviet fashions or military clothing and using mainly local products (Gerth 2020). Once they had a chance to come into contact with foreign fashion and goods, in the late 1980s, that were either contraband or factory overruns, they were impressed. As a result, a supply chain for anything foreign was rapidly developed to meet that demand.

The Rapid Development of Counterfeiting

According to my research subjects, the counterfeiting of luxury fashions and accessories had already started in China by the 1990s. However, because the counterfeiters did not have the technology, the trade was not well developed. The market for counterfeits was small. China became a member of the WTO in 2001 after fifteen years of negotiations (Boden 2012; Friedberg 2022; Nylander 2020; Shirk 2022). Once China joined the WTO, many Western firms entered the Chinese market (Boden 2012; Harney 2009). As reported by Thomas (2007, 197–202), even though some name brands, such as Coach, had arrived in China before 2001, the accession of China to the WTO prompted other leather goods firms to follow suit:

> Yes, luxury handbags are made in China. Top brands. Brands that you carry. Brands that deny outright that their bags are made in China make their bags in China, not in Italy, not in France, not in the United Kingdom. The change came in the mid-1990s when Coach decided to move a small portion of its production from the United States to China. . . . Emboldened by Coach's trailblazing success, other luxury brands quietly began to look into producing leather goods in China. . . . The small Italian leather goods firm Furla said it began to produce some of its wallets and handbags in China in 2002. . . . Celine produced its denim and leather Macadam handbags the following year [2005]. . . . Prada had already been producing leather goods in China [in 2004].

In addition to leather accessories, the counterfeiting of footwear took off after China acceded to the WTO, primarily with the copying of New Balance shoes. Mr. Tian (F2), a supervisor of a contract manufacturer in Houjie, said:

> Counterfeiting of shoes started in 2003, even though contract manufacturing of foreign-brand shoes in China had begun in the 1990s. During that time [the 1990s], many Taiwanese-owned shoe factories that had been contract manufacturers for Western shoe companies in Taiwan began to operate in the Pearl River Delta area. They came to China when the country embarked on the economic reform and opening up policy because labor was cheap here. . . . When the copy-

ing of name-brand shoes started in China in 2003, New Balance was the number one target for counterfeiting. NB shoe styles or samples could be used for many years because they remained the same, and that is why many people here copied them. Besides, NB shoes looked great and were simple, and comfortable.

Before long, the counterfeiting of global brand products became a formidable industry in China (Thomas 2007). When Western brand owners became aware of the problem, they began to prevent counterfeiters from accessing the materials for producing their merchandise. Jane (G1), a Taiwan-born fashion entrepreneur, explained how important it was to get one's hands on genuine materials so that one could produce high-quality counterfeit goods:

> When brand owners came to China looking for contract manufacturers, they were not careful. Foreigners from Europe and the U.S. were naive. They did not control who could access the raw materials and allowed contract manufacturers to source the raw materials in China. This was why the contract manufacturers could produce above and beyond their orders without the knowledge of the brand owners. The manufacturers produced for the brand owners during the daytime, and for themselves at night. Only after the brand owners found out that their products were circulating in the underground market did they begin to control the flow of raw materials. It started with the control of the fabrics, and later this practice was also applied to all kinds of raw materials and metal fittings.

Xiao Yuen (G12) recalled how some brands tried to prevent counterfeiting by using only imported materials and were very strict with the amount of materials they would provide: "Name brand owners were very good at controlling raw materials. For example, they might import all the manufacturing materials from overseas and would give you only the exact amount of materials to meet the required quota." As an alternative, some name-brand owners would designate a small number of local suppliers for raw materials. According to Xiao Yuen, if the raw materials were produced in China, counterfeiters like him would have a better chance of acquiring the materials.

Besides using only imported materials and providing manufacturers with the exact amount of material for a particular order, brand owners might destroy any defective goods to prevent them from being sold on the underground market. According to Xiao Peng (G8):

> After a brand owner picks up the finished goods from a producer, he will cut the neck label into two and cut the whole garment into piec-

es, so that the extra garments will not enter the market. Nike and Adidas also began to punch a hole in leftover or defective shoes so that these shoes would be treated as trash. To their surprise, Chinese manufacturers were brilliant. They filled in the holes and sold the shoes. When customers saw filled-in holes in a pair of shoes, they knew that the shoes were yuandan goods produced by a contract manufacturer.

Regardless of what brand owners did to prevent the flow of unauthorized merchandise, once the demand and supply for these goods gained momentum in China, it was almost impossible for foreign firms or the Chinese authorities to stop it. Not only that, but the counterfeiting industry, like many other legitimate businesses in China at that time, also began to transform itself into a sophisticated business, providing high-quality point-by-point counterfeits as well as less exact look-alikes to increasingly demanding and diverse customers.

From Ordinary Imitation Goods to High-Quality Counterfeits

According to my research participants, the counterfeits produced in China were initially intended for local consumers. Local demand for counterfeits emerged because the extras or defective goods from contract manufacturers could not satisfy the needs of the Chinese consumers. However, as the counterfeiting industry began to expand, globalization, especially what the anthropologist Gordon Mathews and his colleagues (2017) called "low-end globalization," occurred when there was a corresponding demand for Chinese counterfeits in some African countries and the former Soviet Union. Before 2008, fangmaopin (ordinary imitation goods) were mass-produced to meet foreign demand. However, foreign demand for Chinese counterfeits began to shrink after the 2008 financial crisis. This coincided with the expansion of local demand for gaofangpin (high-quality counterfeits), and there was a significant change in the direction of the counterfeiting industry in China as it shifted from fangmaopin to gaofangpin. John (F3), a former shoe factory manager who was my high school classmate when we were in Taiwan, explained:

> You have to differentiate fangmaopin from gaofanghuo. Fangmaopin means someone copies brand name shoes haphazardly; that is, the two products look similar, but the raw materials are different, plus the workmanship for fangmaopin could be better. Fangmao was the norm in the past. Now, it is gaofang. Not only are the raw materials the same as in the original, but the workmanship is also very high, and

there is little difference between gaofangpin and the original. People do not buy fangmaopin anymore; they only want gaofangpin.[1]

Xiao Ma (H4), a leather supplier who was born in China but grew up in Hong Kong, described a similar change in the counterfeiting of leather handbags:

Initially, buyers expected little when they purchased counterfeit leather handbags. Later, as more and more people began to travel overseas and more authentic luxury goods appeared in China, customers began to demand that counterfeit bags be yibiyi (one-to-one) copies. If they weren't, it would be embarrassing if the counterfeit bag a person was carrying was recognized as a fake. At any rate, counterfeiters began to make sure the leather was very similar to, or the same as, the original. In the beginning, they imported the leather from abroad; later, they produced it in China. As long as there is a strong demand for a specific type of leather, there will be someone in China who will produce it.

Ah Bao (F12), a worker at Xiao Ma's shoe leather business, stressed that there are ordinary fakes ("fake fakes") and high-quality fakes ("real fakes") in the world of counterfeiting:

There are two kinds of counterfeit businesses. One is ordinary and copies the original's style. The materials used in the manufacture of these fakes are not the same as those used for the genuine products. The two only look alike. The second type of fake is a high-quality imitation. It is a one-to-one replica; the manufacturing materials are the same as the original, and the quality of the fake is excellent.

Xiao Qin (H16), a thirty-three-year-old handbag merchant, recalled how this transformation from fangmao to gaofang occurred when the center of leather handbag counterfeiting was moved from Shenzhen to Guangzhou. The shift was prompted by the enhanced anti-counterfeiting enforcement in Shenzhen and the decline of Louhu Commercial City, the city's fake goods distribution center:

In the past, imitators could copy by examining the photo of the original bag. As long as the copy looked similar to the original, it was good enough. Even if the copy was far from being a look-alike, once a Chanel or Louis Vuitton label was affixed to the bag, people bought it, regardless of how poorly it was made. Among those who moved to Guangzhou from Shenzhen was a business owner who had been active in Shenzhen for ten years. This man was the first to buy an authentic bag, dismantle it, and copy it. At that time, Celine was making its first appearance in the Hong Kong market. There were Celine advertisements all over Hong Kong, which inspired the man to copy Celine bags. He decided to invest some money in buying an authentic Celine bag before he copied it. It was a major investment; it cost him thousands of dollars. After this gentleman took apart an actual Celine bag and studied the structure and the parts carefully, he came up with a perfect fake Celine bag. Once the fake bags came out, they were a hit. That also brought the quality of counterfeit handbags to a new level. The copies were very close to the original; they used the same leather, metal fittings, and materials as the originals. I immediately bought one of his bags, disassembled it, and copied it. I lowered the price for my bags to beat him out. Let us say he sold his bags for $173, I sold mine for $115. My cost was only $43, and I was content with making $72 per bag. Many other people also copied his Celine bags, so we dragged him down. It did not matter to him because I heard that he had already made $29 million from copying the Celine bags.[2]

Xiao Qin's interview suggests the coexistence of ordinary and high-quality imitations. When someone is involved in high-quality imitation, there is always the possibility that another person will imitate the goods produced by the high-quality imitator (Zaichkowsky 2006). In essence, there was not a complete shift from ordinary to high-quality imitation but a development of a bifurcated counterfeiting industry, where two or more levels of counterfeiting exist side by side to meet the different demands for quality in local and foreign markets.

There are no reliable statistics for the size of local versus overseas markets for China-made counterfeits. A shoe counterfeiter in Dongguan believed that for every two pairs of fake sneakers produced in China, one pair was for the Chinese market and one was for the overseas market. However, according to Peter (G7), a clothing merchant, the Chinese market for counterfeit fashion, fueled by the demand from the large number of sex workers who want to look glamorous but cannot afford the original garments, is much bigger than the overseas market. But it is clear that the local demand for counterfeit luxury goods has continued to grow.

There is also the question of whether there was a corresponding shift from ordinary brands to luxury brands as the counterfeiting industry moved from ordinary to high-quality imitation and from overseas markets to local markets. According to some of my research subjects, this did happen. Xiao Yuen (G12), a fashion business owner, has this to say about his experience:

"When we began to be involved in the counterfeiting of apparel, we were not copying designer brands. We were copying brands like Lee, Levi's, and Tommy Hilfiger, and they were not considered name brands in the United States, even though they were treated as name brands in China. These brands are not copied here anymore, although maybe some people are still copying Levi's jeans." Danny (H3), a leather handbag manufacturer in Dongguan, said: "In China, at one point, many people were copying Coach products, but gradually they stopped because customers here began to buy genuine Coach products. Coach products are not that expensive, so they are affordable for many people here." Chinese consumers often identify international brands as first tier or second tier. According to one source, brands such as Bally, Prada, Burberry, and Miu Miu are considered first tier, and Coach, Tory Burch, and Michael Kors are treated as second tier or light luxury. Ling Jiang and Veronica Cova (2012), business school professors, have observed that the most desirable brands for Chinese consumers are Louis Vuitton, Gucci, and Burberry. Regardless of shifts in demand, in general, at the very beginning, most counterfeits were of American brands because they entered China first after China's economic reform. In sum, by the 2010s, after several stages of evolution, the counterfeiting of luxury goods in China had developed into a large-scale industry.

Types of Trademark Violations

In Chapter 1, I briefly discussed the meaning of counterfeiting as we know it in the West and the differences between deceptive versus nondeceptive counterfeiting. However, it is essential to note that there are many types of trademark violations. My research subjects and key informants in Guangzhou and other parts of China suggested four types of activities in the "counterfeiting" trade. Those four types are explained in the following list, and the similarities and differences among them in terms of their level of imitation of the style and trademark of the original product are summarized in Table 2.1.

1. Yibiyi (one-to-one or point-by-point) counterfeiting: the counterfeit product is almost the same as the original, including trademark, logo, style, materials, metal fittings, and packaging. It could be ordinary or high quality, deceptive or nondeceptive, but, if the item is traded in China in physical markets, it will likely be nondeceptive: buyers will know they are buying an exact copy. Regardless of whether a buyer is deceived, it is illegal in China to produce and distribute one-to-one copies.
2. Cabianqiu (edge-ball) infringement: a product is not the same as the original, but the label, the logo, and the elements are very similar to the original. My research subjects called this type of activ-

TABLE 2.1. A CONTINUUM OF BRAND IMITATIONS

Type of Brand Imitation	Similar Style?	Similar Trademark?
yibiyi (one-to-one or point-by-point) counterfeit	Yes, identical.	Yes, identical.
cabianqiu (edge ball) infringement	Yes, but approximate.	Yes, but approximate.
shanzhai (knockoff)	Yes, but the product can be quite different from the original.	No, the product has its own brand.
fayangguangda (supplemental copying)	No, the imitated brand does not produce merchandise in this style.	Yes, identical.

ity cabianqiu, meaning "hitting an edge ball." In table tennis, a popular sport in China, hitting an edge ball means a player hits a ball that touches the edge of the table and changes direction so that the other player cannot return it. In real life, hitting an edge ball means doing something the legality of which is hard to determine and, therefore, connotes operating in a gray area. According to Kal Raustiala and Christopher Jon Sprigman (2012, 36), these products are derivative works, "Designs that are inspired by the original, but which add some new creative elements." Most buyers of infringing products are aware that these products are not originals. Infringers are trying to protect themselves from the authorities and do not set out to confuse buyers. Infringement is not illegal in China; however, when there is a major crackdown on counterfeiting, people who are involved in this type of activity may also be targeted.

3. Shanzhai (knockoff): a product that is similar to merchandise produced by a well-established brand but has its own label and logo. It is highly unlikely that consumers will be confused between a knockoff and an authentic product. Producing knockoffs is not considered trademark infringement, and it is legal in China. Shanzhai is probably China's most pervasive type of counterfeiting.

4. Fayangguangda (supplemental copying): the literal translation of fayangguangda is "to sustain and expand something good." In the counterfeiting business, to engage in fayangguangda is to take a brand, manufacture a variety of products that are unrelated to the brand, and affix to them the trademark or logo of the brand, even though the brand itself does not produce such products (Zaichkowsky 2006). This is illegal in China and likely to be the least prevalent form of counterfeiting in China.

In this section, I examine these four types of counterfeiting, even though differentiating among them is not always easy. More than forty years ago, in a *New York Times Magazine* article titled "The Big Couture Rip-Off," Susan Heller Anderson (1981) pointed out that there were many forms of counterfeiting, ranging from "out-and-out reproduction of the total product and its labels to the copying of just a signature or initials to simply slapping designers' names on items with which they have never had any association." She also stated that "counterfeiters often change name spellings by a letter to two, counting on the similar look of the lettering to carry an association with the real thing." Since Anderson was writing about the counterfeiting of luxury goods in countries like Italy, Taiwan, South Korea, and Hong Kong more than four decades ago, it is clear that yibiyi (one-to-one reproduction of the total product and its labels), cabianqiu (changing name spellings by a letter or two), and fayangguangda (slapping designers' names on items unassociated with them) are counterfeiting activities that had existed for a long time before China became a dominant player in the counterfeiting business. She did not refer to shanzhai (knockoff).

Yibiyi (One-to-One or Point-by-Point) Copying

Of the different types of trademark violations, yibiyi, or one-to-one, copying is the most often discussed activity and the most likely to draw the attention of brand owners and law enforcement authorities. According to Andrew Mertha (2005, 168), a political scientist, it is essential to differentiate between counterfeiting and infringement:

> There are two general types of trademark violation: counterfeiting and infringement. . . . The rule of thumb in distinguishing the two is that a counterfeit is indistinguishable from its legitimate counterpart, at least as far as the outside packaging is concerned. A trademark-infringing good has outside packaging that is intended to confuse the consumer into thinking that it is a legitimate product; it is similar, but not identical, to the latter.

A yibiyi product, also known as a "genuine fake," is a 100 percent direct copy of a luxury-brand good (Jiang and Shan 2016) and is certainly indistinguishable from its original. We can say yibiyi is counterfeiting, but we also need to keep in mind that, under most circumstances, yibiyi products are marketed as fakes and no deception is involved. A small percentage of yibiyi goods, especially those of exceptionally high quality, might be sold as genuine articles through e-commerce platforms (Zuccaro 2016).

Not all one-to-one fakes are of high quality. According to Jane (G1), there are different qualities of counterfeit products for different markets, selling for different prices:

There are different levels of counterfeiting. Counterfeit leather handbags can be categorized into various classes: Super A, AA, A, B, C, and D. Super A–class handbags come from two sources. First, "originals" from a contract manufacturer. For example, a name brand owner asks a contract manufacturer to produce 1,000 handbags. The manufacturer makes an additional 200 in private without the brand owner's knowledge and sells them. Second, Super A–class handbags are produced by a manufacturer who has no working relationship with a brand owner. The materials are the same as the genuine, and these items all have a barcode. Super A–class handbags typically sell for up to $1,000. AA-class handbags usually go for more than $150, and A-class handbags for between $80 and $150. The price of B-class handbags is between $30 and $80. C- and D-class handbags, in general, cost less than $30. Exported counterfeit handbags are mostly B, C, and D classes, with some A-class in the mix. There are few Super A and AA-grade handbags in the market because only a few people can afford to buy them. That is why the market for these two classes of handbags is small.

Other research subjects did not come up with such a meticulous grading for exact copies. For them, point-by-point fakes are either ordinary or high quality. Laoban (G2), a Taiwanese fashion business owner, remarked: "Yibiyi goods can be categorized into shichanghuo (market goods) and gaofanghuo (high-quality imitations). It is much more difficult to produce high-quality imitations, especially when these items require special or hard-to-make fabrics or other materials. The market for high-end fakes is not big." It is important to note that Laoban's shichanghuo is essentially the same as fangmaopin (ordinary imitation goods). Even though Laoban divided yibiyi fakes into market and high-quality goods, not all market goods are of the same quality. The same is true with high-quality replicas. During my fieldwork in Guangzhou and other cities, I noted that a 25 in. Hermès Birkin handbag sold for many different prices, from a high of more than $1,440 in a store in Baiyun Leather City to $30 in a stall inside the Yisen Leather Market, which is located across the street from Baiyun Leather City. The handbag in Yisen was made of PVC, not leather. Other stores were selling 25 in. Hermès Birkin bags for prices that ranged from $144 to $870.

Laoban (G2) also revealed how the manufacturers of market goods and high-quality goods differ when it comes to "brand loyalty," that is, deciding which and how many brands to copy: "Those who manufacture market goods produce things that are popular in a particular season, regardless of what brand these popular items belong to. High-quality goods producers are different; they specialize in one or two brands and stick with them for a long time. They will not shift to another brand simply because that brand is trendy."

Xiao Ma (H4) described how some handbag makers worked very hard to produce high-quality fakes:

> Some authentic designer handbags are made of exquisite leather. As a result, those involved in the high-end counterfeit business will go all out to find the same leather that is used to make the originals. To do so, they must locate the supplier of the sought-after leather and offer the supplier double the amount for it. All suppliers are going to accept this type of offer. After all, the supplier is a businessman whose main objective is to make money. If the counterfeiter can get ahold of the authentic leather, his handbag can be better than the genuine one. The counterfeiter may also spend more than $43 just for the metal fittings and hire the best artisans to ensure the handcraft is as good as on the real one. That is why the counterfeiter dares to sell his handbag for $1,440. Remember, the real one will cost $9,800 to $10,130, so $1,440 for a really good fake is worth it.

The business school professors Ling Jiang and Juan Shan (2018, 184) comment that, after years of development and improvement, counterfeits from China are not limited to shoddy goods: "The outsourcing of manufacturing technology and the advent of new technologies have greatly improved the quality of counterfeits. Because many of the genuine luxury brands are outsourced to manufacturers in China, some Chinese counterfeiters argue that the products are 'real copies' that are produced by the same factories that have contracts with genuine luxury brands."

Consequently, some of the high-quality counterfeits produced in China, also known as "supercopies" (Naim 2005), may be marketed as genuine articles by unscrupulous sellers. Lau Fang (G21), owner of an apparel business, said: "Nowadays, you can find high-quality, one-to-one copies in Hong Kong that are made in China, and counterfeiters are selling these fakes as originals."

Regardless of whether high-quality counterfeits are marketed as genuine or fake, the market for these goods is relatively small, according to most of my research subjects. Lau Fang (G21) commented, "In terms of business volume, yibiyi counterfeiting is not high, but the demand for these goods is always there."

Cabianqiu (Edge-Ball) Infringement

The second type of imitation is called cabianqiu or "playing edge ball." According to Minghuan Li (2012, 207), a professor in China:

In Chinese, "playing edge ball" is a popular saying meaning an activity intended to challenge the existing rules and avoid punishment. Originally, "edge ball" was a term used in table tennis. If the on-coming ball hit only the edge of the tabletop, it would be almost impossible for the receiver to return the ball; thus the player who successfully hit the edge ball would win the point. It is a great challenge to both hit and receive an edge ball. Therefore, the term "playing edge ball" is often used to connote people who try to gain a profit at the edge of the law or regulation while avoiding punishment.

In his research on the out-migration of Chinese nationals, M. Li (2012) explains how illegal-labor export agencies in China have adopted the tactic of playing edge ball to evade the exit control of Chinese authorities. In my study on the smuggling of Chinese nationals to the United States, I also found that many human smugglers were good at playing edge ball in the process of clandestinely moving undocumented migrants overseas (K. Chin 1999). In fact, playing edge ball is a practice widely used in China for people from all walks of life, referring to any act that cannot be categorized as clearly legal or illegal. In the counterfeiting industry, instead of copying an original point by point and affixing the exact trademark of the original on the copy, a producer duplicates the style of the original but not its trademark. However, to make the product appealing, the producer will apply a trademark very similar to that on the authentic good. This way, the producer can claim that he is not involved in counterfeiting. Jane (G1) explained with a smile: "Playing edge ball is what we in this business call 'teeth clenching and grinding' counterfeiting. This is because brand owners cannot do anything about these activities even if they are upset. These activities do not break the trademark law." There is also the possibility that a producer may duplicate an original's style and logo, but not the label. In a meeting at his office, Zhao Zong (G14), an owner of an apparel business, explained how he played edge ball:

All my garments have my label; I only borrow the styles and logos of various name brands. [He got up, walked over to a rack, pulled out three men's T-shirts, and showed them to me. Each garment had the word Burberry, Balenciaga, or Moncler labels prominently displayed across the chest.] Look at these garments I made. The fabrics are excellent, just like the fabrics of the genuine products. Also, the styles, the symbols, and the trademarks are all the same, except that the neck label bears my company's name. This is called "playing edge ball," which will not be a problem. I even use my brand on the hangtag. When we mass-produce these garments, we spell the name of the luxury brand incorrectly by replacing one letter of the alphabet with another. Balenciaga will become Belanciaga, and Moncler, Mancler. It is done intentionally, and this is again "playing edge ball." This way, there will be no problem.

Ah Lan (G18), a twenty-eight-year-old designer who once worked for Laoban, told me how Laoban engaged in infringement when she was working for him: "When I was with Laoban, he did not do yibiyi; he did not copy name-brand garments point by point. He designed T-shirts and polo shirts with elements of foreign brands, and he also used the logos of name brands, like Dior's Little Bee. However, the logos were slightly altered."

Ah Min (G5), a woman from Taizhou, Zhejiang, also played edge ball. When I visited her store in Kinbo Market, I saw hundreds of men's T-shirts and polo shirts on display. Her garments, produced in her brother's factory, are considered high end and have the logos, trademarks, and elements of name brands such as Chanel, Burberry, and Moncler. However, all her garments have neck labels with her own brands. Moreover, on closer look, one will notice that the name on the right side of the chest was Burberrys—an extra "s" was discreetly added to the original brand name Burberry. Most people would not have noticed the "s" placed at the end of the brand name.

In sum, playing edge ball, or trademark infringement, is one way for entrepreneurs in the counterfeit trade to "legitimize" their business activities and evade law enforcement authorities. Mr. Han (G9), a sixty-five-year-old Taiwanese in Humen who was in the business of shipping apparel from China to Taiwan, jokingly remarked how copycats are very good at imitating name brands: "As far as counterfeiting is concerned, you can say there are so many ways to copy something. Take the logo of Ralph Lauren polo shirts, for example. Some copies have a player carrying the polo mallet with the right hand, some with the left hand, and some carry a small flag instead of a mallet. The same is true with that brand with the crocodile logo. The crocodiles on some copies have their mouths open, some closed, some have their tails up, and some down. No matter what, everybody was hitting edge ball." However, as mentioned earlier, this evasive tactic may or may not protect a business owner from police crackdowns, mainly because there is a thin line between outright counterfeiting and infringement.

Shanzhai (Knockoff)

The third type of imitation is the so-called shanzhai (knockoff). According to Jason Carpenter and Karen Lear (2011, 1), "An item that bears a brand name or logo without the permission of the registered owner is counterfeit, or 'fake.' . . . Unlike counterfeits, the production and sale of 'knockoffs' or 'imitations,' which may look identical to designer originals but do not bear the brand name or logo of another owner, does not violate U.S. law." Raustiala and Sprigman (2012, 5) also comment, "Fashion trademarks are fiercely policed; it is illegal to copy brand names such as Gucci or Marc Jacobs, and expensive lawyers aggressively sue those who try. But the underlying clothing designs can be copied at will."

In China, the word shanzhai is widely used. In her book, *Fake Stuff: China and the Rise of Counterfeit Goods*, the anthropologist Jessica Lin (2011, 13) notes that shanzhai "literally refers to 'mountain fortress' and figuratively refers to bandits in mountain hideaways taking potshots at the established giants in Robin Hood fashion." In a sense, designing, producing, or distributing shanzhai goods is a way for small business owners to jump-start their businesses by being creative and innovative in the process of following in the footsteps of well-established business empires and not breaking any laws. In the same sense, for the poor and the underprivileged, buying and consuming shanzhai goods is a way to show their determination to possess and enjoy things that they usually would not be able to afford. In a country where there are still hundreds of millions of people with modest incomes, the shanzhai phenomenon is much more than the mere production or consumption of goods that resemble name-brand luxury goods. It is a mentality, an attitude, a defiance deeply embedded in the minds of large numbers of people struggling to make ends meet.

Shanzhai entrepreneurs are good not only at copying but also at making their products much more functional than the originals (Beebe 2015). According to Jiang and Shan (2016, 182), "Similar to counterfeit goods, Shanzhai products attract consumers with inexpensive pricing; unlike counterfeit goods, however, Shanzhai products provide interesting additional features through imitation and local innovation. In addition, Shanzhai products are usually sold under another brand name, thus considered legal under trademark laws, at least to some extent." The same points about similarity and legality are observed by Colleen Jordan Orscheln (2015, 254), as he comments: "A knockoff is a good that is similar in design to another good, and the similarity is so apparent that it is evident what item the knockoff is copying. Knockoffs are not protected underneath trademark infringement laws, as currently most fashion designs are unable to be trademarked."

One example of a successful shanzhai business is Xiaomi, a cell phone manufacturing company founded in Beijing in 2010. Xiaomi phones are very similar in style and function to Apple's iPhone. Affordable and reliable, Xiaomi phones have become a good option for many young people in China who cannot afford a genuine iPhone. After establishing itself in China, Xiaomi quickly expanded its overseas markets, and its cell phones became iconic for customers in many countries (Tabassum and Ahmed 2020). In 2021, Xiaomi became the second-largest manufacturer of smartphones in the world, behind Samsung, surpassing Apple (Dean 2021). In December 2023, Xiaomi entered the electric vehicle industry by introducing its first car, the Xiaomi SU7 (starting at $30,000). The car became an instant hit in China, even though it was considered to be a copy of the Porsche (called Baoshijie in China) Taycan (starting at $90,000). Chinese netizens jokingly called the SU7 a Mische (Mishijie).

Fayangguangda (Supplemental Copying)

Fayangguangda (literally, to foster and enhance) and cabianqiu (playing edge ball) are different. The former means manufacturing luxury goods that are neither designed nor produced by a name brand but applying a name brand's trademark and logo to the goods. Legally, it is a form of counterfeiting, also called "fake fakes." Laoban (G2) reiterated that there is no patent for apparel design and that only trademarks are protected. He was active in designing, producing, and distributing men's T-shirts or polo shirts, imitating the products of Armani, Ralph Lauren, and Dior. At one point, he devoted most of his time to designing and producing fayangguangda products that these name brands did not produce. He just attached the brand labels to his finished goods. He explained:

> It means a person designs and develops his own products, puts a name brand's trademark on them, and sells them like hotcakes. Take Armani, for example. Every summer, it markets only about ten different styles of men's T-shirts, but clothing manufacturers here may design more than a hundred styles. Some resemble the originals, some are newly designed and developed, but all of them are branded with Armani labels. Of these more than one hundred styles, the best-selling style could be the one that is an entirely new design that is very different from any of the ten originals. This was my experience.

Compared to the markets for point-by-point, edge ball, and knockoff products, the market for fayangguangda goods is small, and few entrepreneurs are involved.

3

Design and Production

In this chapter, I examine the first stage of counterfeiting: design and production. According to the anthropologist Sara Liao, there are four crucial moments in the production chain of knockoff fashions: "The first moment is sorting through and selecting images and looks for an item to be copied. The second moment is about purchasing the identified original product. While the third moment focuses on in-house production, the fourth moment of feedback creates a circuit back to the first moment where women designers can again initiate reproduction or a new round of selection-purchase-copying/production-distribution" (Liao 2020, 59). Production may or may not involve designing, depending on the type of imitation. Point-by-point copying typically does not need designing, whereas trademark infringing or playing edge ball requires a designer to create a product similar to the original but not an exact duplicate. Nevertheless, some of my research subjects engaging in the production of point-by-point garments said they had "designers" in their firms who were responsible for the "development" of various products. I explain this later in this chapter.

It is hard to categorize the many people who participate in a replica design and production because many roles overlap. Even so, based on my data, I focus on four groups of people who are critical in the design and production stage: organizers or chief designers, manufacturers, materials suppliers, and facilitators or business associates. An organizer is a business owner who takes the initiative to copy luxury merchandise. He is also most likely to be the chief designer of this fake product. A manufacturer is the person who produces the fake goods. A supplier provides the required materials (leather, fabric, metal fittings, etc.) to the organizer or manufacturer. A facilitator or a business associate provides services to the organizer or manufacturer to complete the production process and prepare the commodity for distribution. Packaging is one such service. A person may simultaneously play the roles of organizer or chief designer, manufacturer, and distributor. However, it is doubtful that the same person would be a materials supplier or a packaging service provider. This will become clear as I examine these many roles.

I want to point out that my research subjects did not call themselves organizers, chief designers, or facilitators. Some identified themselves as manufacturers or leather or fabric suppliers, but the vast majority identified themselves simply as business owners.

Organizers/Designers

In this section, I explore how organizers or designers in Guangzhou and Dongguan take the initiative to copy a luxury-brand product. I focus on how they engage in point-by-point (yibiyi) or edge-ball (cabianqiu) copying because only some of my research subjects were involved in the production of supplemental copying (fayangguangda) or knockoff (shanzhai) goods.

Point-by-Point Counterfeiting

All kinds of name-brand garments are counterfeited in China, including T-shirts, polo shirts, dress shirts, jackets, sweaters, suits, and overcoats. Over the past several years, there has been an explosion in the copying of Canada Goose jackets (Vanderklippe 2018). However, T-shirts and polo shirts for men and women are the garments most frequently counterfeited. The reasons are many. According to Peter (G7), a clothing business owner: "The copying of luxury brand T-shirts is the main activity in apparel counterfeiting because it is easy to duplicate a T-shirt, and the market for T-shirts is the largest fashion market in China. Many people own many T-shirts, and they wear them often. Of course, suits, jackets, and winter coats are also copied, but not as much." Xiao Guan (G13), another garment business owner, said there was a noticeable change in menswear in China in the early 2000s. According to him, "In 2002, many men wore dress shirts and ties. It was considered fashionable at that time. Not long after that, T-shirts and polo shirts became very popular." Ah Xiang (G3), owner of a clothing retail and wholesale store, explained why copying men's and women's T-shirts was popular:

> In China, both men and women buy T-shirts because they are practical. The T-shirt market is vast because a person often owns quite a few. Skirts and formal gowns are less likely to be counterfeited be-

cause the market for them is small. It is relatively easy to counterfeit a T-shirt. Whenever a new T-shirt is released, it will be counterfeited. Once you have an original T-shirt, finding a factory to counterfeit it is not difficult. The fabric is a critical component, but there is an abundance of fabrics in China. Usually, the factory will find the fabrics rather than the person who places the order.

Laoban (G2), a Taiwanese, described how he was engaged in point-by-point copying of men's T-shirts:

> We purchased designer brand men's T-shirts abroad, including Louis Vuitton and Chanel, brought them back to our company in China, and copied them. In our sample room, our patternmaker drew a paper sample based on the original. Only an experienced patternmaker can carry out such an assignment. After the patternmaker prepared the paper sample, he would give it to our sample pattern cutter and machinist [or sample sewer]. There are many things a sample pattern cutter/machinist has to do, and that is why if a piece of garment is complicated, he can only sew one piece a day. The sample pattern cutter would cut the fabric according to the paper sample. After sewing, there would be test trying on and then finalizing the sample. After all the samples for a season were ready, we would organize a meeting with our buyers, and based on order quantities, we would decide how many pieces of a garment to produce. After that, my patternmaker would prepare another paper sample for the factory for mass production. My sample pattern cutter would sew another set of pre-production samples, and sometimes, he would also prepare samples for the dangkou [distribution outlet or store].

Counterfeiters may also buy an original in China. Once, I asked a saleswoman in an Armani store in Guangzhou whether Armani products are being copied, and she replied: "Of course, our products are widely counterfeited. I encounter many buyers in this store who are in the counterfeiting business. But what do I care? I am a salesperson, and the only thing that matters to me is whether the person will buy or not. These people are clever; they always buy something they can wear later and pick garments that fit them. After producing the fake garments, they wear the real ones."

Sonny (H10), a business owner with many years of experience in the leather goods industry, explained how leather handbag counterfeiters decide what to copy and how:

> Well, it is simple. A person in this business will send a half-a-million-dollar prepaid card to a friend in Paris and ask the friend to buy

a handbag once it is released and forward it to him immediately using an express delivery service. The other method is for him to travel overseas, visit many cities, buy as many handbags as possible, and bring them back to China. After he has a handbag he wants to copy, he will ask all the potential suppliers to come over, including those who supply leather, zippers, metal fittings, fabric lining, and other components. At the meeting, they will take apart the handbag, and he will ask all the suppliers whether they can provide the same materials. If the leather supplier says he cannot produce the leather, the counterfeiter will have to find a way to import it. If he has money, he can buy whatever he wants. After the sources for all the materials are arranged, he will find a factory to produce the handbags. Some businesspeople have their own factories, so they do not have to outsource.

I am not sure whether Sonny was exaggerating the amount of money on the prepaid card. However, I am sure he was correct in making the point that counterfeiters in point-by-point copying of luxury-brand leather handbags are very generous in spending money to have name-brand handbags as soon as they are released in Europe. Otherwise, they will not be able to embark on a new business endeavor. Xiao Qin (H16), the owner of a leather handbag business, proudly claimed that "the reason for the booming of the genuine luxury-goods market is because people like us buy half of the products."

Counterfeiters in the footwear industry echoed the sentiments of those in the clothing and handbag businesses. According to Mr. Jin (F14), a forty-eight-year-old man from Jiangsu Province: "Our main activity is copying name-brand shoes. It is simple; go out and buy a pair of name-brand shoes, take a good look, and then duplicate them. If you only have a photo of the shoes, it is hard to copy them because you cannot feel the quality of the materials. The best approach is to have a pair of original shoes in front of you when you copy."

Kenny and Gigi (G23), a couple in Dongguan, offered the most detailed answer on how point-by-point counterfeiters decide what products to copy and how they find the originals of those products to use as samples. They were engaged in copying various luxury fashion goods, including clothing, handbags, footwear, sunglasses, scarves, and cosmetics, but they did not have their own factories. They were online distributors who did not have any brick-and-mortar stores in which to market their products:

> If we want to copy something, we will buy the original first. We spend about $150,000 to $300,000 a year purchasing authentic luxury goods. For our business, we are willing to spend this kind of money.

We paid $1,200 apiece for these two articles of clothing by Gucci. That was because the store required us to buy two pieces at the same time. They are somewhat different. [From a stack of clothes on a sofa behind me, Kenny picked two pink Gucci women's shirts in a simple style.] After we bought them, we discovered that we could not find the same fabric, so we gave up copying them. That is why these garments are lying here. The other reason for not copying something we already bought is because we found out that other people had already copied it.

When we are shopping for the originals, we do so openly. Once we step inside a store, we will ask the sales assistant to bring us a tape measure, and then we will measure the merchandise thoroughly. We will examine it closely, take photos, and then buy it. Because we plan to produce the copies in many sizes, we need to do the measurement in the store. The staff there know why we are buying their goods.

Sometimes when we walk into a luxury goods store, the staff there take one look at us, and they know what kind of business we are engaged in. They will whisper to us, ushering us to go upstairs to a VIP room so that we do not need to shop downstairs with other customers. We often fly to Beijing to shop. Some stores will call us occasionally and ask us why we have not been there for so long. They tell us about new arrivals and urge us to visit them.[1]

People involved in producing ordinary point-by-point or market goods do not need to deconstruct an original (or engage in reverse engineering) to know how to copy it. They say they check the websites of luxury fashion houses to get an idea of what to copy. Jane (G1), a fashion business owner and chief designer from Taiwan, proudly claimed: "When I was a fashion student in Japan, our teacher asked us to go to a store, look at a garment, come back, and make a replica. His purpose was to develop our ability to copy something after a quick look."

Edge-Ball Infringement

Entrepreneurs engaged in point-by-point copying aim to produce a duplicate of an original. Thus, their main activities involve: (1) gaining access to the original and figuring out how to reproduce it, (2) obtaining the same materials as the original or, if that is not possible, finding similar materials, and (3) finding a manufacturer who can not only produce high-quality counterfeits but also be flexible and responsive to market demands. For point-by-point counterfeiters, designing is not critical because not much designing is involved. This is not the case with playing edge ball or engaging in trademark infringement. Infringers, most of whom are also chief designers, pay special attention to design because they have to make a product very similar in style and elements to a name-brand item but not a point-by-point replica. Lin Jun (G17), a clothing business owner from Sichuan Province, said: "When designing a men's T-shirt, we like to mix a few letters from the English alphabet on the chest of the shirt and see how the word looks and feels. We adopt it if we think it is fine, regardless of whether the word has any meaning." He wore a black T-shirt with the word SREAL prominently displayed across the chest.

Lau Fang (G21), a hard-working woman from Jiangxi Province, has a reputation for designing luxury fashions that resemble the style, pattern, color, and other features of global brand products. She has her own brands affixed to all her garments. However, when there is a strong demand for point-by-point products, she can promptly meet the demand by shifting from producing and distributing edge-ball copies to point-by-point reproductions. Ah Lan (G18), one of the three designers working for Lau Fang, said:

> We are now designing T-shirts and polo shirts for next summer. At this moment, I am working on a design mimicking a collection of Gucci T-shirts. The Gucci design has two cats, and the word "Kind" is above the cats, and "Strangers" is beneath them. It is a colorful design with two cartoon characters. I got rid of the cats and replaced them with other characters. I sent the photos with several alternative animals to my boss and our clients and asked them to decide which design they prefer for next year. They selected the design with two hugging Donald Ducks; they are colorful and cartoon-like, like the Gucci cats. The bottom line is that our design is very similar to Gucci's in terms of style and elements. To retain the elements of the original, the English words need to look similar to the original. However, we also intentionally misspell the brand name or turn one of the letters upside down.

Manufacturers

There is no reliable data on what proportion of organizers/designers in the counterfeiting business are also manufacturers. Of the twelve fashion organizers/designers I interviewed, nine were also engaged in manufacturing. However, as mentioned in Chapter 1, my sample is small and nonrandom; it would likely be inaccurate to apply this percentage to the general population of apparel counterfeiters. The data from my fieldwork suggests that it is difficult to tell whether a store owner or distributor produces the goods he or she is selling. Generally, whenever store owners are asked where their goods are from, they will respond, "My factory produces them" or "I have a contract manufacturer," depending on the circumstances and the person who poses the question. Production facilities can be categorized into factories or workshops, depending on the scale of the operation.

Factories

A factory, especially a legitimate one, is a relatively large manufacturing site with hundreds, or even thousands, of workers and a clear division of labor; it is located within a so-called industrial district and has a dormitory for workers. Counterfeit-producing factories can be divided into legitimate and illegitimate factories.

Legitimate Factories

Mertha (2005, 171) reports that "sometimes the production of trademark-violation merchandise takes place in factories that also produce legitimate merchandise. Either these factories sell production overruns illegally or they maximize profits by simply manufacturing the same merchandise for the legal trademark owners and, after hours, for the counterfeiters in 'fly-by-night' operations." Peter (G7) said it is possible to find a legitimate contract manufacturer for luxury-brand owners to do the dirty work, but it is uncommon: "There are two ways to produce counterfeits. One way is to buy the raw materials yourself and then find a small factory to produce for you. The second way is to find the contract manufacturer who works for the brand and ask them to produce for you. Some daring contract manufacturers might be willing to take a chance and do it for you, but it is rare."

Besides asking a contract manufacturer working for an international brand to produce the counterfeits, there is also the option of finding a legitimate factory with no connection to name-brand owners to make copies. According to Mertha (2005, 171), "In most instances, the factories make perfectly legal 'generic' merchandise that violates trademarks only when the offending mark is affixed." According to Xiao Xin (G15), owner of an approximately thirty-five hundred square foot clothing factory, she and her husband were mainly involved in the manufacturing of garments for local brands, but the couple would also occasionally work with customers in the counterfeiting business:

> In general, we do what our customers want us to do. We produce goods that resemble the samples they give us and do not worry about whether we are copying name brands or not. If they want us to put international labels on the garments, we will do so. It all depends on what our customers want. We will not charge our customers more simply

because they ask us to copy international brand merchandise. Our workers prefer copying name brands because, usually, these customers are less demanding than those who own local brands.

Illegitimate Factories

Besides the legitimate factories that are occasionally involved in producing counterfeit goods, there are small factories that are exclusively engaged in counterfeiting. According to Peter (G7), these small factories that make only counterfeit goods are unlikely to simultaneously produce goods that are not counterfeit. This is because, if they do, their involvement in counterfeiting might be discovered. His point is that people in the counterfeiting business will limit their interactions with legitimate businesspeople to minimize the risk of their illegal activity being discovered. However, Mr. Song, a private investigator, rejected this point: "Handbag factories cannot be categorized into those that produce only legitimate goods and those that produce only fake goods. Many regular handbag factories will accept contracts from counterfeiters to produce fake goods if they have no other contracts. The most important thing for them is to ensure their workers have work to do. Besides, they are simply doing what their clients ask them to do."

Ah Xiang (G3), owner of a clothing store, explained how a contract factory produced her counterfeit clothes. Her case supports Mr. Song's point:

> I have a clothing store and deal with a contract factory with which I have a cooperative arrangement. If I want to manufacture something, original or fake, I will ask that factory to produce it. I do not own anything in the factory and am not involved in its operation. This kind of working relationship means I am a preferred customer; the factory will prioritize my orders. If store owners say they own a factory, they are lying. For them, "owning" actually means they have an arrangement with a contract factory. Also, not all store owners have such an arrangement. Only a small number of them do so, and among them, only a tiny percentage have a relationship with a contract factory that is willing and capable of producing counterfeit garments.

I had the opportunity to visit a few factories that were involved in the production of counterfeit goods. Most of these factories were small and rudimentary, with no more than a dozen workers. They were mostly operated by a husband and wife team who were both responsible for finding and negotiating with customers and involved in the day-to-day production activities, working side by side with their workers. These men and women spend almost all their waking hours in their small offices or on their factory floors. An embroidery factory owner, with his wife (and business partner) at his side, complained: "This is a grueling business; my wife and I work seven days a week. We work from early morning until late night; there is very little time to rest."

Working Conditions
There are many manufacturing factories in Guangzhou and the surrounding area, and it is hard to pinpoint where the counterfeiting factories are located. However, it is no secret that most manufacturing factories, regardless of whether they are involved in counterfeiting, are congregated in the Baiyun District. With a population of about 2.7 million, Baiyun is dotted with tens of thousands of factories and a large number of wholesale markets. People who live or work in other districts of Guangzhou have a negative impression of the district. In the next chapter, I explore this district in greater depth when examining the wholesale markets for counterfeits.

According to my research subjects, working conditions at manufacturing factories, legal or not, have improved significantly over the past several years due to labor shortages. Mr. Tian (F2), a Sichuanese supervisor at a well-established Taiwanese-owned shoe factory in Dongguan, explained how things have changed:

> Now, we close on Sundays; if we didn't, our workers would complain. In the past, it did not matter how loudly they protested; now it is a different story. That is because we cannot find enough workers, so we are now more accommodating. Before, they started to work at 8:00 A.M., ate lunch at noon, returned to work at 1:00 P.M., worked until 6:00 P.M., had dinner, and worked until 10:00 P.M. or midnight. When we needed to speed up, we forced them to work until dawn or to work 48 hours nonstop. When we were under pressure to produce, we locked the factory gate and did not allow people to leave.

Mr. Tian's factory is a contract manufacturer for a major U.S. shoe company and employs thousands of workers. Smaller factories in Guangzhou, however, still require their workers to work on Sundays. Lao Su (G24), a forty-nine-year-old manager of a clothing factory, explained his factory's work schedule as follows:

> My factory allows only one day off every month, and that is payday. Every day, we start at 8:00 A.M., eat lunch at noon, resume work at 1:30 P.M., have dinner at 6:00 P.M., return to work at 6:30 P.M., and work until 10:00 P.M. The evening shift is called the "overtime shift," but there is no overtime pay because workers are paid by the piece. Employees in management positions receive a fixed salary, so there

is no overtime pay for them either. On Sundays, we do not have to work after dinner. The dining hall is above the factory; a cook prepares lunch and dinner for about 60 workers. We make men's T-shirts.

A worker for another clothing factory in Guangzhou reiterated what Lao Su said: "Every day, I go to work around 9:30 A.M., eat lunch, and then take a nap between noon and 1:30 P.M., go back to work and have dinner at 6:00 P.M. Dinner time is only 30 minutes. I then work overtime until 10:00 P.M. Even though it is called overtime, there is no overtime pay because we are piece workers. We work seven days a week every week; the only break we have is that we do not have to work overtime on Sundays." Regardless, she thinks workers are treated better now than before: "Employers treat their workers better than they did in the past. That is because it is not easy to find workers anymore. Now, we do not have to pay for our meals and lodging. If a worker does not want to live in the dorm and wants to rent a place elsewhere, he or she will be compensated about $50 a month. Bosses are also much nicer to their workers."

Some reports on counterfeiting suggest that forced labor and child labor were once rampant in the counterfeiting industry (Naim 2005; Phillips 2005). My findings from interview data and field observations indicate that this is no longer the case. As mentioned earlier, factory workers can be subjected to long hours of work, but they are not underage, forced into labor, or trafficked.

Workshops

In addition to the small factories in industrial parks or zones, workshops in urban villages also play a critical role in manufacturing counterfeit goods. In China, most major cities have their share of so-called urban villages, or villages-in-the-city (chengzhongcun), but the largest number of such urban villages exists in Guangzhou and other parts of Guangdong Province (Al 2014; Zhanguo Liu and Lo 2020; M. Zhou, Xu, and Shenasi 2015). Urban villages are simply original villages that, due to rapid urbanization, have been surrounded by city structures. Zhanguo Liu and T. Wing Lo (2020, 2–3), authors of the book *Understanding Crime in Villages-in-the-City in China*, explain the ramifications of a dual land system in China:

> In China, many poor settlements in urban areas are found in villages-in-the-city because of the existence of a dual land system in which urban land is owned by the state, whereas rural land is owned by rural collectives, thus creating different property rights within the same territory. Villagers remain villagers, not city residents, although

the villages are somewhat merged into the city. Moreover, farmland still belongs to rural collectives and is not considered urban land. The city government can neither control the villagers nor plan what to do with their land. Moreover, the social organization, social networks, social culture, and architectural styles of villages are dramatically different from those of the city.

Under the dual land system, city residents have better social security and welfare systems than the villagers. During the process of urbanization, when the rural farmland is no longer in use but is not yet under requisition, the indigenous villagers need another means to earn a living. To protect their own interests, maximizing the benefits from their remaining and unused farmland becomes the inevitable choice. They use the village space to build as many rental houses as they can afford, but they have no integrated plan. The rental houses are built in high density areas, and thus all buildings in villages-in-the-city are in a state of serious disorder.

These rented buildings become the sites of small and midsize factories or the dwelling places of migrant laborers (Zhanguo Liu and Lo 2020). The buildings are called "kissing buildings" or "handshake houses" because, as one researcher described it, "you can literally reach out from one building and shake hands with your neighbor" (Al 2014, 1) (see Figure 3.1). These buildings are constructed in violation of local building codes. Zhanguo Liu and Lo (2020, 3) characterize urban villages as follows: "Streets are narrow and congested; electricity, telecommunication routes, and water and gas pipelines are disorganized; lighting, ventilation, and drainage are insufficient; and sanitation is poor. Overall, villages-in-the-city give people an impression of being 'dirty, chaotic, and poor.'" Al (2014, 3), quoted at the start of this paragraph, observes that "often a village is dominated by a special industry, be it information technology, ceramic production, replica products, or massage parlors." The populations of these villages range from several thousand to more than a quarter of a million. Hundreds of urban villages in big cities such as Shenzhen, Beijing, Chongqing, and Guangzhou exist outside of municipal land laws and regular planning jurisdictions.

Mr. Fu, an investigator with a private firm that provides a variety of investigative services, including collecting information on counterfeiting activities, commented on the power structure of urban villages and the tensions between village leaders and local or central government administrators:

In some of the urban villages in Guangzhou, there are many factories and workshops. Village residents built many buildings and rented them to people from outside for commercial or residential

Figure 3.1 The handshake buildings in an urban village.

purposes. Village residents elect a village head, and under the head, there are different groups. Some villages have more than a dozen groups. Group leaders are also elected. A village may have thousands of residents, but the smaller ones are only a few hundred. A village also has a village party secretary, and the groups have group party secretaries. Party secretaries represent the Party; they are assigned from the top. Generally speaking, a village's power structure comprises a head, a party secretary, and a bookkeeper. The three have to work together if they want to accomplish anything. Of course, there could be a power struggle among them. Village heads often take the lead in mobilizing residents to challenge the power of the central or city authority and to engage in collective resistance to the police force. They will not hesitate if they have to shut down their villages, and will not let any outsiders enter. In China, the one place the CCP cannot control is the villages. The elected village heads always try their best to promote the interests of their residents, and they will do whatever it takes to help their residents make money. Whatever these village leaders are doing is not a reflection of the central or local government policies.

Panda Village (A Pseudonym)

Of all the urban villages in Guangzhou where many IP-infringing workshops are located, Panda Village is probably one of the best known due to the thousands of footwear workshops there. It is located in Baiyun District. It is also close to the Guangda/Guoda Shoe Market of Shijin, an area that functions as a clearinghouse for excess inventory of fashion merchandise and accessories. It is where many buyers from Africa find cheap but new clothing, shoes, handbags, and other goods from past seasons.

Mimi (F7), a twenty-four-year-old petite woman from Zhanjiang, Guangdong Province, owns a shoe workshop in Panda Village. She dropped out of middle school when she was sixteen and moved to Guangzhou. She became a bookkeeper for Laoban (G2). After Laoban closed his business, she worked for a fake shoe workshop for six months before starting her own shoe business. She rented a site in Panda for $290 a month. She started with only a $7,200 investment, spending about $3,000 on secondhand machines and equipment. She has eight workers who are paid by the piece. Her workers make $1,000 to $1,150 a month working from 8:00 A.M. to 10:00 P.M., taking a lunch break between noon and 1:00 P.M., and a dinner break from 6:00 P.M. to 7:00 P.M. Her workshop, and all the workshops around her, are closed only once a month, on the first day of the month. She revealed how she, with the assistance of her brother, was running the business:

> After I opened the workshop, I asked my brother to join me in Guangzhou. He is only 18, and he is in charge of production. I am responsible for design, development, and distribution. I work from early morning to late evening every day, rushing to send the merchandise out. I work seven days a week; I never have time to rest. It is a very demanding job, for sure. I sell about 1,000 pairs of shoes a month.

My cost is about $15 per pair; I sell them for $21. I copy mostly Chanel shoes, and that is because the brand has many styles, unlike Hermès. Plus, the market for counterfeit Hermès shoes is dominated by those who have been in this business for a long time; it is not easy for a newcomer like me to participate in this line of business because they have already established their distribution channels. Although I retail my shoes on WeChat [a popular messaging and social media app], most of my goods are sold to store owners. Several of them are regular customers, and they give me an order after seeing the photos I send them using WeChat. Store owners purchase my shoes only after they receive orders from their customers. Their orders are small, just a few to a dozen pairs per order. I can copy shoes based on photos of the originals; I do not need to see the actual shoes.

A year after the interview, I returned to Guangzhou to continue with my data collection, and I heard that Mimi was doing well with her business. She had received a "big order" from a buyer in Dubai and had bought a new car, something many entrepreneurs in China do after they make money. Her brother was also getting more familiar with the business. A healthy competition had developed between Mimi and her brother, both of them working hard to find out who is a better entrepreneur. This rivalry between them had become a catalyst for their success.

I visited a workshop in Panda Village that was owned by Ah San (F16). Ah Yun (F13), who supplied dust bags to counterfeit shoe manufacturers, brought me to the workshop, which was located on the second floor of a six-story building, and introduced me to Ah San. There was a dirty small elevator at the end of a dingy narrow hallway, but we decided to use the stairs. Even though there were windows, it was very dark inside because there was so little space between the buildings. All the lights were on, even though it was around 2:00 P.M. I could not tell whether it was bright or dark outside when I was inside the building.

At the time of my visit, there were no workers in the workshop. Ah San said business was slow, so he had asked his workers not to come in. His workers came in on short notice and were not regular employees. The place was small (about one thousand square feet), and dirty, and the toilet did not work. When I asked him later why these workshops were so unkempt, Ah Yun told me: "No workshop operator is going to keep his workshop nice and clean, because he might have to move somewhere else at any given time." Ah Yun's point was that due to unexpected crackdowns from the authorities, no workshop owner could be sure how long his workshop would continue to be in operation.

When I asked him how he copied name-brand sandals, Ah San said: "Copying these sandals is very easy; I can do so just by examining their images. We check the international brands' websites to see what new products have come out and then copy them. Of course, if we have the original in front of us, it is much easier to copy, plus the quality will be better." As for who his customers are, he said:

> They are store owners, WeChat vendors, or Taobao [an e-commerce website] operators around Guangzhou. They come to my workshop to pick up the goods. We do not do express or hand delivery unless the buyers are from the Guoda or Guangda shoe markets. They need my shoes but do not have the time to pick them up, so we ask a *modi* [illegal motorcycle taxi] driver to deliver the shoes. When the *modi* arrives there, the driver will call the cell phone number I give him, and after the buyer receives the shoes, he gives the driver $1.50 as a delivery fee.

I ordered one pair of men's Adidas Yeezy shoes and two pairs of women's Louis Vuitton Lock It Flat Mules from Ah San as a token of appreciation for participating in my research. When I visited his workshop the second time, the three pairs of shoes were lying on the floor. I tried on the Yeezys and found they were too tight, so I asked him to get me a larger size (see Figure 3.2). I quickly looked at the two pairs of Louis Vuitton Lock It sandals and thought they were fine. I gave him $44 for the two pairs of sandals. He told

Figure 3.2 A copy of a pair of Adidas Yeezys.

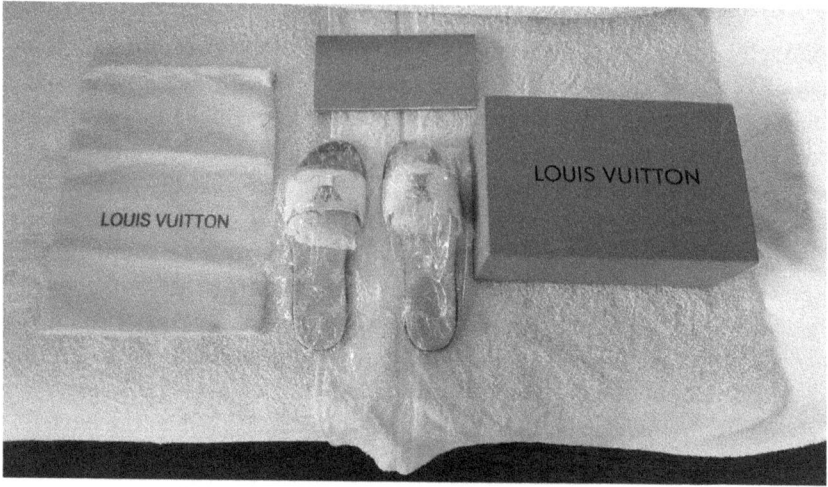

Figure 3.3 A copy of a pair of Louis Vuitton Lock It Flat Mules.

me they were made by a workshop next door. Inside each of the beautiful orange boxes with Louis Vuitton labels was a pair of sandals wrapped in plastic and stuffed with tissue paper, a yellow dust bag, and a receipt in English inside an envelope. The receipt was supposedly issued by a boutique inside the Peninsula of Hong Kong, an iconic five-star hotel (see Figure 3.3).

Other Manufacturing Centers

Besides the Baiyun District, there are other manufacturing hubs for counterfeits in Guangzhou. Other well-known centers include Shiling for leather goods and the Zengcheng District for denim jeans.

Shiling

Shiling, dubbed "Capital of China's Leather Goods," is a town in the Huadu District of Guangzhou, located twenty-four miles from the city center. The Shiling International Leather Goods City, a large market complex with forty-two hundred stores is located there. Before the emergence of the Baiyun District as the preeminent center for leather goods manufacturing and distribution in 2003, most people visited Shiling for leather products. According to the private investigator Mr. Fu: "The fake handbag market in Shiling is unique: there is a strong connection between the distribution outlets and the factories. The factories there are relatively large and are mostly located in industrial complexes. These factories have workers ranging from a few dozens to hundreds. These factories produce all kinds of fake name-brand handbags, including Louis Vuitton, Chanel, Gucci, and others, but they do so in turn. They will make Louis Vuitton products for a few days, and after completing the job, they will switch to producing Chanel for a few days."

I visited a village in Shiling where almost every household was involved in the leather goods business. Mr. Hung (H14), a village resident who owns an old Buick, explained how he utilizes his house to conduct his business and how he and his relatives work together:

> This is how I operate my business. Several years ago, I built this three-and-a-half-story house. I converted the first floor into a factory, and my family and I live on the second floor. The third floor is now empty, but at one point, I let my workers live there. Some workers are from this village, so they return home after work. I provide lunch and dinner for my workers, and my wife cooks. At this point, I only have three workers.
>
> My cousin has a store at Guihuagang [a handbag market across the road from Baiyun Leather City in central Guangzhou]. His wife goes to the store early in the morning every day to take orders from customers. She remains there until late afternoon. Then, my cousin picks up the orders, returns to Huadu, and goes to the markets to buy leather, other materials, and metal fittings. After that, he delivers all the stuff to my home in Shiling, and I immediately begin working. If the order is urgent, I work until dawn so he can deliver the goods to his buyer the next day. In general, the orders are small. Of course, sometimes it may take several days to complete a particular order. I make whatever bags my cousin wants me to make. I do not know anything about international labels. Sometimes, we produce bags with no labels. We make only a tiny amount of money from manufacturing fees.

Zengcheng

The Zengcheng, a district of Guangzhou, has a population of 1.4 million, only slightly less than the population of Huadu, which is estimated to be around 1.6 million. In her book *Fashioning China: Precarious Creativity and Women Designers in Shanzhai Culture*, Sara Liao (2020, 34) remarks: "Xintang, a small town in Zengcheng District, Guangzhou, . . . emerged as the world's 'blue jeans capital' during the 1980s. Shops, stalls, street vendors, and factories from one end of the town to the other produced export goods, primarily denim garments. . . . To this day, Xintang continues to be known for denim production, but most of the factories now recycle designs and styles from off-the-rack foreign brands and produce everyday clothing for the domestic market. These factories employ many patternmakers but not many fashion designers, and few of the region's brands are widely known, partly because of the rampant knockoffs."

Mr. Wang, a young prosecutor in Zengcheng, characterized the denim jeans counterfeiting industry in his jurisdiction as follows:

> The district where I work is a hub for the counterfeiting of denim jeans. Many small factories, wholesale outlets, and retail stores exist for jeans. The place is also dotted with small businesses related to the denim jeans industry, including button manufacturing, washing, and packaging. More than 50% of our counterfeiting cases involve denim jeans. Our district's well-established larger factories are contract factories that produce denim jeans for foreign brands. They have regular customers, so they are unlikely to be involved in counterfeiting. Besides, it is just too risky for them. If they take a chance and get into legal trouble, they will lose all their investment. For these large businesses, it is not worth taking the risk. The small factories are a different story. They do not have legitimate regular customers, so they must rely on outlet owners who want them to produce fake jeans. Most small factories are located in the urban villages.

Moving Out of Guangzhou

Of the many manufacturing hot spots for counterfeit goods in Guangzhou, the Baiyun District is where most factories are located. As mentioned earlier, it can be challenging to differentiate between legitimate factories and those engaged in counterfeiting. In addition, factories and workshops in Baiyun frequently move from one village to another to avoid government crackdowns. Initially, counterfeiters would set up their factories and workshops in an urban village near their distribution center in the Sanyuanli area. However, as that village became a hub for counterfeit goods manufacturing, the authorities intervened and tried to push the factories and workshops farther away from Sanyuanli, presumably to make the counterfeiting problem less noticeable. After two decades, underground factories and workshops are being pushed farther and farther away from the center of Guangzhou, even though they remain within the larger Baiyun District.

Moreover, some of my research subjects pointed out that many counterfeiters are moving their manufacturing operations out of Guangzhou. Xiao Xin (G15) explained how and why she had diverted most of her production activities to her husband's hometown, which is far away from Guangzhou:

> I am using this place [the factory in Guangzhou] mainly to take orders. Three years ago, we opened a factory in my husband's hometown in Jiangsu Province. We are now using that factory to fulfill the orders we receive here. At any rate, transportation is not an issue anymore;

we can pretty much deliver goods and materials very quickly nowadays. Besides, there are more workers in the rural areas, and labor and expenses are also relatively low. Workers also prefer to work near where they live.

Mr. Sun, a policy researcher with the city government of Guangzhou, also said many counterfeit factories have left Guangzhou: "Many counterfeit goods manufacturing facilities moved to inland provinces like Hunan and Yunnan. Regarding counterfeiting, the authorities there are not as aggressive as in Guangzhou. Besides, wages and other business costs are lower there. The only downside is that counterfeiters have to spend money to transport the finished products back to Guangzhou."

In sum, when I asked him the whereabouts of factories and workshops that are involved in the manufacturing of luxury counterfeits, Mr. Tang, an officer with the Economic Crime Unit (the key police agency responsible for the investigation of counterfeiting), responded as follows:

It is hard to say where the majority of the factories are located. They are everywhere in Guangzhou, but, in general, there are more in the districts of Baiyun and Panyu. Some are located outside of Guangzhou. There are also many in Huadu. These factories can survive only in large districts where rents are low. If they try to operate a factory in a district like Yuexiu, due to its small size and high rent, they will not survive. Some factories had moved out of Guangzhou, or they were set up away from Guangzhou at the outset. Take, for example, some of the villages in the Chaoshan area. Entire villages are manufacturing counterfeits, and it is difficult for an outsider to sneak into these villages.

Materials Suppliers

No matter how good a counterfeiter is at copying a product, he needs high-quality materials to produce a replica indistinguishable from its original. If an imitator does not have access to materials that are the same as or similar to the original's materials, he will not produce a so-called Super A point-by-point counterfeit, regardless of how exceptional his artisans and machines are. Thus, materials suppliers play a crucial role in the high-end counterfeiting industry.

Fabric

Participants in the garment industry stressed how convenient it is for them to do business in Guangzhou due to the ease of finding materials they need there. Anyone who has visited the Zhongda Garment City will agree. The market is located across from the main entrance to the campus of Zhongshan University (also known as Sun Yat-Sen University), one of China's elite universities. The market is surrounded by many megamarkets catering to businesspeople in the fashion industry. According to Xiao Peng (G8), a Wenzhounese who bought Laoban's business after the latter returned to Taiwan:

> Guangzhou is heaven for the ready-made garment industry. Here, you can buy all kinds of fabric at the Zhongda Garment City. It is not only a one-stop shopping area for everything you need, but it also lets you quickly get what you want. Unbelievably convenient for people like us. Let us say you are producing a ready-to-wear garment here for a cost of $7.20; you are not going to find another place in China where you can produce the same garment for the same amount of money. That is why Guangzhou is the number one hub for the ready-made garment industry in China.

Leather

There are many leather suppliers in Guangzhou, especially in the Sanyuanli area. The authorities do not target these establishments even if they do business with counterfeiters. Xiao Ma (H4), a leather supplier, described his role in the leather business as follows:

> I "research and develop" all kinds of leather for handbag producers. I pay attention to what kinds of name-brand handbags are popular. I also travel overseas to buy original bags and find a leather manufacturer to produce the leather. This is what "research and development" is all about: finding a leather manufacturer to produce the same leather as is used in the original, authentic handbags. A handbag counterfeiter will not be able to ask a leather manufacturer to develop a particular type of leather because any single counterfeiter needs only a small amount of leather. As a leather supplier, I can ask a manufacturer to produce a large quantity of leather. It will then become stock in our warehouses, and then I will sell it to individual counterfeiters. That is why the counterfeiters come to us for leather. I was heavily involved in researching and developing leather for Prada and Gucci handbags. Later, I began to develop leather for Hermès products, but I was arrested for tax evasion.

Xiao Ma also explained why he is so successful at what he does: "In the past, I visited Baiyun Leather City at least once a week. I checked every store to see what they were selling, what goods were popular among buyers, and what color was trendy. This way, I knew what leather to import or develop. I also invited store owners to come to my office. While sipping tea and chatting, I showed them my leather. Unlike other leather suppliers, I was very aggressive. That was why I did very well in this business."

Since leather is one of the most critical components of a good-quality counterfeit handbag, many leather goods copycats envied Xiao Ma. He recalled how, at one point, the demand for leather was so strong that he did not have to worry about not selling his leather:

> In the past, when the counterfeit leather handbag business was good, I was a key player in the leather supply industry. Many people came to me for leather, begging me to sell to them. One of my clients said: "I want to buy a new Mercedes this year, and I am counting on you to help me to do that." At that time, it was a seller's market. As long as you got the stuff, you did not have to worry about not finding a buyer. It was a time when demand was much stronger than supply. Now, it is a different story.

Xiao Ma revealed how he had both counterfeiters and noncounterfeiters as clients, how these two types of buyers differed, and how crucial it was for him to have both types of clients to expand his business:

> While selling leather to counterfeiters from Baiyun Leather City, I was also doing business with buyers who were outside the counterfeiting business. For me, it was the same; I did not care what my buyers did with the leather they bought from me. The differences between the two types of buyers were delivery speed and order size. When counterfeiters made an order, they wanted you to deliver the goods right away. Besides, their orders were small because they were afraid to produce a large number of fake handbags all at once. They would be in deep trouble if the authorities were to catch them with so many counterfeit handbags. From the get-go, I was involved in the buying and selling of large quantities of leather. That was why I did not focus on catering only to fake handbag makers. If you specialize in the fake handbag leather market, you cannot manage large quantities because the market is not that big, even though the profit margins are high.

Ah Bao (F12), who had been a hairstylist before being hired by Xiao Ma to run his shoe leather business, underscored that a leather supply firm needs to be proactive and well stocked to be successful.[2] A passive supplier with limited inventory could never become a key player in the leather supply trade and most likely would be just a broker, selling a small quantity of goods obtained from a well-established supplier:

> If you are serious about your business, you must invest lots of money. Not only do you have to stock your warehouses with a large inventory, but also you need to develop new products continuously. You have to have a strategy, like predicting what types of leather will sell, doing your research, producing the goods, and putting the goods in your warehouses. You must do more than just buy a certain amount of materials, store them in your warehouse, and sell whatever you get.

Xiao Lai (H15), a relative of Xiao Ma, owned a leather supply store in the Dragonhead Leather Market, a prominent leather supply market inside an impressive building in the Sanyuanli area. Before I interviewed Xiao Lai, Xiao Ma briefed me about Xiao Lai's business:

> Xiao Lai's store primarily serves people who are producing fake handbags. Not only does he sell leather to these counterfeiters when they come to him, but he also takes the initiative by buying authentic designer bags, showing the bags to his customers, and persuading them to copy these bags. If one of them is interested, he will be responsible for providing the leather. Xiao Lai may also do this along with a metal fittings supplier. This way, he can share with the metal fittings supplier the expense of buying the original, authentic bags. He and the metal fittings supplier will meet a customer together. Metal fittings suppliers have the most risk in the counterfeiting business because all their products have trademarked labels. That is why if a counterfeiter is assured that there will be support from both a leather and a metal fittings supplier, he will be much more confident in copying a certain bag. It is not true that the counterfeiters initiate all the counterfeiting activities.

Metal Fittings

Of all the suppliers, metal fitting providers are the most at risk because when the authorities catch them with their merchandise, they cannot deny their engagement in trademark infringement. Mrs. Gao, a sixty-year-old owner of a small store that sells metal fittings and charms for handbags inside Baiyun Leather City, has this to say about her life and her business:

> I was born in Chongqing in 1958. I am married; my husband was in the Air Force. As someone who was born in the 1950s, I went through

hell. People born in the 1950s were unlucky enough to have experienced so many disasters. I used to work as a cashier for a government unit, so I can tell the difference between real and fake currency. After I retired from my unit, I moved to Fuzhou because my husband was stationed there. In 2006, we moved to Guangzhou.

I "bought" [buying a long-term lease] this small store many years ago. Even though I do not have to pay rent, I still have to pay around $650 monthly for maintenance. Because I own the store, I am not afraid to sell trademarked metal fittings. If I rent, I would not be able to do so. [Probably because the owners would not allow their renters to do so.]

People from the gongshangju [AIC] often come to check on us. A few years ago, I was fined more than $7,200 for counterfeiting. At that time, I was making good money, so the fine was not a big deal. However, the authorities shut down my store for one month. Gongshangju people come here because most of the stores in this building sell counterfeit goods. It is illegal here. Stores like mine that sell trademarked metal fittings are particularly vulnerable because they pay more attention to us.

Shoe Materials

According to an employee of a local shoe firm, there are four shoe capitals in China: Jinjiang/Putian in Fujian Province; Chengdu, Sichuan Province; Wenzhou, Zhejiang Province; and Guangzhou. There are also many shoe materials suppliers in Guangzhou. However, if a buyer is looking for a better price, he is likely to travel to Jinjiang because the materials there are cheaper than in Guangzhou.

There are also many shoe materials suppliers in Dongguan City, especially in and around Houjie Township. Mr. Zeng (F10), a shoe uppers supplier, told me how his company was willing to do business with both name-brand owners and counterfeiters:

This upper became popular after Adi [a shortened name for Adidas] began to use it on their shoes. The unique thing about this type of breathable mesh fabric upper is that stitching is unnecessary. It is one whole piece that attaches to the shoe's sole. Plus, there is no shoelace; you have to slip it on. We sell our uppers to Prada's contract manufacturer, and they ask us to sign a contract prohibiting us from providing the same uppers to anyone else. Of course, [to avoid breaching the contract] we sell something very similar to other buyers. At any rate, it is hard to tell the difference between the two types of uppers, those we sell to Prada's manufacturers and those we sell to others.

John (F3), an expatriate from Taiwan who had worked in the shoe industry in Houjie for more than thirty years, explained how easy it is for counterfeiters to find a way to obtain the materials they need:

> As a contract manufacturer for Skechers, we have to work with them in deciding how to procure the shoe materials. Generally, they will select two or three local suppliers for each type of material, and we will pick one. Many departments in our company have access to this list of suppliers. When they see a pair of shoes, counterfeiters can immediately tell which contract manufacturer produced the shoes. Then they will try to obtain the supplier list from that contract manufacturer. Once they get the list, they approach these suppliers to buy the same materials. Of course, Skechers will tell these suppliers not to sell the same materials to other buyers, but the problem is that even if the owners of these firms will not sell, they cannot stop their employees from doing so. Counterfeiters may also ask employees in the purchasing department of a contract manufacturer to buy the materials for them. At any rate, there are many ways for counterfeiters to gain access to the same materials as those used in authentic products. They would consider using similar materials only if they failed to source the same materials.

Other Facilitating Businesses

Besides materials suppliers, various other businesses provide crucial support and services to counterfeiters. I discuss only three types of facilitating businesses: packaging, embroidery, and textile printing.

Packaging

Regardless of whether they produce the counterfeits in their factories or subcontract the work to one or more other factories, counterfeiters are not involved in packaging. They focus on production and distribution and let another business take care of the packaging. According to Ah Yun (F13), a thirty-four-year-old owner of a shoe bag factory located in Panda Village:

> Shoe factory operators are only involved in the production of shoes. After the shoes are produced, these manufacturers will find a shoebox factory to provide shoeboxes. The same factory will also recruit

other suppliers for such items as shoe bags, labels, certificates, and packing paper. The shoebox factory operator will collect all these items from the various suppliers and deliver them, along with the shoeboxes, to shoe factory operators. That is why, in the shoe counterfeiting business, shoebox producers are the key players in the accessories business; they are the ones that shoe manufacturers rely on to find other suppliers. Besides, of all the supplemental materials, shoeboxes are the most expensive; they cost from 85 cents to $1.40 per box, depending on the quality. I rarely deal directly with shoemakers; I only maintain a close relationship with more than a dozen shoebox providers. The modus operandi for packaging is the same for both the shoe and handbag counterfeiting businesses. That is, shoe and handbag counterfeiters outsource the packaging of their products to a shoe or handbag box manufacturer and let that person decide who will provide dust bags, labels, certificates, and packing papers.

Ah Yun took me to a shoebox factory he does business with. The factory, about four thousand square feet, is near Panda Village. Ah Yun said a shoebox factory is noisier than a shoe workshop, so it is important for the factory to be located in an industrial complex to prevent neighbors from reporting it to the authorities. On the factory floor, I saw three women working. With the help of a gluing machine, two of the women were making Louis Vuitton shoeboxes. The other woman, also operating a gluing machine, was producing Fendi shoeboxes. The machines were relatively old and simple, and much of the work was done by hand. Regardless, the finished boxes were similar to the authentic shoeboxes used by the name brands.

Embroidery

Another type of facilitator in the counterfeiting industry is the person who provides embroidery services to garment manufacturers. A typical embroidery factory or workshop is a family business located in a residential area and employs only several workers to manage a few machines. These small firms do business with both legitimate garment makers and counterfeiters. It is not easy for the authorities to find out whether or when an embroidery service provider engages in illicit activities.

According to the owner of such a workshop, Mr. Gu, most of his investment was spent on embroidery machines. A men's shirts counterfeiter told me that an imported embroidery machine may cost more than $144,000, but a locally produced machine costs only a few hundred dollars. However, these two types of machines produce embroideries of very different quality. I visited Mr. Gu's workshop, a family business he and his wife run. Their two adult children were also there, and it seemed that their children were helping their parents with the business. They were living in the building where the workshop was located. The area was only about two thousand square feet. There were several computer-controlled embroidery machines that can produce embroideries by applying thread or other materials such as pearls. Mr. Gu said this is a very competitive business because Guangzhou has so many small embroidery firms. The market price for embroidery service is very static; there is little room for price negotiation because when the two parties meet to discuss business, both have a very good idea of what the going price is. If a provider tries to raise the price, the other party will go somewhere else.

Hundreds of embroidered-patch suppliers exist in and around the Guangzhou Zhongda Garment City. These suppliers provide all kinds of embroidered patches to garment makers, including those involved in counterfeiting. Take Mrs. Jia (G11), for example. She is from Kaiping, Guangdong Province, and her husband is from a Hakka area, also in Guangdong. She rents a store in a market across the street from Zhongda for $4,300 a month. She also rents a store inside Zhongda for $11,500 a month, and a close relative manages that store. Her husband is in charge of a factory that produces embroidered patches. She said their factory has about eighty workers. Most of the patches on display were not trademark infringing; however, she can quickly provide whatever a customer wants.

Textile Printing

Textile printing is the process of applying color to fabric in definite patterns or designs. For garment manufacturers, textile printing can be an essential service. Textile printing businesses, especially those that do work for counterfeiters, are generally small family businesses located in some of the worst urban villages in the Baiyun District. I visited one such printing firm, and the following is from the field notes of my visit:

> Our car missed the entrance to the village. As a result, we had to find the entrance on the other side of the village after driving around in a big circle. The village's main road was long, narrow, and filled with potholes. Garbage was strewn everywhere along the roadside. After much effort in evading the potholes and motor vehicles coming from the opposite direction, we turned onto a side road, and, not long after, into a narrow, crooked alley. There were cars parked in the alley, and cars coming and going on both sides. When we arrived at the printing workshop, there was no place to park our car, so we parked it in front of a house and partially blocked the alley. Xiao Wen (G6) stayed in the car in case he had to move it. Obviously, the buildings there

were built haphazardly, and I don't think there was any planning at all. All the buildings there seemed to be factories/workshops or living quarters for migrant workers. There were dogs lying in the middle of the alley, and they did not even bother to move when an approaching car honked its horn in a frenzy. The driver had to get out of the car to shoo the dogs away.

The printing facility was located on the third floor of a dilapidated building. The space was about three thousand square feet and was filled with rows and rows of textile printing tables. The business belonged to a couple from Guizhou Province, one of the poorest areas in China. The husband said that he had worked for a textile printing plant when he arrived in Guangzhou more than ten years earlier. After working there for a few years, he opened his own printing business. Initially, the business was located somewhere else; he moved to this spot because authorities often came to check for environmental protection violations in his first plant. Many businesses in that area were forced to move due to strict environmental protection regulations. Here, in this village, the enforcement of environmental protection regulations is relatively lax. When I was walking around, I saw rats running underneath the tables. Xiao Wen's wife, a fashion designer and distributor, discussed with the couple the possibility of cooperation between them. The couple showed us some women's T-shirts they were working on. One of the garments was a red T-shirt bearing the word Misochino in big white letters. I believe the misspelling was intentional.

In addition to packaging, embroidery, and textile printing, many other auxiliary businesses provide vital services or goods to luxury goods counterfeiters. I cannot list all of these businesses here. For example, some entrepreneurs provide self-adhesive films to textile printing facility owners; some businesspeople specialize in supplying hangtags to garment makers. They are called auxiliary material suppliers, and they, like the suppliers of fabric, leather, metal fittings, and shoe materials, conduct business with both legitimate firms and counterfeiting enterprises. This dual role allows them to publicly present their businesses as legitimate, and, yet, if need be, they can be involved in the facilitation of counterfeiting.

4

Distribution

fter counterfeit products are manufactured, they need to be distributed to customers both in China and abroad. In this chapter, I examine how counterfeit goods are distributed through brick-and-mortar
physical markets. I also explore the rapidly expanding online markets. I focus
on the markets in Guangzhou because the city is not only the most important manufacturing hub for counterfeit goods in China but also the preeminent distribution center for them. The distribution of counterfeits, like the
designing and manufacturing of fake goods discussed in Chapter 3, is deeply
embedded in the legitimate business sector. A casual observer can hardly differentiate between the two amid the bustling commercial activities in China.
Moreover, the modus operandi of the two business worlds are almost identical,
with the exception of risk management. The counterfeiters are more concerned
about the authorities than are the legitimate businesspeople, and thus they
pay more attention to risk management. This is explored in Chapter 7.

In Guangzhou, the two most essential distribution centers for fashion
and accessories are Zhanxi Road in the Yuexiu District and the Sanyuanli
area in the Baiyun District. The former is a well-known shopping area for
clothing and watches, and the latter for handbags and shoes. Other major
markets for fashion and fashion accessories include clothing distribution
centers such as Baima, Shisanhang, and Shahe; handbag markets such as
Huadu; and shoe malls such as Gouda and Guangda. There are one or more
major distribution centers in Guangzhou for every type of merchandise one
can imagine. During my stay in Guangzhou and trips to other parts of

Guangdong, I visited outlets for electronic devices, toys, children's clothing, cosmetics, furniture, lighting, Christmas decorations, and paintings, not to mention dozens of markets for men's and women's clothing, leather goods, and shoes. Unlike other shopping outlets, I have visited in other parts of the world, the markets in China are humongous, made up of several huge buildings near one another. These markets are open seven days a week, from early in the morning until late in the evening. Foot traffic in and around these markets can at times be mind boggling, especially when thousands of customers and employees leave the buildings at closing time.

It is no secret that the local authorities own many of these markets. Andrew Mertha, a political scientist and the author of *The Politics of Piracy: Intellectual Property in Contemporary China* (2005, 172), characterizes distribution centers in China as follows: "'Distribution centers' can range from small nondescript warehouses to operations that encompass entire towns and local economies. These distribution centers are often managed by local government agencies (such as the AIC), or that have quasi-private ownership but include officials such as former vice mayors or former AIC directors on their boards of directors."

Physical Markets

Jane (G1), from Taiwan, noted that many counterfeit dealers in Guangzhou were operating out of hotel rooms before the emergence of well-established brick-and-mortar physical markets for counterfeit goods: "Many years ago, retailers simply checked into a hotel and used their rooms as showrooms. They advertised heavily, saying they were selling excess goods from contract manufacturers of foreign brand owners, or their goods were foreign-made products smuggled into China. Because their goods were cheap, many people were willing to buy them. Sellers did not say they were selling fake goods, and buyers did not care. Hotel operators knew what was happening, but they turned a blind eye." The hotels were located in Zhanxi Road or Sanyuanli. Some of them were later demolished and replaced by newly built distribution centers or markets.

In this section, I examine some of Guangzhou's major physical markets for clothing, leather goods, and footwear. Both counterfeit and noncounterfeit goods are traded in these markets, and the proportion of counterfeit to noncounterfeit goods varies by market.

Apparel

Zhanxi Road (Station West Road)
Guangzhou is one of China's major textile distribution centers. For ready-to-wear garment buyers from out of town, Zhanxi Road is the place to go for

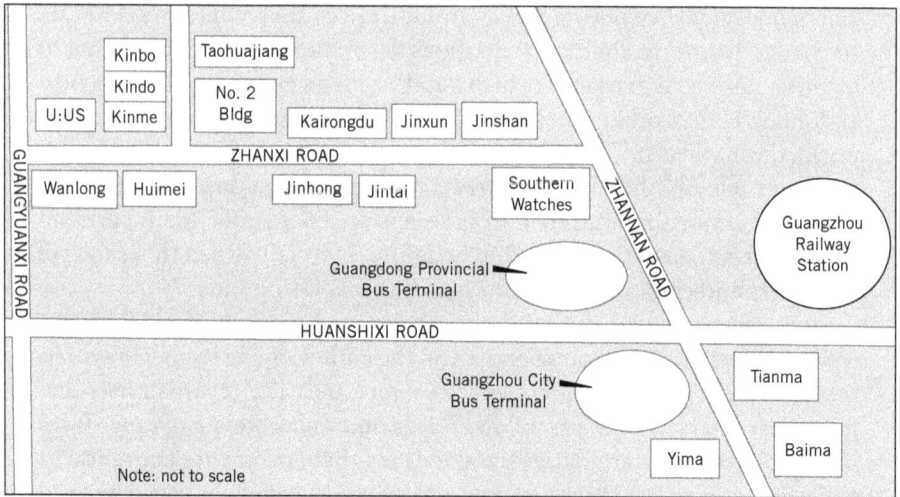

Figure 4.1 The Zhanxi Road area. (*Map by Rutgers Cartography*)

fashion and accessories. It is a narrow street to the west of the Guangzhou Railway Station (see Figure 4.1). There are two bus terminals just south of the street: the Guangdong Provincial Bus Terminal and the Guangzhou City Bus Terminal. Before air travel became widely accessible, this was the area on which most visitors to Guangzhou, from all over China, first set their feet. Nowadays, the road is dotted with more than a dozen fashion and fashion accessory markets, including many markets for counterfeit watches. Zhanxi Road is also very close to an area that includes the Baima, Yima, Liuhua, and Kapok (or Hongmian) fashion markets. The "old" shoe city of Guangzhou is not far away. In sum, the markets on and around Zhanxi Road play a crucial role in the distribution of fashion goods in Guangzhou. The office of the USTR designated the Zhanxi Area Markets as a notorious physical market in its annual reports for six consecutive years, between 2017 and 2022 (see Table 4.1). According to the USTR, a "notorious market," either online or physical, is a place where a large number of counterfeits are traded. The 2022 USTR *Out-of-Cycle Review of Notorious Markets* identified thirty-nine online markets and thirty-three physical markets worldwide as notorious markets.

Zhanxi Road became a hub for the distribution of counterfeits after some of the government guesthouses there were converted into wholesale markets. According to Laoban (G2), a clothing business owner:

Initially, the distribution center for garments in Guangzhou was Baima. Later, as rent in Baima increased rapidly, people in the fashion industry gradually moved their businesses to Zhanxi Road. Many buildings on that road were originally guesthouses owned by the Chinese People's Armed Police (a powerful paramilitary organization primarily responsible for internal security). There were many barracks in the area, and it was rumored that powerful and influential people protected the neighborhood. Many clothing traders stayed in these guesthouses and sold garments from their rooms. Some of the guesthouses were later transformed into apparel distribution centers and formed two main markets: Jinxiang and the No. 2 Building. Taohuajiang Market followed. At that time, most manufacturers were contract manufacturers for foreign firms, and they had plenty of leftover goods. Store owners from Zhanxi Road went to these factories to buy excess goods. Their business was brisk, and their profit margins were huge. These leftover goods belonged to American brands such as Tommy Hilfiger and Ralph Lauren. In 2003, many manufacturers established distribution outlets on Zhanxi Road, and this marked the beginning of the era of this road as a major clothing market.

There are many market buildings along both sides of the Zhanxi Road. Besides the three major markets for counterfeit watches (and there are many more on nearby streets), there are a dozen or so apparel markets, including U:US, Kinme, Kindo, Kinbo, Taohuajiang, No. 2 Building, Kairongdu, Jinxiang, Jinshun, Wanlong, Huimei, Jinhong, and Jintai. The buying and selling of counterfeit garments are hidden in the seemingly routine and legal business activities of these markets on Zhanxi Road.

Kinme, Kindo, and Kinbo Markets: Of all the clothing markets on Zhanxi Road, the three interconnected and recently renovated Kinme, Kindo, and Kinbo markets play a prominent role in retailing and wholesaling counterfeit apparel (see Figure 4.2). Of the three malls, Kinbo is the newest and the most upscale. It caters to the sellers of men's clothing. Kinme and Kindo have clothing, shoes, sunglasses, and leather goods stores. According to Ah Min (G5), who owns a store in Kinbo, Northeasterners (people from the three northeastern provinces of Liaoning, Jilin, and Heilongjiang) and Wenzhounese are very active in the Kinbo market. She also said: "The monthly rent for the stores here is more than $5,800. When the lease is signed, you pay a two-month deposit and one month's rent. The lease is renewable every year. In the past, when business was good, the rent here was about $10,000 to $11,500 a month. If you want to 'buy' a store here [a long-term, such as five or ten years, lease without rent, although you still need to pay a monthly management fee], it will cost you about $260,000. It is not worth it; leasing is better than buying."

TABLE 4.1. USTR-LABELED NOTORIOUS MARKETS IN CHINA: PHYSICAL (2009–2022)													
	09	10	11	12	13	14	15	16	17	18	19	20	21	22
Asia-Pacific, Shanghai													X	
Baiyun Leather Goods Market, Guangzhou								X						
Chenghai District, Chaozhou							X	X					X	X
Cheng Huang Cheng Int'l Auto Parts Market, Beijing								X						
Fu'an (An'fu) Footwear and Accessory Market, Putian				X								X	X	
Garment Wholesale Center, Guangzhou					X									
Hongqiao Market, Shanghai									X					
Huaqiangbei Electronics Markets, Shenzhen										X	X	X	X	X
Jin Long Pan Garment Market, Guangzhou						X	X	X	X					
Jinshun Garment Market, Guangzhou					X	X			X					
Jinxiang Garment Market, Guangzhou									X					
Jiulong (Joulong) Shoe Market, Guangzhou					X									
Kindo (Jindu) Garment Market, Guangzhou									X		X	X	X	
Kinbo Garment Market, Guangzhou					X									
Louhu Commercial Center, Shenzhen			X	X	X		X			X	X		X	
PC Malls, Shanghai and Beijing		X												
Ritan Office Building, Beijing													X	
Silk Market, Beijing	X	X	X	X	X		X	X	X	X	X		X	
Southern Watch Trade Center, Guangzhou											X	X	X	X
Wu Ai Market, Shenyang									X		X	X	X	X
Yiwu Small Commodities Market, Yiwu	X	X	X	X		X					X	X	X	X
Yulong Garment Wholesale Market, Guangzhou											X	X		
Zengcheng Int'l Jeans Market, Guangzhou					X	X								
Zhanxi Area Markets, Guangzhou									X	X	X	X	X	X

Figure 4.2 Kindo and Kinbo Markets on Zhanxi Road.

Laoban (G2) recalled how costly it was to secure a place at Kinbo after 2009 and explained why the high rents do not deter potential store operators:

> When I signed a lease with a Taiwanese businesswoman managing Kinbo, it was a five-year lease from 2005 to 2009. Zhanxi Road at that time had become a center for apparel wholesale and retail businesses, so many business owners began to show up. Of course, that was also the golden era for the booming Chinese economy. When the first lease expired in 2009, I signed a second lease for a ten-year term, but the price had increased dramatically. At that time, the way Zhanxi Road had expanded was incredible; every day, the place was packed. Even though the rent for a stall at Kinbo continued to rise exponentially, someone would replace anyone who lost money and left. Many entrepreneurs are not afraid to die.

Kindo was listed as a notorious market by the USTR Office in 2017, 2019, 2020, and 2021. Kinbo was designated as such only once in the past, in 2013. Kinme was never mentioned in the USTR's notorious markets reports.

Huimei International Clothes Market: Located across the street from the Kinme, Kindo, and Kinbo complex, Huimei (opened in 2008) is another major garment market on Zhanxi Road. It is a twelve-story building, with stores for retail and wholesale businesses in the basement and on the first five floors, and with "offices," for wholesale businesses only, on the rest of the floors. Foot traffic in Huimei is often better than in other markets. The stores in the market feature local brands' trendy high-end women's clothing.

Kairongdu Costume Wholesale Center: This market is one of the most popular destinations for buyers from Africa. Many stores on the first floor of Kairongdu sell African-style garments with bold designs and colors (see Figure 4.3). Some salesgirls speak English, Portuguese, and French, in addition to Chinese. The stores sell counterfeit clothing, scarves, and shoes. The market has seven stories: retail stores are on the bottom three stories and offices for wholesale businesses only are on the top four floors.

Guangzhou Baima Garment Market and Neighboring Markets: People in the fashion industry view the Baima Garment Market as the place to go for high-quality fashion. The first page of a brochure (Guangzhou Baima Special Edition, May 1–5, 2018, 1) in English and Chinese placed at the main entrance of the market characterizes the establishment as follows:

> Guangzhou Baima Garment Market, founded in 1993, is China's first modern commercial specialized clothing market. Its constructive area is about 60,000 square meters, gathering over 1,000 clothing manufacturers from the Pearl River Delta, Yangtze River Delta and other regions, including Hong Kong, Macao, Taiwan, and South Korea. . . . Baima's annual turnover is about 10 billion RMB [$1.44 billion], of which the export proportion accounted for up to 30%. Guangzhou Baima Market belongs to Yuexiu Group, one of the biggest local state-owned enterprises.

Every day, buyers from near and far come to Baima to shop. After they purchase their goods, they seek help from transporters waiting outside the market to deliver the goods to their destinations. Buyers only need to tell sellers who their transporters are and continue with their shopping. The saleswomen will hand deliver the packages to the designated transporters waiting outside the building. Most of these buyers are female entrepreneurs from the outskirts of Guangzhou, other cities, or neighboring countries such as Vietnam.

Across the street from Baimai, there is the Yima Market for men's clothing and the Guangzhou World Trade Clothing City. Not far from Baima, there is the Guangzhou Liuhua Garment Wholesale Market, for inexpensive garments for African buyers, and the Hongmian International Clothing Wholesale Market. In sum, the Zhanxi Road area is dominated by many

Figure 4.3 Dangkous (stores or outlets) in Kairongdu Costume Wholesale Center.

wholesale and retail markets for fashion and accessories. Every multistory building is a market, and every market has hundreds of stores.

Shisanhang
Shisanhang (Thirteen Hongs of Canton or Thirteen-House) is another major garment distribution center in Guangzhou (see Figure 4.4). It comprises

Figure 4.4 Long-distance trucks loading in front of a market in Shisanhang.

several malls for women's clothing and an entire street of menswear stores. It started as a distribution center for women's fashion. Then, some stores selling men's clothing opened on a street near the entrance. All the stores in the area sell trendy but affordable garments. Profit margins for sellers are low; they are willing to make a sale if they can get a profit of 30 to 45 cents per item, and they do not care how many items a customer buys. They cater to distributors from third- or fourth-tier cities or retailers from first- and second-tier cities. These distributors and retailers come to the center early in the morning to make purchases. The stores opened at 6:00 A.M. and closed by 1:00 P.M. Laoban (G2) characterizes the market this way:

> In the very beginning, the unit prices for clothing at Shisanhang were low, and so was the quality. However, the garments were trendy, and the sellers did not require their distributor buyers to purchase a specific volume. Even so, business was brisk for some stores; they sold more than a million garments a season. I heard that one seller there sold five million pieces in a season. It was a low-profit-margin, high-volume business. A group from Beijing came in 2005, bought the market, and renovated it into a completely new establishment. The rent increased dramatically, from $350 to $500 a month to at least $2,500 to $5,000 a month. Because of the expensive rent, the original business strategy of selling cheap but at high volume gradually changed. Now, businesses in Shisanhang are striving to develop their own brands.

According to one of my subjects, there has been a change of fortune in the garment business in Shisanhang. Xiao Yuen (G12), a clothing merchant, had this to say about the establishment:

> Shisanhang has been getting very popular lately. People looked down on this market in the past, saying the goods here were all junk. Now, sellers from Baima come here to buy stuff and resell it at Baima. They buy it here for $4 per piece and sell it there for $8. Now, poor-quality goods are in Shahe. The stores here mainly sell their goods under their brands; they do not counterfeit that much. Typically, a store will design its clothes, find a factory to manufacture them, and then distribute the goods through the store. Rent here is very high; it costs from $7,200 to $11,500 a month now [in 2019].

Shahe

Shahe is also a garment distribution center in Guangzhou, especially for low-end fashion. Like Zhanxi Road and Shisanhang, Shahe is bustling with people at any given time, and taxi drivers usually refuse to drop their customers at the entrances of the more than a dozen markets there because of the heavy traffic. Shahe was originally a distribution center for garments for customers from rural areas. The clothes were cheap and of poor quality, but the trading volume was enormous. However, by 2005, Shahe began to change because of the increase in people's earnings. The markets there were revamped, and many commercial developers came to build new market buildings. After Shahe went through a facelift, the rents began to rise. However, its reputation as a place for cheap goods remained mostly unchanged. Some stores that had been in Zhanxi Road but moved to Shahe to take advantage of the cheaper rent could maintain a good amount of business because their regular customers followed them to Shahe.

A female worker at a clothing factory has this to say about Shahe:

> We call merchandise from Shahe maohuo (unpolished rough goods). The quality of these goods is very poor, and they are mostly for export. The stores there do not have either their own or contract factories. The stores are predominantly run by couples who sew the garments in their homes with the help of a few machines. Entrepreneurs from Shahe often go to other markets to learn what other people are selling and then come back to copy the styles.

In sum, there are many garment distribution centers in Guangzhou, each composed of a dozen or so markets. Each market is a seven- to twelve-story building occupied by hundreds of retail and wholesale stores, called dangkou on the first three to four floors and so-called xiezilou, or "offices" for wholesale only, on the rest. I cannot discuss all the clothing distribution centers and markets in Guangzhou, so I focus on those that my research subjects thought were the main markets. None of these markets are exclusively for shoppers only interested in buying counterfeits, even though some of them are labeled as notorious markets by the USTR Office. There are more legitimate fashion and accessories being traded than counterfeits in some of these markets. For most business owners, the involvement in counterfeiting is fluid and opportunistic, constantly crossing the line between legal and illegal, depending on business opportunities and market demands. The process is as simple as affixing or removing a trademark or a label from a product or adding or deleting a letter of the alphabet from a brand's name.

Leather Goods—The Sanyuanli Area

There is a saying that reflects the significance of the leather trade in Sanyuanli: "When it comes to leather goods, the world looks up to China, China looks up to Guangzhou, and Guangzhou looks up to Sanyuanli." Located in the Baiyun District, Sanyuanli is close to the Guangzhou Railway Station. It is estimated that there are up to thirty-four commercial buildings or leather markets in Sanyuanli, with ten thousand stores and an annual revenue of $4.3 billion. To avoid being viewed as a place where there are lots of goods but no brands, the Baiyun District Government in 2011 initiated a strategy of encouraging leather goods entrepreneurs to develop their own brands.

According to Xiao Ma (H4), a leather supplier born in China but raised in Hong Kong, the transformation of Sanyuanli into a preeminent leather center took many years. The leather trade in Sanyuanli began to take shape in 1987. Xiao Ma recalled that before Baiyun Leather City opened in 2003, the three major leather goods markets in Sanyuanli were Guihuagang, Zhongau, and Shengjia.

Baiyun Leather City

Of all the leather goods markets in Guangzhou, Baiyun Leather City (see Figure 4.5) is the most well-known and popular place to go for high-quality replicas of designer handbags, even though it has been listed only once, in 2016, by the U.S. authorities as a notorious market. It has two eye-catching look-alike commercial buildings (Phase I and Phase II). Colorful billboards hang high on the exteriors of the tall structures, and slogans in Chinese, such as "You Pay the Wholesale Price Even If You Buy Only One Handbag" and "Whatever You Dream Of, You Can Find It Here in the World of Luggage and the Ocean of Leather Goods," are prominently displayed. The establishment of the Sanyuanli Leather Market (with Baiyun Leather City as its main component) in September 2003 was listed as one of the twenty-five most significant developments and events in Guangzhou since the late 1970s. The mar-

Figure 4.5 Baiyun Leather City.

ket received the nationwide Leather Commerce Center Award in 2012 (Xiaojing Huang, Li, and Feng 2018).

Outside the Phase I building, along the wide boulevard called Jiefangbei (Liberation North) Road, many young men and women working as lakezai (solicitors or peddlers) roam the street looking for customers. The stores the solicitors represent are located in the residential buildings next to Baiyun Leather City, and these stores sell counterfeits already affixed with labels and trademarks. As I explain later, stores inside Baiyun Leather City display only generic replicas of leather products without trademarks to avoid being targeted by the authorities. After a customer buys a generic handbag, the trademarked bag will be sent to the customer's home or hotel in the evening. The customer must pay the seller the full price plus a delivery fee. If the buyer wants to pick it up the next day, he or she needs to make a down payment of about $100–$200, depending on the price of the handbag. Some buyers prefer to purchase trademark counterfeits on the spot rather than viewing a generic copy, because they cannot tell how the bag they order will look and feel after the trademark is affixed to it. These are the buyers who follow the solicitors into the stores in residential buildings near Baiyun Leather City.

The stores on the lower levels of Baiyun Leather City are called dangkou (see Figure 4.6). Most are small, ranging from one hundred to two hundred square feet. Some are divided in half, and one side is sublet to whoever is interested in squeezing into this highly congested and competitive business premise. A store owner on the second floor revealed that she was paying a monthly rent of $2,900 (in 2019), substantially less than the $7,000 she paid a few years back. Regardless of how tiny these outlets are, a member of a market management group said laughingly: "Do not look down on the people in those booths; all of them have a factory behind them." Most of the outlets sell leather handbags, and all the handbags on display are generic designer handbags. None of the handbags have any trademarks, such as labels or logos, or metal fittings bearing the name or logo of the brand. Most of the handbags resemble the products of Hermès, Louis Vuitton, Chanel, Gucci, Celine, Prada, and Loewe. Inside the stores, there are generally two saleswomen. Some owners come and go without a trace; some spend a substantial amount of time in their stores.

Most of the products on display in Baiyun Leather City have no price tags. People I talked to about the place said that one should bargain when shopping there. A Guangzhou resident gave me the following advice when I asked him how to shop at Baiyun: "When you visit Baiyun, you bargain as hard as you can. Whatever the saleswoman says, you pay only 30% of the asking price. If she says no, you go to another store and offer 35%. If it does not work, you then do this with another store and raise it to 40%. The bottom line is you do not pay more than 50% of the asking price. The store makes money

Figure 4.6 A dangkou (store or outlet) inside Baiyun Leather City.

from selling the item to you for a 50% discount." This is easier said than done because, while so many stores carry similar items, they may not be the same in terms of size, color, materials, metal fittings, or workmanship. Once, I was asking a saleswoman about a Hermès handbag. She showed me what appeared to be two identical handbags; the size, color, and materials looked the same. However, one was selling for $460 and the other for $320. She said the two bags used the same leather and the same metal fittings, but the first was hand stitched, and the other was stitched by machine. She then explained how to tell the difference by examining the stitches, and said it was not easy for most people to notice and appreciate the difference even after being shown.

Moreover, not all stores in Baiyun are willing to accept bargaining. I saw a high-quality Hermès Birkin bag at a store in Baiyun with a price tag of $940, and the sales assistant told me the price could not be reduced by even a penny. I returned to the store at least three times over the next several weeks, and every time I asked for the price of that Birkin bag, it was always $940, regardless of who was tending the store. When I asked a saleswoman why the bag was so expensive, she showed me a crocodile Birkin selling for $1,700. Her point was that if you think $940 for a fake handbag is expensive, we have other fake handbags that cost much more.

Zhonggang Leatherware Mall

After Baiyun Leather City, Zhonggang Leatherware Mall is the most popular place to shop for leather handbags in Guangzhou, especially for buyers looking for less expensive but good-quality bags. Stakeholders of the establishment promote Zhonggang as the birthplace of local brands that become name brands after many years of innovation and excellence. The implication is that Sanyuanli has been viewed as a marketplace where businesspeople are only interested in making quick money and not in spending the time it takes to establish their brands. Business owners in Zhonggang want to change this perception. According to a brochure (in Chinese and English) placed at the mall entrance: "Zhonggang Leatherware Mall is a specialized market of mid-to-high-end original leatherware . . . with a total construction area of more than 40,000 square meters. Since it was founded in 1998, more than 700 leatherware brands or merchants have joined and its annual turnover has exceeded 3 billion RMB [$430 million]."

Many stores in Zhonggang sell counterfeit handbags, even though, as in the stores in Baiyun, these stores do not display handbags with the trademarks of name brands. In my field notes, I recorded one of my visits to Zhonggang as follows:

I was talking to a saleslady (probably the owner as well, even though she would not admit it) in a store about buying a Chanel flap bag. As a friendly gesture, she offered me a chair to sit on. When I walked in, a woman had just finished buying three handbags, and the saleslady was patiently repacking the dozen or so handbags that the buyer had examined. The store had about forty handbags on display, primarily black Chanel look-alike leather handbags. Like other stores, this store was about nine by eleven feet. It had four rows of shelves against the walls and a stack of boxes underneath them. There were about sixty boxes. There was a small table near the entrance from which the saleslady conducted business.

While I was chatting with the saleswoman, a young man walked in and promptly ordered twelve fake Chanel shoulder bags. Later, the saleslady told me the man had been in her store a few times that day, and that all buyers shop around for a while before they make a final decision. The saleslady asked the buyer whether he was in wholesale or retail. The man said wholesale. Later, the saleslady told me the price for a wholesaler is lower than for a retailer but not by much. After the buyer examined the bags he was going to buy that were on display, he asked the saleswoman to show him the same bags in the boxes. Again, the saleswoman later explained to me that what the man was trying to do was to make sure the bags on the shelves were the same as the bags that were not on display and would be delivered to the buyers. Many buyers are concerned that the samples on the shelves are quality-wise better than the actual goods received by the customers.

The man said he came to Guangzhou to purchase because his wife was busy taking care of their children during the summer when the schools were closed. Otherwise, his wife would take the trip as she was the one who was in charge of their business. He said he came from a small place in Shandong, a province in the north, and he only sells black handbags because it is a cold area.

After the man placed the order, the saleswoman said she would deliver the bags to him in Shandong and waive the shipping fee. The man said she could charge him for delivery, but the saleslady insisted that there would be no shipping fee. At one point, the two seemed to be flirting with one another as the saleslady (herself a married woman) joked: "Too bad you are married." The man was good-looking, humorous, and gentlemanly.

Later, the man asked the saleslady whether she could affix the (Chanel) trademarks on the bags, and she said yes, but he needed to make such a request in advance. The man said that some stores attach trademarks on the spot using a small machine and that it was not difficult. The saleslady responded by saying that her business has a machine in their factory to adorn the trademarks, but it is a big machine. The man did not continue with the discussion.

Before I left, I bought a Chanel Classic Double Flap Lucky Charms handbag from the saleslady for $30 (see Figure 4.7). She told me the wholesale

Figure 4.7 A copy of a Chanel Classic Double Flap Lucky Charms handbag.

price for the bag was $23. A wholesale price is offered when a customer buys five or more of the same bag. However, a buyer has to purchase thirty or more small items like coin purses to receive the wholesale price.

Other Leather Goods Markets

As mentioned earlier, there are more than thirty leather goods markets in Sanyuanli, and these markets can be categorized as high end (e.g., Baiyun), midrange (e.g., Zhonggang), and low end (e.g., Yisen). Bags sold at Baiyun and Zhonggang are made of genuine leather, and those sold at Yisen are made of artificial leather. The prices at these markets are very different. When I was inquiring about a Hermès bucket bag in a store in Yisen, a saleslady told me:

> We are selling this Hermès bucket bag for $13. It is a PU (polyurethane) leather bag, not natural leather. Plus, there are no Hermès trademarks. It is a very ordinary bag, and also very cheap. If you go to Zhonggang, you can find a bag like this in genuine leather, but it will not have any Hermès trademarks either. It sells for $29 to $43 there. If you want a Hermès bucket bag with genuine leather and Hermès trademarks, you have to go to Baiyun. The bags there are considered gaofanghuo (high-quality imitations), but for the same bag, you will have to pay more than $430.

Besides Chanel and Louis Vuitton, Hermès handbags are the most often counterfeited in Sanyuanli. As noted by Dana Thomas (2007, 170–171), the author of *Deluxe: How Luxury Lost Its Luster*: "In the world of luxury handbags, as in automobiles and clothing, there is a pyramid of quality: made-to-order down to mass-manufactured. The best—the equivalent of a Rolls-Royce or a Chanel couture suit—is a Hermès handbag. Made of the finest leather and fabrics, sewed by hand, and with starting prices of more than $6,000 and years-long waiting lists, Hermès handbags are considered by many to be the last true luxury goods in the luxury fashion industry." Thus, it is no surprise that the most expensive fake handbags I saw in the area were crocodile Hermès Birkin or Kelly bags. However, as mentioned earlier, there were also inexpensive Birkin or Kelly bags.

Footwear

Guangzhou's Zhanxi Shoes City

Guangzhou's Zhanxi Shoes City is close to Zhanxi Road. Shoppers can get there by crossing the pedestrian bridge in front of U:US Market at the end of Zhanxi Road. The two distribution centers are divided by Guangyuanxi Road. Like other distribution centers in Guangzhou, Zhanxi Shoes City is made up of several large malls, including Buyuntiandi and Metropolis.

Shijing

Shijing is a well-known clearance center for unsold fashions and accessories. It is where many local and foreign buyers purchase leftovers for resale. There are many garment, leather goods, and shoe markets in Shijing, and one of the best known is the Guangda/Guoda Shoe Market. According to Ah Bao (F12), a shoe leather supplier, Guangda and Guoda, originally two separate markets, were at first located near the Guangzhou Railway Station. When there was a crackdown on counterfeiting in 2008, the two markets moved to Shijing.

Ah San (F16), a Louis Vuitton sandal manufacturer, described how the market evolved after moving to Shijing:

> Guangda was, at one point, a bustling market. It was so crowded that to get in or out of it was a huge challenge. That was before 2015. At that time, even if you were willing to offer more than $150,000 for a store, you would not get it. One day, a reporter from CCTV [China Central Television, a state-owned broadcaster] arrived at the market to work on a special report, and he interviewed a store owner there. The owner answered all the questions in detail, saying something like: "We have all the brand name shoes here," "We have all the shoe styles here," "We can deliver the goods to our buyers very quickly," and "We can give you any kind of receipt you want." After the CCTV report was aired, the authorities conducted a major crackdown. From then on,

business here was very different from the past. Now, the stores open only at night; there is little foot traffic during the daytime.

There are clothing and leather handbag markets in Shijing as well. A store there sells men's T-shirts and polo shirts for $4 each. If someone buys more than one hundred items, the price becomes $3 per item. The price for children's T-shirts is $1.50 apiece. Some of the markets sell only children's wear or underwear. Most of the markets there are at street level, and, in front of the stores, there are mountains of cheap goods, plus expensive cars such as BMWs, Range Rovers, and Porsches. Judging from the way the cars are parked, they probably belong to the store owners.

After an overview of some of the major physical markets in Guangzhou, it is pertinent to ask who the stakeholders in these markets are. A number of my research subjects told me that many markets were on sites where armed police or government guesthouses had once been located. During that time, those areas were considered off limits for ordinary people. After the guesthouses were demolished, the government unit that owned the land subcontracted with a developer to build markets and found a property management company to manage them.

No matter who owns a market or who is running it, there is no question that markets are developed with the blessing of the local authorities, and, in turn, the local authorities are supported by authorities one level above them. According to Ah Yun (F13), a dust bag producer, "The development of Shijing was closely tied to counterfeiting, and the local authorities condoned it because they wanted to boost the local economy."

Operating Entities

There are many operating entities engaging in the distribution of counterfeit goods, including dian (stores), dangkou (outlets), xiezilou (offices), and gongsi (companies). Unlike the first three types of operating entities, companies are located far away from the physical markets, presumably for larger spaces with lower rent and for being more active in designing, marketing, and management than distribution. Later, I examine both how these entities are set up and function and the working relationship among them.

Dian (Stores or Shops, Stand-Alone, Retail Only)

The simplest way to sell counterfeit goods is to operate a stand-alone retail store in a residential area, an urban village, or a neighborhood produce market. The owners of these retail stores will visit specific wholesale markets regularly to purchase merchandise, transport it back to their stores, and sell it to their customers. These stores usually sell both counterfeit and noncounterfeit goods and cater to the mostly working-class people who live nearby. Ah Hua (H6) is the owner of one of them. A twenty-six-year-old single woman, she has a small retail store in the Huangpu district of Guangzhou. Her store, located at the entrance to a produce market in a working-class neighborhood, is only about five by eight feet, so tiny that only Ah Hua can move around in there. Customers must stand outside the store, on the sidewalk, to talk to her. The store has no door, no window, no air-conditioning. According to her:

> I was a street vendor selling women's clothing in an urban village, but I quit after being chased frequently by the para-police.[1] The authorities wanted to stop street trading. I went to work as a beer sales-girl in a restaurant and became a KTV [karaoke television] hostess after some people urged me to do so. I entertained clients inside the KTV nightclub and also went out with them for sex. Later, the police forced the KTV to close its doors, and the owner dismissed all his employees. To make a living, I opened this store.
>
> The store has been in operation for only three months. I invested $3,000 to $4,000. At first, business was good and I made money. However, when the market owner decided to install an escalator between the first and second floors, my business went down. Because of the construction, the sidewalks are closed. Now, I consider it not bad if I can make enough money to pay the rent.
>
> I primarily sell shoes; handbags are just supplemental. I carry mainly Louis Vuitton, Gucci, and Coach handbags. My location determines what level of goods I can sell. After all, this is a food market in the Huangpu area [an impoverished area], so selling anything that costs $50 to $100 is impossible. Some customers will say they cannot afford an item if it costs more than $30. I buy most of my shoes and bags for $15 to $30, and I sell them for $30 to $45. This Louis Vuitton Petit Bucket bag is my most expensive bag; I buy it for $41 and sell it for $50. At Baiyun [Leather Market], this bag costs more.
>
> I get my goods from Guangzhou and Dongguan, from the dang-kou. A small store like mine cannot buy stuff directly from factories. They do not want to bother with a person like me. If I go to Dongguan, I close my store. It takes me only five to six hours for the trip. I go to Dongguan because they have better quality products plus trendy styles.
>
> I do not have a warehouse to store my goods; everything I have is in this store. I have more than three hundred pairs of shoes, but not that many handbags.

When Xiao Ning (H7, the person who introduced me to Ah Hua) and I were about to leave Ah Hua's store, Xiao Ning said she would like to buy the red Louis Vuitton Petit Bucket bag and asked Ah Hua to sell it to her for $44. Ah Hua graciously agreed to sell it for 288 yuan ($42), eight being a lucky number. The bag had a yellow dust bag, a certificate, and everything else that comes with a genuine Louis Vuitton bag. Xiao Ning, a young woman with good taste in fashion and accessories, thought that the bag was a high-quality replica because not only the materials and the handicraft but also the metal fittings were superb.

Dangkou (Stores or Outlets for Retail and Wholesale)

Of all the operating units for distribution, dangkou are the most likely places to conduct business transactions, whether retail or wholesale. Dangkou, meaning a business window, is originally a Cantonese word. A person who is interested in selling goods, especially in large quantities, needs an outlet. That outlet is most likely to be a dangkou located within a market that is known for a particular type of commodity. In China, it is common for a market building to host hundreds or even thousands of outlets because most are small.

As mentioned earlier, a person interested in the distribution of goods can "buy" or rent a store. "Buying" means buying a long-term right to use a store for commercial purposes without rent, usually for three to ten years. It may cost a buyer up to $140,000. Many counterfeiters say they and other businesspeople they know become involved in investing in dangkou after they make a significant amount of money from their counterfeiting businesses, meaning they "buy" one or more stores and rent them out. When the prices of their dangkou go up, they sell them to other buyers and make a handsome profit. Some people get rich by investing their money in the dangkou. Owners and managers of the dangkou do not prohibit original buyers from "selling" the stores if they want to.

The many counterfeiters who buy and sell stores to make a profit are taking quite a risk because no one can tell in advance whether a market will be successful or how long it will remain a success. The business environment in these markets can change rapidly, due to, in part, both the illicit nature of the business and law enforcement constraints. When there is a major crackdown, a market can collapse overnight. In brief, the markets are fluid and unpredictable.

Most start-up entrepreneurs do not have the money to "buy" a store, so they rent one for a few hundred or a few thousand dollars a month. Usually, the renter has to pay a two-month deposit and one month's rent when the lease is signed. All dangkou are subject to a monthly maintenance fee of several hundred dollars paid to the management of the building. This fee is always paid by the person who "owns" the store. Even though the price to "own" or rent a dangkou has increased astronomically over the past two decades, there are still millions of people in China who want to get rich fast. This is one of the reasons for the continued high demand for commercial distribution outlets. If a newcomer cannot afford to pay for an entire store, he or she will still go ahead and rent it but sublet half of it to other vendors.

Every store must pay a predetermined fixed amount of municipal tax every year, regardless of its revenue. The amount of the tax depends on the size of the store and the types of goods it sells. According to Prosecutor Wang, "Dangkou owners have to pay a lump sum of tax every year regardless of whether they make money or not, or how much they make. That is because their business transactions are in cash, and there is no way the authorities can figure out the real volume of their businesses. The lump sum amount is not the same for all dangkou; it depends on the type of business, the location of the dangkou, the level of foot traffic, the size, and other factors."

Some stores sell products manufactured by their own factories or contract manufacturers, and some sell merchandise they purchase from other distributors because they do not have their own factories or contract manufacturers. There are advantages and disadvantages associated with both business strategies. Xiao Zhen (H13), a leather handbag manufacturer, disclosed how he and his wife worked together to distribute the handbags he produced, plus handbags from other distributors or producers:

> After I started my manufacturing plant, my wife opened an outlet store at Baiyun Leather City. She sold the Fendi and Dior handbags I produced, as well as other brands manufactured by other factories. There were two advantages to this strategy. First, you sell whatever bags are popular, and you are not constricted by the few brands you make. Second, if you are selling a variety of brands, you are less likely to be the target of private anti-counterfeiting investigators hired by a particular brand, and thus you can avoid being subject to a crackdown by the authorities.

In general, the stores get busy after the gates are closed. That is when they begin to process the orders they receive during the day. After the items are packed, they are taken out through the back doors. Often, this will go on until midnight.

Xiezilou (Offices, Wholesale Only)

As mentioned earlier, the first few floors of most of the markets are occupied by dangkou, and these stores are involved in both retail and wholesale. Dangkou are relatively small; the size of the vast majority of them is only a few hundred square feet. They are not suitable places for sellers to have a long discussion with their clients because there is so much commotion inside and outside of these stores. As a result, some store owners also operate a xiezilou (offices) on the upper floors of the same building, where they receive wholesale buyers. Xiao Peng (G8) explains the different functions of dangkou and xiezilou as follows: "You can do retail business in a dangkou, and you pay the rent with the money you make from retail. Renting a dangkou will cost you up to $8,800 a month. Rent for a xiezilou may be between $3,000 to $4,500 a month, but no individual buyer is going to a xiezilou to buy things. That means you can only do wholesale business in a xiezilou. With dangkou, you can do both retail and wholesale. In general, dangkou are located on the lower floors and xiezilou on the upper floors."

Xiezilou are, in general, much bigger than dangkou. Some of the xiezilou are about six hundred to seven hundred square feet and normally have space to display products to customers in an attractive way. For example, Sonny (H10) has both a dangkou and a spacious xiezilou in Zhonggang. He even has a big private office inside his xiezilou, and there is an area outside his private office for his staff to work. In that area, there are also many shelves where his leather handbags are beautifully displayed.

Gongsi (Companies, Wholesale Only, with Showrooms)

A gongsi, or company, is most likely to be located in a commercial complex where other companies are also situated. It functions as the headquarters for owners of dangkou and xiezilou; it is there where the various departments of a business are located, including design/development, accounting, customer service, purchasing, and others. Xiao Guan (G13) explains how his gongsi, which has an impressive showroom, is connected to his dangkou and xiezilou on Zhanxi Road and to a warehouse near the gongsi:

> This place is my gongsi. I also operate a dangkou and a xiezilou in a market on Zhanxi Road. The rent here is lower than in Zhanxi Road. My rent here is about $1,100 a month, and the gongsi is a large place. I hired someone to manage the xiezilou in Zhanxi Road and rarely go there. The rent for the xiezilou is high, about $3,600 a month. Some xiezilou cost more, like $10,300 to $11,800 a month, depending on the location. In general, xiezilou are small, and dangkou even smaller. Dangkou rents for about $1,500 to $3,000 a month. I have two salespeople in my dangkou and hardly anyone visits the store. I also have a warehouse with four workers. In sum, I have ten people working for me.

The four operating entities mentioned here—dian, dangkou, xiezilou, and gongsi—are not unique to the counterfeiting industry. All the small and large legitimate businesses in China also adopt one or more of these four operating units to distribute their products. Again, like the manufacturing phase discussed in Chapter 3, there is not much difference between a counterfeiting business and a legitimate business in terms of distribution.

Exports

Counterfeit luxury goods produced in China are distributed locally and internationally. It is common to see vendors selling cheap fakes on the streets of urban centers worldwide. There are also many shops in poor and rich neighborhoods across the globe where copies from China are sold. In New York City's Chinatown, there are many Chinese and non-Chinese vendors selling fake leather handbags, watches, sunglasses, jewelry, and other fashion accessories to New Yorkers and tourists alike (Shao 2019; Staley 2013). According to a 2021 indictment, four Chinese from Brooklyn and Queens were arrested and charged for importing sneakers, sweatsuits, boots, slippers, and headphones from China to the New York metropolitan area. The indictment described how the group conducted its business: "The defendants first imported the goods in generic form from China to the Port of New York and New Jersey. The goods were then delivered to workshops and storage facilities controlled by some of the defendants in Queens and Long Island. In those workshops, insignias, emblems, trademarks and other brand signifiers were applied to the generic goods, converting them into purported brand name merchandise. These counterfeit goods were then sold as a part of the scheme directly to consumers and to wholesale buyers. The estimated retail value of the counterfeit-branded goods, had they been genuine, was in excess of $130 million" (U.S. Attorney's Office Eastern District of New York 2021, 2).

It is unclear what percentages of counterfeit luxury goods produced in China are for export or local consumption. Some of my research subjects thought it was fifty-fifty, and some guessed the foreign market was bigger than the local market, but most agreed that there had been a gradual shift from catering to foreign buyers to catering to local consumers. However, a 2018 report by Alibaba on counterfeiting suggests that the aggressiveness of Chinese authorities in anti-counterfeiting efforts might have forced counterfeiters to become more active in selling their products overseas (Alibaba 2018, 16).

My research participants were also not in agreement when I asked them whether there were differences in quality between fakes that were exported and those that were not exported. Some suggested that exported counterfeits are primarily low-quality yibiyi replicas. Xiao Cai, a person with many years of experience in the fashion industry, said: "Overseas orders mostly involve yibiyi goods, but not high-quality yibiyi. Local orders generally do not entail yibiyi goods, but if they do, they are for very high-end fakes." Zheng Hua (G19), a thirty-four-year-old from Hubei, also claimed that, when his firm switched from focusing on the foreign market to the local market, he also decreased the number of exact replicas he produced. Jane (G1) echoed: "The majority of the exported counterfeits are B, C, and D class fakes; there may be a small number of A class fakes, but no Super A or AA fakes whatsoever."

Peter (G7), Jane's husband, explained why counterfeit goods destined for overseas are generally low-quality fakes: "Why is the majority of the faked stuff overseas of low-quality? There are many reasons for this. One, if you transport high-end copies abroad and they get seized, you will have to absorb a huge loss; two, the cost of producing high-quality copies is already very high, so there is a limit to your profit margin. When you have high risk and low profits, it is not good for business; three, foreigners are unlikely to be willing to spend much money buying fake luxury goods; if the price for a copy is very high, they would rather buy a genuine one."

Jane also revealed that Wenzhounese are key players in the shipment of counterfeit goods out of China, mainly because they enjoy an excellent relationship with Chinese customs officials: "The transnational transportation of counterfeits is controlled by the Wenzhounese, regardless of whether the destination is Europe or the United States. Even though there are many Cantonese living abroad, they are not able to enter the transportation business, and that is because they cannot hook up with Chinese customs officials. Only Wenzhounese have this connection." In their book on the development of courier services in China over the past two decades, Xiaojun Zhu and Liping Yang (2017) note that China's top four courier service firms all belong to hard-working risk-taking entrepreneurs from a small town in Zhejiang Province. Wenzhou is the provincial capital of Zhejiang. My interactions with counterfeit vendors in New York City's Chinatown indicated that the vast majority of them originated from Wenzhou City and other parts of Zhejiang Province.

Regarding exports, the demand for counterfeit goods in Africa must be considered. During my fieldwork in Guangzhou, I noted that many individual entrepreneurs from Africa were active in various businesses. According to the sociologist Zhou Min and her colleagues (2015), an estimated fifty thousand to one hundred thirty thousand African migrants, mostly self-made entrepreneurs, were in Guangzhou in 2015, most of them from Nigeria, Mali, Ghana, Guinea, Cameroon, Congo, Tanzania, and Zambia. Gordon Mathews and his colleagues characterizes Africans in Guangzhou as follows: "I considered these entrepreneurs through the lens of 'low-end globalization'—not the globalization of multinational corporations with all their lawyers and advertising budgets, but of traders sending relatively small amounts of goods under the radar of the law, bribing customs agents on different continents, and getting these goods back home to stalls and street vendors" (Mathews, Lin, and Yang 2017, 2).

Mr. Bai, a deputy chief of a police station in Guangzhou, suggested that Africans play a vital role in the luxury goods counterfeiting industry in Guangzhou:

> This business now relies mainly on Africans. They like Guangzhou a lot, maybe because the weather here is similar to their weather back home–very hot and no snow. They are also crazy about buying counterfeits. If a product is not a fake, not a brand name, they do not want it, regardless of how good the quality is. Once you apply the name of an international brand, they want it, even if it is shoddy. Maybe there was strong local demand for fakes in the past, but now not so many people here are buying them, especially not the Guangzhounese. That is why most fakes are now for the overseas market.

In contrast, according to Mathews and his collaborators, African buyers are not interested in copies with international brand names. According to them, "Most [80%–90%] of the goods sold in Xiaobei or Guangyuanxi are knockoffs, copying the style or design of a product, but are using a different brand name, or no brand name" (Mathews, Lin, and Yang 2017, 93). Thus, there is no clear-cut answer to the question of whether African buyers are going after point-by-point fakes or edge-ball knockoffs that mimic the style or design of a brand-name product. Maybe this is not the most important issue for them to consider when they arrive in China to bring merchandise back to their home countries for resale. As Mathews et al. (2017, 94) points out, "Knockoffs are in demand throughout the developing world because people in those countries want the goods of the developed world but can't pay developed-world prices."

E-Commerce

The distribution of counterfeit goods has changed dramatically since the emergence of e-commerce in the new millennium (Antonopoulos et al. 2018; Forgione 2016–2017; Greene 2019). According to Anita Radon (2012, 74), a Swedish researcher, "The problem with counterfeit goods has become even more pressing for luxury brands with the entrance of the Internet as a new market actor." Esther Zuccaro (2016, 146–147), a legal scholar, suggests that "Online shopping permits consumers to buy and sell counterfeits from the comfort of their living rooms, eliminating 'dark alleys and basements from the buying equation.' E-commerce marketplaces can provide a successful setting for counterfeiters: low operating costs to sell on websites, less risk of legal action, and the ability to easily open another store, should one be shut down." A report by Alibaba (2018, 16), the "Amazon of China," concludes that enhanced anti-counterfeiting measures adopted by the Chinese authorities "forced counterfeiters . . . to move their operations from one e-commerce platform to many other platforms to avoid being detected."

China was home to 890 million mobile internet users in the first half of 2018 (Y. Zheng 2018). Moreover, Zuccaro (2016, 151) notes that "unlike in the United States, many large cities in China do not offer shopping malls or large retail centers, resulting in Chinese residents turning to shopping on-line for their retail needs." As a result, Chinese consumers have already developed the habit of buying almost everything online (Ma 2018). A college professor in Guangzhou shared her online shopping experience as follows: "I buy stuff online every day; I buy everything online. Whatever I need, I buy on Tianmao (TMall) or JD.com. I also buy things from Taobao. If I run out of rice, I buy it from Tianmao, and it will be delivered to my door right away. I do not have to go outside to carry it back. In the past, my husband had to go across the street to a supermarket to buy rice; there's no need for him to do that anymore."

The professor compared the chance of inadvertently purchasing counterfeit goods on JD.Com and Alibaba's Taobao:

> JD.Com is a perfect e-commerce platform for shopping. It is very aggressive in preventing counterfeit products from penetrating its site. Not only does it keep a close eye on counterfeiting, but it also levies a heavy fine on violators. The platform is a third-party platform; it does not sell goods itself. The platform is heavy on electronic appliances but has almost everything. On the other hand, Taobao is saturated with fake goods, and many of these goods are sold as if they were genuine items.

According to a report by the U.S. DHS (2020, 7), an online third-party marketplace "means any web-based platform that includes features primarily designed for arranging the sale, purchase, payment, or shipping of goods, or that enables sellers not directly affiliated with an operator of such platforms to sell physical goods to consumers located in the United States." The report also suggests that e-commerce sales are growing faster than brick-and-mortar retail sales and that counterfeit goods "are now marketed to consumers in their homes through increasingly mainstream e-commerce platforms and third party online marketplaces that convey an air of legitimacy" (U.S. DHS 2020, 8).

Peter (G7), a Guangzhounese who has many years of experience in the clothing business, explained how the well-established express delivery service industry in China plays a critical role in the explosion of e-commerce: "Nowadays, express delivery service is a well-developed industry in China, and it is a big help in promoting business transactions. Here, the fee for delivering a package anywhere in China is only 73 cents for up to one kilogram. If the consignment is large, the courier can reduce the delivery fee to 50 cents a kilogram. Very cheap! Also, the package will arrive the following day, no matter what. Very fast!" Peter explained how he had completely changed his business operations from selling goods in physical markets to online outlets:

> I do not operate any brick-and-mortar outlets anymore. I ask a contract manufacturer to produce goods and then I sell them online. E-commerce has revolutionized the counterfeit trade, and the distribution of fakes has changed dramatically.
>
> On Taobao, you can ask online influencers to help you to sell things. Some of them are big stars online, and some are lesser stars. These influencers have many followers, from hundreds of thousands to millions, and that's why their marketing capabilities are outstanding. They can also do live-streaming, attracting up to hundreds of thousands of people watching at the same time.
>
> Besides Taobao and TMall, I also market my merchandise on WeChat. It is easy to do business on WeChat. Let me give you an example. You know I have the stuff, and I am the yuantou [main source, meaning either the designer/organizer or the manufacturer of the products]. I sell you an item for $15, and you sell it to people on your online social network. I send you pictures of the item, and you post them on your network site. You sell the product for $30. If someone wants to buy it, he or she pays you $30, you give me the buyer's address, and I send the item to that person. You keep $15 and give me the other $15. You do not even have to touch the product. I will let all the people in my online social network know what goods I have, so they know what they can buy from me. They, in turn, let people in their social networks know what they have. When this kind of information circulates from one network to another, it spreads rapidly and reaches people near and far.

Alibaba's Taobao

Of the major e-commerce platforms in China, Taobao is the most prominent and the most likely place to find counterfeit goods. According to Zuccaro

(2016, 156), "In 2013, Columbia Sportswear purchased hundreds of listings claiming to be genuine Columbia products on Taobao, and determined that 82% of products purchased were counterfeit." In her work, Zuccaro (2016, 149–150) makes a detailed introduction to Alibaba, as follows:

> Founded sixteen years ago, Alibaba is China's largest e-commerce company, utilized in eighty percent of online Chinese commerce. Alibaba is an all-in-one e-commerce marketplace, bank, and search engine. Alibaba offers services on its platforms conceptualized as a mix of eBay's user-generated listings and Amazon's wide product availability, with additional features such as product search functions and online payment systems, similar to those [of] Google and PayPal. The Alibaba company offers three main e-commerce websites: Taobao, TMall, and Alibaba.com. Taobao is Alibaba's largest business, on which vendors may list items for free of charge, but pay for services such as advertising so that their products stand out. . . . TMall is a more upscale e-commerce website on which large brands such as Nike or Proctor and Gamble pay a hefty fee to list their products. . . . Alibaba.com connects Chinese companies with exporters throughout the world.

According to Zuccaro (2016, 153, 155), Alibaba and its various e-commerce websites are often used by counterfeiters to sell their products and, as a result, have become targets for U.S. and Chinese anti-counterfeiting agencies:

> Alibaba, which has been called "the Internet's Mecca for Counterfeit Clothing," has a history of counterfeiting and knockoff items for sale. The Office of the United States Trade Representative ("USTR") compose[s] a Notorious Markets List every year, identifying certain marketplaces, both on and offline, "that reportedly engage in and facilitate substantial copyright piracy and trademark counterfeiting." Alibaba's websites are no stranger to the notorious market[s] lists. Alibaba.com was listed in 2008, 2009, and 2010, and Taobao was listed in 2008, 2009, 2010, and 2011, but were subsequently removed. . . . In January 2015, China's State Administration for Industry and Commerce ("SAIC") estimated that two thirds of products offered on Taobao were counterfeit.

Mr. Jin (F14), a shoe counterfeiter, recalls how he at one point was bringing in a sizable amount of money selling counterfeit shoes on Taobao: "In 2003, I began to do business on Taobao, selling the fake shoes I produced. I did that until 2009. At that time, I earned more than $44,000 a month. However, I did not save much money because I was having a great time every day and squandering money. At any rate, it was easy come, easy goes."

The popularity of Taobao prompted the emergence of so-called taobaocun (Taobao Villages) all over China. Certain areas were labeled taobaocun because of the many entrepreneurs in them who specialized in producing merchandise for the sole purpose of selling it on Taobao (Cui 2019).

Tencent's WeChat

Not long after the emergence of Taobao, WeChat (the Chinese equivalent of Facebook) became a platform for small-time sellers to market their goods. Unlike Alibaba's Taobao, Tencent's WeChat allows netizens to conduct their businesses without any charges. According to Lau Fang (G21), a clothing business owner, this practice by WeChat transformed China into a country where "everybody is a merchant" (quanmin jieshang), as opposed to "everybody is a soldier" (quanmin jiebing), a popular slogan of the Mao era (1949–1976) (Dikotter 2016; Macfarquhar and Schoenhals 2006). Ordinary people who sell products on WeChat are called weishang (WeChat vendors). Xiao Yuen (G12) recalled how a man amassed a fortune selling fakes on WeChat: "Between 2015 and 2016, many people got very rich because of WeChat. I knew a young man from Chaoshan who earned more than $1.47 million in three months as a weishang. He sold all kinds of counterfeit products; he had everything. He bought Diesel men's T-shirts from me for $4.40 apiece and sold them for $8.80 on WeChat. I knew what he was doing, but I could not do what he did because not everyone can be a successful weishang. Not only do you have to know how to do it, but also you need to have connections. Otherwise, you cannot make it." Xiao Peng (G8), also a garment businessman, thought that WeChat was a godsend for counterfeiters: "WeChat makes it easier for people to sell counterfeit goods. All they need to do is post photos of Gucci or Chanel products on WeChat, claiming that these are the images of their counterfeit goods, and viewers have no idea what is happening. Besides, it is almost impossible to prevent the buying and selling of fakes on WeChat."

Mr. Liu (G20), a full-time self-proclaimed "professional" weishang, explained how he sold all kinds of copies on WeChat:

> I sell a variety of things on WeChat, including men's and women's clothing, handbags, footwear, watches, sunglasses, and other products. They are all copies. I also sell Canada Goose jackets. Look at this (showing several photos of the jackets on his cell phone). They look exactly like the originals. I am selling them for a little over $147 apiece. I frequently send text messages to people in my group and

tell them what goods I have. And they contact me when they are look-ing for something. That is because they know I am a professional WeChat vendor. There are three types of WeChat vendors. The first type is a person doing it full-time and professionally. The second type is someone who works, but for only a short amount of time in the morning, and spends the rest of the day selling goods on WeChat. The third type is a housewife doing it part-time or someone in it for fun. I belong to the first type, which is why people will ask me for things they want, knowing that I can find them even if I do not have them.

I have more than four hundred suppliers to source my goods. I can find all kinds of fake goods, and they are high quality. My buyers are primarily wealthy people, and most also buy genuine luxury prod-ucts. They buy high-quality imitations because they feel like they do not have to wear their originals all the time; for them, it is fine to wear replicas occasionally. At any rate, from their viewpoint, they only wear high-quality fakes, so nobody is going to notice if they are wearing fakes.

Those who provide me with merchandise are not first-tier whole-salers. My suppliers have their suppliers, and who knows how many tiers there are on top of my suppliers. I can't buy stuff directly from factories. Factories are not going to deal with an individual WeChat vendor. I rarely go to my suppliers to pick up the goods; they usually send the goods to me. I pay my suppliers only after receiving the goods and ensuring they are in good condition. However, it is a dif-ferent story with my buyers. My buyers have to pay me first before I send them the goods.

Leslie (H9), a twenty-six-year-old college graduate who was working full-time for a computer chip company in Shenzhen, revealed how he sold coun-terfeit goods on WeChat, how his business expanded, and how he moved up the ladder of WeChat vendors. Moreover, he recalled both how he was not allowed to use WeChat for three months and how he then returned to be-come a low-profile vendor after he was "punished." While selling fakes on WeChat, he worked full-time and earned more than $1,500 a month, a de-cent wage in China:

Initially, I got my leather handbags from a Chaozhou woman called Mary and sold them to my friends on WeChat. I posted pictures of the bags on WeChat and listed the prices. If someone was interested, he or she paid me, I asked Mary to send the bag to my buyer, and then I paid Mary. I did not have to touch the bags. After a few months,

I realized that business was not good, and after I came to know two brothers who were selling fake watches, I switched to the watch business. I was mainly selling Rolex, Armani, and Daniel Wellington watches. I got a Rolex Submariner from the brothers for $60, sold it for $220, and made a $160 profit. My cost for a Daniel Wellington watch was $30, and I charged $73 to $88.

As my business grew, I became a second-level *yuantou* (source). I recruited a bunch of sellers to be my downstream operators. I had more than twenty of them, but only about ten were major sellers. I offered them Daniel Wellington watches for $44 each and made only $14 per watch myself. They could sell them for $73 to $88 and earn $29 to $44 per watch. My profit margin became smaller, but my sales quantity increased, so in the end, I made more. My downstream operators might have their downstream sellers, and that was not a concern for me because our motto was, if there is money to be made, let's make it together. When business was good, I made $442 a day, and after a few months, I earned more than $14,750.

In September 2017, I received a notice from WeChat telling me that I was involved in selling counterfeit goods and that they were going to shut down my account for three months. That scared the hell out of me because if you do not have a WeChat account, it is incredibly inconvenient. I had no choice but to wait for them to resume my account. Now, I do not dare to be a "source" anymore; I just do what I did before, selling only to my friends. This experience is a big deal for me, so I am now laying low.

Leslie showed me the Chinese notice from WeChat, which I translated into English:

DISCIPLINARY NOTICE FROM THE WECHAT TEAM CONCERNING THE SELLING OF COUNTERFEITS

Due to users' complaints and our verification, we have found that you have very often used your WeChat account to market counterfeit goods to your friends. Therefore, we are terminating your friend circle function. It will be resumed on 2017–12–15. During this termination period, your friends cannot read the messages you send them.
Infringed name brand: Daniel Wellington
Please pay attention to how you use your account; otherwise, we will impose more restrictions on your account, and you may be subject to a lawsuit by the property rights owner. For details, please refer to "Regulations on the usage of WeChat personal accounts."

Pinduoduo

Another e-commerce platform notorious for cheap merchandise and counterfeit goods is Pinduoduo (meaning striving for more and more). According to Hu Yongqi (2018, 7), a journalist with the English-language *China Daily*, "Established in 2015, Pinduoduo claims it now has more than 300 million users. Though it went public on Nasdaq, thousands of goods sold on the platform were found to be counterfeit." Another *China Daily* reporter, Fan Feifei (2018), reported that Pinduoduo's shares rose by more than 40 percent on the first day of trading when it debuted on the Nasdaq in New York. The Chinese media have criticized the e-commerce platform for distributing cheap fakes (*Southern Metropolis Daily* 2018a). Temu, an online marketplace in the United States, is owned and operated by the holding company of Pinduoduo.

The Impact of E-Commerce

Xiao Yuen (G12) explained how the rapid development of e-commerce in China has shifted the focus of sellers and buyers from product quality to price:

> E-commerce platforms have utterly changed our shopping patterns. Nowadays, people do not leave home to buy anything; they do it online. When you buy things online, you do not see or touch the actual goods; you buy after viewing their images. That is why many entrepreneurs pay less and less attention to quality. As long as the merchandise is cheap, that is all that matters. Because consumers can check and compare the prices of a product online, they buy from the vendor who offers the lowest price. Buyers from third- and fourth-tier cities are proud of their ability to find the lowest price and see this as an accomplishment. They are not concerned about receiving useless merchandise. That is why the goods nowadays are getting cheaper and cheaper, and their quality is getting poorer and poorer.

According to Peter (G7), e-commerce has established a direct link between manufacturers and end users and, in the process, eliminated the retailers and wholesalers. This has imposed enormous pressure on business owners to keep prices at a minimum to be competitive:

> In the past, we conducted business the traditional way; which was to have a headquarters and then have an authorized wholesale distributor in every province. The provincial distributors would have their city-level authorized distributors, and city-level distributors would deal with county-level distributors. Of course, when a product goes through different levels of distributors, its price will increase many times be-

cause each of these distributors needs to make a profit. Now, the many levels of distributors are gone, and that is because of the emergence of e-commerce and express consignment carriers. Now, the source can sell his or her products directly to customers and bypass all the intermediaries. Under such circumstances, competition is fierce, and prices are transparent, comparable, and kept to a minimum.

The development of e-commerce also allows counterfeiters in China to sell their products to buyers around the globe (U.S. DHS 2020; USTR 2021). According to a report by the U.S. Intellectual Property Enforcement Coordinator (IPEC 2019, 8), "A small package is charged less to be shipped by air from China to the United States than when it is shipped entirely within the US," and "this artificially low postage has significantly contributed to the rapid growth in recent years of counterfeits being shipped from China to the United States."

5

INDIVIDUAL CHARACTERISTICS

In this chapter, I examine the individual characteristics of counterfeiters, both business owners and employees. I also explore how they entered this line of business and how they perceived themselves and their everyday lives. At the end of this chapter, I provide the profiles of several counterfeiters I interviewed. Considering the magnitude of counterfeiting worldwide, there is a need for more systematic empirical data about the individuals who engage in it. This study is the first step in examining the backgrounds of counterfeiters based on data collected from face-to-face interviews with a limited number of them in their natural surroundings.

The Counterfeiters

In this section, I examine the individual characteristics of my research subjects. I focus on their age, gender, education level, marital status, place of origin, and nationality. The fifty-seven research subjects are divided into three groups depending on which industry they belong to: garment ($N = 24$), handbag ($N = 17$), and footwear ($N = 16$). The individual attributes of members of each group are presented in this chapter's tables: Table 5.1, for participants in the garment industry; Table 5.2, for those in the handbag industry; and Table 5.3, for those in the footwear industry.

TABLE 5.1. RESEARCH SUBJECTS FROM THE GARMENT INDUSTRY (N = 24)

Name	Sex	Age	Marital Status	Education	Place of Origin	Role	Remarks
G1 Jane	F	40s	Married	College (Australia)	Taipei, Taiwan	Organizer/designer	Also manufacturer and distributor
G2 Laoban	M	68	Married	College (Taiwan)	Taipei, Taiwan	Organizer/designer	Also manufacturer and distributor
G3 Ah Xiang	F	50s	Unknown	Unknown	Unknown	Distributor	Both retail and wholesale
G4 Wendy	F	30s	Unknown	Unknown	Unknown	Organizer/designer	Also manufacturer and distributor
G5 Ah Min	F	40s	Divorced	Middle school	Taizhou, Zhejiang	Organizer/designer	Also manufacturer and distributor, ex-wife of Zhao Zong (G14)
G6 Xiao Wen	M	39	Married	Unknown	Henyang, Hunan	Organizer/designer	Mainly for exports to Russia
G7 Peter	M	49	Married	College (Australia)	Guangzhou, Guangdong	Organizer/designer	Married to Jane, also manufacturer and distributor
G8 Xiao Peng	M	Early 50s	Married	Unknown	Zhejiang	Organizer/designer	Also distributor
G9 Mr. Han	M	65	Married	Unknown	Jiayi, Taiwan	Maritime transporter	None
G10 Mr. Xia	M	40s	Unknown	Unknown	Zhangzhou, Fujian	Hangtag supplier	None
G11 Mrs. Jia	F	40s	Married	Fashion vocational school	Kaiping, Guangdong	Embroidered patch supplier	None
G12 Xiao Yuen	M	49	Married	Unknown	Weishan, Yunnan	Organizer/designer	Also manufacturer and distributor
G13 Xiao Guan	M	40s	Married	College	Mianyang, Sichuan	Organizer/designer	A former employee of Jane (G1)

(continued)

TABLE 5.1. RESEARCH SUBJECTS FROM THE GARMENT INDUSTRY (N = 24) (continued)

Name	Sex	Age	Marital Status	Education	Place of Origin	Role	Remarks
G14 Zhao Zong	M	40s	Divorced	Unknown	Taizhou, Zhejiang	Organizer/designer	Ex-husband of Ah Min (G5)
G15 Xiao Xin	F	40s	Married	Fashion vocational school	Unknown	Manufacturer	Works with counterfeiting and noncounterfeiting customers
G16 Xiao Meng	F	30	Married	Middle school	Henyang, Hunan	Designer/worker	A former employee of Laoban (G2), sister of Ah Lan (G18)
G17 Lin Jun	M	34	Married	Middle school	Nanchong, Sichuan	Organizer/designer	Also manufacturer and distributor
G18 Ah Lan	F	28	Married	Middle school	Hunan	Designer/worker	A former employee of Laoban (G2), works for Lau Fang (G21), sister of Xiao Meng (G16)
G19 Zheng Hua	M	43	Married	Middle school	Hubei	Organizer/designer	Also manufacturer and distributor
G20 Mr. Liu	M	40s	Unknown	Unknown	Unknown	WeChat merchant	E-commerce
G21 Lau Fang	F	40s	Married	College (major in fashion design)	Jiangxi	Organizer/designer	Also manufacturer and distributor; Ah Min's (G5) sister-in-law
G22 Ah Ting	M	35	Married	Vocational school	Guangxi	Distributor	None
G23 Kenny and Gigi	M	34	Married	Unknown	Henan	Distributor	None
G24 Lao Su	M	49	Married	Unknown	Chongqing	Factory manager	A former employee of Laoban (G2)

Note: Jane and Laoban are from Taiwan; the rest are all Chinese nationals.

TABLE 5.2. RESEARCH SUBJECTS FROM THE HANDBAG INDUSTRY (*N* = 17)

Name	Sex	Age	Marital Status	Education	Place of Origin	Role	Remarks
H1 Li Bing	F	46	Married	Elementary school	Wenzhou, Zhejiang	Distributor	A devoted Christian; married to Mr. Mu (H8)
H2 Ah Leung	M	30s	Married	Unknown	Zhanjiang, Guangdong	Manufacturer	None
H3 Danny	M	42	Unknown	Unknown	Unknown	Manufacturer	None
H4 Xiao Ma	M	45	Married	Middle school	Chenghai, Guangdong	Leather supplier	Grew up in Hong Kong
H5 Chen Jian	M	Late 40s	Married	College	Taishan, Guangdong	Distributor	Visited New York City, Boston, and San Francisco
H6 Ah Hua	F	26	Single	Unknown	Shaoyang, Hunan	Shoe and handbag retailer	A former street vendor
H7 Xiao Ning	F	20s	Single	Graduate	Unknown	Organizer/designer	Taobao vendor
H8 Mr. Mu	M	49	Married	Elementary school	Wenzhou, Zhejiang	Distributor	Married to Li Bing (H1)
H9 Leslie	M	26	Single	College	Hebei	WeChat vendor	Has a full-time job in a chip company

(continued)

TABLE 5.2. RESEARCH SUBJECTS FROM THE HANDBAG INDUSTRY (N = 17) (*continued*)

Name	Sex	Age	Marital Status	Education	Place of Origin	Role	Remarks
H10 Sonny	M	36	Married	Graduate school	Chaoshan, Guangdong	Organizer/designer	None
H11 Xiao Jen	M	30s	Married	Unknown	Leizhou, Guangdong	Warehouse worker	None
H12 Mrs. Lin	F	49	Married	Unknown	Henan	Saleswoman	Works for her sister
H13 Xiao Zhen	M	35	Married	Vocational school	Guangzhou, Guangdong	Manufacturer	Also distributor
H14 Mr. Hung	M	50s	Married	Unknown	Shiling, Guangzhou	Manufacturer	None
H15 Xiao Lai	M	40s	Married	Unknown	Chaoshan, Guangdong	Leather supplier	Husband of Xiao Ma's (H4) cousin
H16 Xiao Qin	M	33	Married	College	Chaoshan, Guangdong	Organizer/designer	Also manufacturer and distributor
H17 Mr. Zhou	M	40s	Married	Unknown	Unknown	Organizer/designer	None

Note: Xiao Ma is from Hong Kong; the rest are all Chinese nationals.

TABLE 5.3. RESEARCH SUBJECTS FROM THE FOOTWEAR INDUSTRY ($N = 16$)

Name	Sex	Age	Marital Status	Education	Place of Origin	Role	Remarks
F1 Mr. Cheng	M	40s	Married	Unknown	Zhanjiang, Guangdong	Workshop worker	None
F2 Mr. Tian	M	40s	Married	Unknown	Sichuan	A supervisor of a Skechers contract manufacturer	Copies Skechers, Timberland, and UGG shoes on the side
F3 John	M	70	Married	College (Taiwan)	Taipei, Taiwan	A supervisor of a Skechers contract manufacturer	Retired; a high school classmate of mine
F4 Mr. Mao	M	40s	Married	Unknown	Jiangxi	Manufacturer	Duplicates Timberland, Ecco, and Keen shoes
F5 Mr. Hu	M	50s	Unknown	Unknown	Hunan	Retailer	Sells New Balance, Yeezy, Nike, Adidas, and Florsheim shoes
F6 Mr. Huang	M	50s	Unknown	Unknown	Quanzhou, Fujian	Retailer	Mainly sneakers
F7 Mimi	F	20s	Single	High school	Zhanjiang, Guangdong	Manufacturer	Mainly Chanel sandals
F8 Mr. Wu	M	40s	Unknown	Unknown	Shangzhi, Sichuan	A supervisor of a contract manufacturer	Copies Skechers shoes with Mr. Liang (F9)

(continued)

TABLE 5.3. RESEARCH SUBJECTS FROM THE FOOTWEAR INDUSTRY ($N = 16$) (*continued*)

Name	Sex	Age	Marital Status	Education	Place of Origin	Role	Remarks
F9 Mr. Liang	M	40s	Unknown	Unknown	Unknown	Manufacturer	An investor who partners with Mr. Wu (F8)
F10 Mr. Zeng	M	40s	Married	Unknown	Chengdu	Materials supplier	Specializes in breathable mesh fabric for uppers
F11 Xiao Fei	M	30s	Married	Unknown	Harbin, Heilongjiang	Materials supplier	Specializes in shoe hardware
F12 Ah Bao	M	40	Married	High school	Zhaoqing, Guangdong	Shoe leather supplier	Works for Xiao Ma (H4), but only responsible for the shoe leather business
F13 Ah Yun	M	34	Married	Unknown	Zhanjiang, Guangdong	Dust bag manufacturer	Mainly for Louis Vuitton and Gucci counterfeits
F14 Mr. Jin	M	48	Married	Unknown	Yangzhou, Jiangsu	Organizer/designer	Also distributor
F15 Sun Lu	F	39	Divorced	Elementary	Henan	Organizer/designer (sneakers)	Also manufacturer and distributor
F16 Ah San	M	33	Married	Unknown	Zhanjiang, Guangdong	Manufacturer	Mainly Louis Vuitton sandals

Note: John is from Taiwan; the rest are all Chinese nationals.

Age

Most of my subjects were in their prime, energetic, and full of hope for a bright future. They had arrived in Guangzhou from other parts of China when they were in their late teens or early twenties, worked in the fashion business for several years, and learned how to run a business. In China, most ambitious migrant workers do not arrive in major urban centers anticipating they will work for someone else for a long time; they are already mulling over the idea of starting their businesses not long after they show up for work. Many research subjects were employed for only a few years before starting their businesses. In China, small business owners know that their employees could one day be their competitors. Thus, when that happens, they take it in stride. Some employers offer outstanding employees partnerships to prevent them from leaving.

Because I did not ask every subject his or her age at the interview, my data on this variable is incomplete. In general, most were in their thirties or forties. The oldest subject (Laoban, G2) was seventy, but, by then, he had already been out of the counterfeiting business for five years. I had the opportunity to interview him several times in Taipei (where he lives) and Guangzhou (where he occasionally returns to meet his former workers). The youngest subject (Mimi, F7) was in her early twenties and operated a shoe manufacturing workshop with her younger brother.

Gender

Women play an important role in the counterfeiting of garments and fashion accessories in China, either as business owners or as workers (Liao 2020). Most distribution outlets, offices, and companies employ predominantly young women for design, sales, and accounting. Most factory workers are also female. Men are more likely to be hired for packaging, warehousing, or delivery.

When a couple runs a business, there is a good chance that the wife is much more active in the business than the husband and that she is the one who makes all the critical decisions. Of the more than a dozen couples I interviewed and became acquainted with, it was always the wives telling the husbands what to do. Some men did work hard along with their wives, but some appeared to be simply tagging along, showing little interest in the business, and were more interested in enjoying a good life or talking about buying a new car.

In my other studies, I have also found that women play a prominent role in facilitating certain types of transnational criminal activities. For example, in two research projects on the smuggling of Chinese nationals to the United States, my colleagues and I discovered that some of the most successful snakeheads (human smugglers) were women (K. Chin 1999; S. Zhang and Chin 2002; S. Zhang, Chin, and Miller 2007). When my colleagues and I examined the drug trade in the Golden Triangle and Southeast Asia, we found that women were active not only as mules or low-level sellers but also as organizers (K. Chin 2009; K. Chin and Zhang 2015). In a study of the transnational movement of Chinese women for commercial sex, my collaborator and I learned that women played a critical role not only in helping other women travel overseas to sell sex but also in the day-to-day operation of a sex venue (K. Chin and Finckenauer 2011, 2012). The important role women play in transnational crime is not unique to the Chinese. Research on gender and crime involving other nationalities or ethnic groups has also confirmed the critical role women play in drug trafficking (Carey 2014; Paluch 2023), drug sales (Maher and Hudson 2007), human smuggling (Sanchez 2015), and sex trafficking (Keo et al. 2014).

Education

Most counterfeiters I interviewed had received little formal education. After spending a few years in an elementary or a junior high school, they quit and began to work. Only a few had completed high school, vocational school, or college. *China Daily*, the most circulated English newspaper in China, reported that most of the counterfeiters processed by authorities in Shenzhen have only an elementary school education and some were illiterate. In their study of counterfeiters of automotive components in China based on published court judgments, A. Shen, Turner, and Antonopoulos (2022) found that most of the counterfeiters had attended only middle school or were uneducated.

With a sense of pride, a research subject told me that, even though she had only two years of elementary school education, she was smart enough to make a handsome amount of money from her handbag business. Some of my research participants acknowledged that, due to their lack of education, they knew nothing about the concept of IPR when they began to copy luxury goods. They were not aware that they were engaged in illegal activity. They said they began to have some knowledge of it after the Chinese government began to educate the public about IPR.

Marital Status

Most of my subjects were married and had children. A few of them were divorced, and two had marital problems because of infidelity by one or both partners. As mentioned earlier, if a couple jointly ran a business, the wife was most likely to be the one who was in charge of it, not the husband. Regardless of who was in charge, a husband and wife business team requires the couple to work together for long hours. As a result, they must leave their young children with their parents in their home villages. Children taken care of by their grandparents in rural areas, far away from their working parents in urban centers, are called left-behind or stay-at-home children, and the many problems associated with their development have often been reported in the media (Yeqing Huang and Gong 2022).

Place of Origin

People from different areas of Guangdong Province, as well as from other Chinese provinces, come to Guangzhou to work, and many of them end up in counterfeiting businesses. The largest groups of migrant workers in Guangzhou come from the Chaoshan area of Guangdong Province; Wenzhou, a city in Zhejiang Province; and Zhanjiang, a prefecture-level city in southwestern Guangdong. The two major cities in the Chaoshan area are the seaports of Chaozhou and Shantou, hence the name Chaoshan (C. Cheng 1997).

Many Chaoshanese say that people from their area do not like working for others. They prefer to be their own bosses, even if their businesses are tiny. Chaoshanese are tight knit, see themselves as superior to other subgroups, and are reluctant to marry anyone not from their area. If one of them does, other Chaoshanese will consider him or her a loser and predict that the marriage will not last. Sonny (H10), an outspoken leather handbag business owner from Chaoshan, characterized his people as follows:

> You need to understand the reasons the Chaoshanese play a vital role in the counterfeiting industry. First of all, they are very united, and counterfeiting is a family business for them. They leave their hometowns to work when they are very young, and they do that for only one purpose: to prepare themselves to be business owners one day. When they are young, they work for others, not because they want to be workers, but to learn how to do business.

Mr. Fu, a private investigator who had many years of experience in anticounterfeiting activities, explained how Chaoshanese present a united front in the counterfeiting industry: "Chaoshan people are close-knit, and they like to form groups. If a counterfeit product is popular, they will all get involved in the production and distribution of it. Besides, they will not compete among themselves in a price war; they all know how to set the price for the product." A Chaoshanese businessman who owned a stationery store suggested that one of the reasons for his people to be active in counterfeiting is because the Chaoshan area was where the smuggling of foreign "garbage" (cheap goods) into China initially occurred, and, as the first group to come into contact with foreign goods, this put them, especially those from the coastal areas, in a position to be the first group to replicate goods smuggled into

China, including cell phones, motorcycles, and a variety of other merchandise. There is a perception among people in Guangzhou that individuals and families from the Chaoshan area play an important role in luxury goods counterfeiting.

Residents of Wenzhou, in Zhejiang Province, are also considered to be very active in counterfeiting. Like Chaoshanese, Wenzhounese are very keen on starting their own businesses and are not content with working for others. Lin Jun (G17), a young man from Sichuan Province who was involved in producing men's T-shirts, said: "Wenzhounese would rather be a boss making 15 cents a day than a worker making $15 a day." However, Lao Zhu, a clothing factory owner and the spouse of Xiao Xin (G15), commented that there is a significant difference between the two groups regarding their role in the fashion industry: "Chaoshan people are good at counterfeiting, and Wenzhounese, at imitating, not counterfeiting." In other words, Chaoshan businesspeople are more likely to engage in point-by-point counterfeiting, and Wenzhou entrepreneurs in infringing.

Xiao Qin (H16), a Chaoshanese handbag business owner, suggested that "although there are many similarities between people from Chaoshan and Wenzhou—residents of both cities have good business acumen and are aggressive risk-takers, hard-working, family-oriented, and cohesive—Wenzhounese are significantly more united than Chaoshanese. Chaoshanese know how to stick together against outsiders; but when you go to a street dominated by Wenzhounese stores and ask for the price of a particular item, you will get the same price from all the stores."

There are also many migrants in Guangzhou from Zhanjiang, a prefecture-level city in southwestern Guangdong Province. Zhanjiang is about 260 miles from Guangzhou, but the launching of an express train connection in 2019 made travel between the two cities much easier. Zhanjiangnese operate many shoe factories or workshops in Guangzhou. They recruit people from their hometowns to join them in these businesses.

In sum, people in Guangzhou agree that most of the hard-working individuals in their city are outsiders, not local Guangzhounese. From their viewpoint, Guangdong Province, especially the province's major urban centers, such as Shenzhen, Zhuhai, Dongguan, and Guangzhou, are incredibly welcoming to outsiders, and this is why businesspeople and workers from all over China flock to Guangdong to try their luck. Most people from outside of Guangdong have to endure years of hardship before improving their economic condition, although some of them do become very rich. In contrast, there is a perception that the indigenous Guangzhounese do not have to work: all they have to do is to collect rent, and that is why so many businesspeople in Guangzhou are from elsewhere.

It is hard to conclude which subgroup dominates which counterfeiting industry in Guangzhou. In general, the Chaoshanese are the most active in the leather goods trade, the Wenzhounese in the clothing industry, and the Zhangjianese and Fujianese in the shoe business. However, according to a prosecutor from Zengcheng, a district of Guangzhou where the counterfeiting of denim jeans is rampant, the jeans industry in his district is not dominated by a particular group from a particular province.

Nationality

According to data from my interviews and fieldwork, most luxury goods counterfeiters and their facilitators are Chinese nationals, and, as mentioned earlier, many buyers worldwide go to Guangzhou to purchase counterfeits for resale in their home countries. Most foreign buyers come from Africa, Latin America, Russia, Turkey, Eastern Europe, India, and Southeast Asia. Only one of my research subjects mentioned that he had conducted business with American and Western European entrepreneurs.

In examining the nationalities of the counterfeiters in China, we need to pay attention to two groups of ethnic Chinese from outside of China because of their roles as pioneers of the Chinese counterfeiting industry—entrepreneurs from Hong Kong and Taiwan (Al 2014; Vogel 2013; Wu 2019). Laoban (G2), a clothing business owner from Taiwan, explained why Hong Kongers and Taiwanese were at one point the leaders in the counterfeiting industry in China and how that changed later on:

> Businesspeople from Hong Kong and Taiwan were the key players in the counterfeiting industry in China in the very beginning. That is because they were able to gain access to authentic products or information about those products. At that time, it was difficult for Chinese nationals to go overseas. After the Chinese authorities allowed their people to travel to Hong Kong and Europe, local Chinese became the dominant players in this business. Since they were locals, they could expand their businesses all over China. For people like us, from Taiwan, doing business in Guangzhou, it is not easy to open a distribution outlet in Beijing.

Chen Jian (H5), a distributor who specializes in infringing Fortune Duck handbags, described why entrepreneurs from Hong Kong and Taiwan were in a better position to develop the counterfeit trade in China: "Hong Kongers and Taiwanese initially developed the counterfeiting business in China. They had more contacts with the West and had access to all sorts of information, and that is why once China began to adopt the reform and open-door policy, they were the first to come over to do business. Initially, they were active in the coastal areas, especially in Guangdong Province."

The sociologist Ezra Vogel detailed how, after decades of stagnation under Communist rule, Deng adopted, in the late 1970s, the reform and opening up policy. He also noted the important role Hong Kong entrepreneurs played at the very early stage of China's transformation:

> When the communists took over China, some industrialists from Shanghai and Ningbo fled to Hong Kong where they helped build up the Hong Kong textile industry and global shipping sector. By the 1960s Hong Kong was becoming a leading international financial center. And in the 1970s talented youth who [had] spent their early years in Hong Kong and then gone abroad to study in England, the United States, Canada, and Australia began returning to the colony with a sophisticated understanding of modern finance, high technology, and international markets. Hong Kong in the late 1970s thus offered China something that the Soviet Union sorely lacked—a treasure trove of entrepreneurs thoroughly knowledgeable about the latest developments in the West who shared the same language and culture as their motherland, and stood ready to help (Vogel 2013, 403–404).

According to Jieh-min Wu (2019), author of *The Rent-Seeking Developmental State in China: The Taishang, Guangdong Model and Global Capitalism*, from 1978 to 1989, Hong Kongers were the pioneers in China's transformation. However, after the 1989 Tiananmen incident, the Taiwanese, the world's largest single group of contract manufacturers (Hamilton and Kao 2018), became key players as Westerners began to impose economic sanctions on China. Taiwan was known as a "pirate kingdom" in the 1970s and 1980s (Freemantle 1986; A. Sun 1998). According to a 1986 report by John Burns of the *New York Times*, "Until a few years ago, Taiwan was the undisputed counterfeiting and illegal-copying capital of the world, a place where millions of dollars of fake goods were turned out with virtual impunity in back-street sweatshops. . . . Not many years ago, in International Trade Commission hearings in Washington, Taiwan was accused of accounting for 50 percent of counterfeiting worldwide." As China became a magnet for manufacturers due to its cheap labor and loose regulation, some counterfeiters from Taiwan moved their operations across the strait to China, in the 1990s, a time when Taiwanese authorities were cracking down on counterfeiting and successfully implementing IP protection reform (A. Sun 1998). Laoban (G2) provided the reasons for the rise and fall of Taiwanese clothing entrepreneurs in China:

When I started my business in China in 2001, the Chinese government had not yet allowed Chinese nationals to visit Hong Kong, which put us [businessmen from Taiwan] in a very advantageous position. Hong Kong was where luxury fashion houses released their new products for the Asian market. By 2004, Chinese citizens were visiting Hong Kong in droves, which also meant the end of our supremacy. Chinese entrepreneurs traveled to Hong Kong faster than we could, and bought many more originals [to copy] than we could. After that, we had to rely on our ability to design to compete with them. However, once our products became popular, many competitors bought our stuff, copied it, and sold it for a lower price. By 2008, the market was saturated, and there was the rise of e-commerce. All these factors disrupted the market's order and prices. Most Taiwanese who came here at the same time as I did are back in Taiwan. The repatriation started in 2010, and the main reason was because local people had learned the trade and joined the race.

Jieh-min Wu, the previously cited scholar in Taiwan, confirmed Laoban's point. According to Wu, after China joined the WTO, in 2001, and firms from all over the world entered the Chinese market, the Taiwanese role began to diminish and was almost gone from China by 2008–2009 (Wu 2019).

Most of my research subjects suggested that Hong Kongers were active in the leather goods business, and the Taiwanese in clothing and footwear. Scholars such as Wu (2019, 137) have also observed that "it was the Hong Kongers who first brought the know-how of leather ware into China." Mr. Tian (F2) said shoe factories in China were mostly operated by the Taiwanese at the beginning and not many Hong Kongers were involved. Xiao Yuen (G12) said the counterfeiting of apparel was brought to China by the Taiwanese. He worked for a Taiwanese when he arrived in Guangzhou from Yunnan. When the Taiwanese quit, Xiao Yuen took over the business.

Becoming a Counterfeiter

In this section, I examine why and how my research subjects entered the counterfeit trade. I explore what prompted them to become counterfeiters, either as employees or as business owners, and what qualifications they needed to become counterfeiters.

The most likely pathway for someone to become an employee of a counterfeit business is to arrive in Guangzhou from a rural area looking for a job and ending up working for a business that is engaged in producing or distributing counterfeit goods. Take Ah Lan (G18), a fashion designer, for example:

"I graduated from middle school but did not attend high school because my grades were not good and I did not like school. That is why, when I was seventeen, my cousin Xiao Wen (G6) introduced me to his boss [Laoban, G2], and the boss hired me. The year was 2008. Initially, I sketched fashions, but after a year, the boss let me design." Ah Lan was aware in advance that her cousin was working for a firm involved in the design, production, and distribution of knockoff apparel.

Becoming the owner of a counterfeit business is more challenging than simply working for a counterfeit business. The question is: What prompts an employee to start his or her own business rather than be content to remain as a worker? Most of my research subjects told me they made the move because the counterfeit business: (1) enabled them to make good money, (2) required little start-up money, (3) offered more freedom than working for someone else, and (4) did not have any entry barriers (although not all subjects agreed on this point).

It is not clear whether the counterfeiting industry is as lucrative as many people thought it would be. However, my research subjects became involved in it due to the belief that it would make them rich quickly if they were lucky enough to come up with one or two hot products. Some personally knew business owners who made millions of dollars from counterfeiting. Plus, even though it is a lucrative business, it does not harm people and society. Mr. Hu (F5), a sneaker retailer from Hunan, explained why he entered this business:

> It is simple: money. If I had not entered it, I could not make money. To survive, I had no choice but to do it. At any rate, it is not murder or arson; it does not harm people. Also, we do not cheat our customers; they know they are not buying authentic goods once they are told the prices of the goods. Yes, we are taking advantage of the achievements of other people. They spent many years researching, designing, and developing something, and we copy that something that has been proven to be good and marketable. We also affix their trademarks on the copies. We know these fake goods are going to be popular among our customers.

For Jane (G1), counterfeiting can be addictive because it is so lucrative. According to her, "Doing fake brands is addictive, just like taking illicit drugs; you simply cannot stop it. Why is it so addictive? It is simple. You produce a [noncounterfeit] T-shirt for $1.45, sell it for $1.88, and make a profit of 43 cents. However, if you take the same T-shirt and sew the label or stitch the logo of a name brand, this slight change allows you to sell the T-shirt for $3. Tell me, if you were me, would you become addicted or not?" Peter (G7), Jane's husband, agreed with his wife: "Why counterfeiting? Simple, to make a huge profit. If I engage in a normal business, a garment will give me a 20 percent profit, but if I counterfeit, my profit is 100 percent. Why shouldn't I become involved in counterfeiting?"

Many subjects said it was easy for them to enter this business because copying something is not difficult. According to Laoban (G2): "It is easy to copy something because if you run into any kind of problem, all you have to do is to buy the original and take it apart; you will immediately find out what the problem is, and figure out a way to overcome it. Before I entered this trade, I never heard of brands like Armani or Versace. After becoming involved, I often visited name brand boutiques or bought luxury products, and I quickly became familiar with luxury fashions."

The other reason for starting a counterfeiting business is the low start-up cost required. A person with limited money can find a way to enter this business. According to Laoban, anyone with a little more than $7,000 can start a small business in this industry. As mentioned earlier, Mimi (F7), the young owner of a shoe workshop, started her business with only $7,200. Laoban (G2) described where Mimi, one of his former employees, obtained the money:

When Mimi was about to start a workshop, she considered finding a business partner who could provide the start-up money. I told her that if you operate a small business with a partner, there could be many problems between the partners, and it would be best to do it on her own. I suggested: "Ask your mother for help and tell her that you will engage your younger brother in the new business. When your mother learns that this new business will benefit her son, she will surely give you the money." She took my advice and did what I said. Her mother gave her the money.

Many people in China prefer to work for themselves and not for others because they like freedom, especially if they have young children. If a migrant couple works for others, they probably will have to leave their children in their hometowns with their grandparents because they simply do not have time to take care of them. According to one estimate, there are approximately sixty-nine million so-called left-behind children in China (UNICEF 2019). So many young children growing up in rural areas without their parents around has become a major social problem in China. For couples from rural areas making a living in coastal cities, one of the appeals of owning a small business instead of being employed is that they can keep their children with them. It is not unusual to see toddlers running around their parents who are minding their stores in Guangzhou. In some cases, female business owners have babies in their arms while talking business with customers. If a person is an employee, it is unlikely that an employer would allow him or her to bring a child to the workplace.

Although most of my research subjects said that a person needs no qualifications to enter the counterfeiting business and that luck is more important than anything else to be successful, a few of them stressed that specific qualifications are needed for a counterfeiter to thrive. Peter (G7) outlines the qualifications:

> First, having a certain amount of money to invest. Second, possessing sensitivity to fashion, a strong sense of smell for clothing, and knowing in advance what styles and colors will become popular. Third, being well-connected and familiar with the industry's supply chain, knowing where to buy fabrics and other materials, where to find clothing factories, and how to distribute the garments. Fourth, knowing how to reduce the manufacturing and operating costs so that the profit margins will be high, including where to buy materials that are good and cheap. Fifth, knowing how to establish a good distribution system. Sixth, possessing a self-preservation consciousness. These are all the qualifications needed; otherwise, the person is going to either lose money or get into trouble.

Danny (H3), a well-established forty-two-year-old leather handbag manufacturer and a former quality-control inspector for Coach in Dongguan, argued that if an individual has never worked for a contract manufacturer for a global fashion house, he or she will not know how to produce quality counterfeit leather goods:

> In the past, those contract manufacturers had thousands of workers, and many of those workers later became counterfeiters. To copy designer luxury goods, a person has to have worked in a contract factory [for an international brand] before; it is impossible to copy such goods just by using your imagination. Even if you have worked in a noncontract leather factory for many years, if you have not had work experience in one of those contract manufacturers, you will not know that these two types of factories have different operating systems. Moreover, you will not know how to make a designer handbag.
>
> In addition, if you have never worked for a contract manufacturer, you will not have the necessary social capital. One essential part of a successful counterfeiting venture is the ability to source the materials. This is a major challenge. Suppliers providing materials to contract factories will not take a risk and sell you their materials because they

rely so much on their business with foreign brands. They would be devastated if they lose a contract with a major brand. They will not risk their arrangements with name brands for the sake of doing business with counterfeiters. Also, a counterfeiter is going to buy only small quantities of materials. In addition to leather, you also need to look for metal fittings, lining materials, threads, and other components of the counterfeited items.

So, what are you going to do? Your only choice is to utilize your social capital. You can ask your former colleagues in contract manufacturing to refer you to a buyer who is working for Coach, and ask him or her to help you to make extra orders. If Coach needs materials for 2,000 bags, the buyer can order materials for 2,300 bags and sell you the extra materials. The alternative is to ask colleagues in the contract factory to steal a few pieces of material daily and sell them to you. If all else fails and you cannot secure the same materials as used in the item you are counterfeiting, you will have to use similar materials. However, the effect is going to be different; you cannot claim that your copies are point-to-point Super A products.

That is why you usually copy the brand your former employer was associated with. If you used to work for a Coach contract factory, switching to duplicating Louis Vuitton bags is hard. There are two reasons for this. One, you do not have the social capital after you switch, and two, the two brands belong to different classes of luxury items.

Mr. Tian (F2), a supervisor at a Skechers contract manufacturer, agreed with Danny.[1] According to him, "If you engage in footwear counterfeiting, you must have some working experience with a brand's contract manufacturer." John (F3), a former supervisor of Mr. Tian, revealed how Mr. Tian and one of his colleagues, Xiao Yao, were involved in counterfeiting while working for the Skechers contract manufacturer:

Xiao Yao is copying Skechers shoes and doing it with Mr. Tian. Neither of them has a factory; they find a factory to produce the shoes for them. Xiao Yao is an assembly supervisor in one of Skechers contract manufacturers, and Mr. Tian is a deputy assembly supervisor. They know who among their workers are counterfeiting Skechers shoes in private. The man who is in charge of Xiao Yao and Mr. Tian knows what the two are doing behind his back. I had a chat with that person a few days ago. He said he knows that Xiao Yao and Mr. Tian are forging Skechers shoes, but he is OK with this as long as it does not get out of control.

John explains why supervisors like Xiao Yao and Mr. Tian were involved in counterfeiting while working full-time for a brand's contract manufacturer:

> Their salaries are meager; even now, they make only a little more than $1,470 a month. They do not have company cars, and the company has not offered any help buying a house. Some companies assist their workers in management in applying for a home mortgage as a way to prevent them from leaving. The Taiwanese boss [who owned the factory] is a penny-pincher. In addition to not helping his employees with the purchase of cars and houses, he investigates any employee who buys a car or a house to find out how the person got the money to do so.

Only a handful of my research subjects were affiliated with brand-name contract manufacturers before they began to copy brand-name luxury goods. They thought that such experience was critical for anyone who wanted to thrive in the counterfeiting business, at least to be able to make quality replicas. They took great pride in their familiarity with how genuine luxury goods are made and looked down on those infringers who had no past experience with how luxury goods are produced. They thought those infringers only knew how to make fast money and did not care about the quality of their products.

Most of my research subjects, however, worked for a counterfeiter, and not a contract manufacturer, before they began their own businesses. Mr. Mao (F4), a shoe manufacturer from Jiangxi, was one of them:

> I used to work for a Taiwanese who copied brand-name shoes. At that time, even though I was involved in the business, I was disgusted by it. However, I changed my point of view about counterfeiting after I saw that the Taiwanese boss made tons of money and I had to work to death just to survive. I was very bitter; that motivated me to start my own counterfeiting business later on. I thought to myself, everything on earth comes from imitating and everybody is imitating one another. I also thought that copying was inevitable in the process of development. After a person or a society is developed to a point where they can establish their own brands, then there will be no need for them to copy.

Among my research subjects, some individuals had no experience in the production of genuine or fake luxury goods before they started their counterfeiting businesses. Wendy (G4), a young woman who counterfeited Japanese T-shirts, described how she entered this business:

In 2005, I worked for a trading company. At that time, my elder brother was a garment store owner. Japanese brand T-shirts were very popular, so I began to explore the opportunity to counterfeit them. I got in touch with a factory in Qingdao that produced basic, logo-free T-shirts for a Japanese company. The basic T-shirts were transported to the company in Japan where they printed the patterns on them. I asked the factory to sell me the basic T-shirts, and they did. After I brought the basic T-shirts to Guangzhou, I found someone here to print the patterns for me. The authentic Japanese T-shirts were selling for $20. I bought the basic T-shirt for about $1.30 apiece, spent 65 cents on printing, and sold them for $3. I did that for three years, between 2006 and 2009, and then stopped. That was how I made my first pot of gold.

Xiao Zhen (H13), a leather handbag manufacturer, described how a classmate became a very successful handbag counterfeiter, even though the classmate had no contract manufacturing experience:

My classmate never worked for a contract manufacturer and yet he was able to enter this business. The reason is simple: once you buy an original and take it apart, you learn everything about the product. You can also hire a handbag maker to help you. Those who say you need to work for a contract manufacturer before you start your own counterfeiting business are simply trying to raise their social status.

Sonny (H10), a straight-talking well-connected leather goods entrepreneur, summed up his observation of why there are so many people involved in counterfeiting in China: "Chinese people are just very good at copying. No matter what type of product you give them, they can come up with a perfect replica. Also, they do not care about the issues of trademark infringement and illegality; they just want to make money." Zheng Hua (G19), a clothing business owner, offered an interesting answer when asked why he preferred copying brand-name products instead of developing his own brand:

I have two sons to support, so I need to make money. Besides, copying designer-brand goods is not an evil act. It is easy; it's like preparing Chinese herbal medicine. You have a wide variety of herbs to choose from, and mixtures of small portions of several different herbs can give you very effective and comprehensive treatments. The same is true with counterfeiting. There are so many brands to copy. If an order contains a few garments from each of these brands, you can easily fulfill it. If you only do your own brand, then it is like taking Western medicine, there is only one pill, and its effects are limited. How many styles can you come up with if you only manufacture your own brand? There are other benefits to copying designer brands. One, copying designer brands definitely makes money. Second, the risk is not that high as long as you are careful. Even if you run into trouble with the law, you will be locked up for only one year.

Some of my research subjects reacted defiantly when asked what prompted them to engage in counterfeiting. Lin Jun (G17), a soft-spoken clothing factory owner, thought that his attempt to make money through counterfeiting was justifiable if one considers how name brands are making such huge amounts of money: "The manufacturing cost for an Armani T-shirt for men should be less than $14. How the hell can they sell it for more than $140?"[2]

In sum, counterfeiting is an informal sector in which many marginalized and underprivileged migrant workers from rural areas attempt at the beginning to earn a wage as a worker and later to get rich as an entrepreneur. According to Scott Rozelle and Natalie Hell (2020), there are large numbers of people in China who enter the *informal* sector because they have no other choice. They characterized the informal sector as "the part of the economy where workers do not have regular salaried jobs with benefits and set contracts. These are generally small businesses (or microfirms), often one person working alone. In some cases, that person may employ a family member, a friend, or a neighbor or two" (Rozelle and Hell 2020, 52–53).

Self-Perception

In general, my research subjects had no qualms about engaging in counterfeiting. They viewed themselves as honest and hard-working people, who, like hundreds of millions of other migrants from the hinterland, arrived in Guangzhou to make a living. They had a positive self-perception, and, even if they knew that counterfeiting is illegal, the idea that they were "criminals" never crossed their minds.

Many business owners I interviewed were proud of their contributions to the fashion industry. They thought that the high-quality replicas they produced paved the way for luxury brands to enter and thrive in the Chinese market. According to Laoban (G2), "The popularity of international luxury brands in China was made possible by the existence of high-quality fakes. Counterfeit goods were widely accepted by Chinese consumers beforehand, so when authentic luxury goods arrived in China in 2004, these name-brand goods were immediately well received. Nowadays, both types of goods are popular." Xiao Yao, a supervisor at a contract manufacturer for Skechers and a partner of Mr. Tian (F2) in copying Skechers shoes, also stressed how imitation not only played a critical role in improving the public perception of Skechers but also benefited consumers who could not afford to buy the genuine goods:

> Skechers shoes are selling in China mainly because their shoes are imitated. Otherwise, who would have noticed Skechers? If someone is copying a brand, that means its products are good enough to be counterfeited. That is why Skechers should thank these counterfeiters. Besides, the business of name brands is not affected by counterfeiting; a person who buys a pair of fake Skechers is not going to buy the real Skechers. On the other hand, this counterfeiting business benefits those who cannot afford to buy the originals. The cost to produce a pair of authentic Skechers is $12 at the most, but the brand is selling them for $74. If there is a pair of fake Skechers selling for $25, and the shoes are not that much different from the real shoes, which pair of shoes are you going to buy? If you can buy a similar product for a lot less, of course, that is a benefit for you.

My research subjects did not feel guilt or shame for copying designer luxury goods. For them, counterfeiting was just a business. They also believed that many popular brands became successful only after they began to imitate the products of those well-established brands and sell their products for a lower price. John (F3) said: "Skechers became popular after they started to copy Nike shoes. Their shoes are very similar to Nike's, but their prices are lower. That's how they took away a large volume of Nike's business." My research subjects also pointed out that counterfeiting luxury goods is very different from counterfeiting food or medicine in terms of harm done to consumers, and thus it is no big deal to produce or sell fake luxury goods.

Not only did they not feel guilty or shameful but some of them were proud of their counterfeit products. Mr. Mao (F4), a shoemaker in Dongguan, said: "The leather for my Timberland 6-inch classic shoes is probably better than the original. I use expensive leather pieces." Laoban (G2) was adamant about the exquisite quality of some of the copies he produced or saw: "Some of the authentic goods produced by fashion houses are not better than high-quality imitation goods. Nowadays, high-quality counterfeiters, to survive, are producing goods that are superior to the quality and design of the originals."

Jane (G1) also had a very positive opinion about both the people who were in counterfeiting and the products they manufactured. As someone who completed her college education in Australia and received formal training in fashion design in Japan, she had the confidence to say something that might sound unreasonably critical of the IPR regulations:

> Counterfeiters are very talented; they can duplicate because they are smart. Moreover, sometimes their products are better than the originals. Take the Apple Watch, for example. It is expensive but does not have many functions. The fake Apple Watch produced in China is a lot cheaper and has more functions. The original does not measure blood pressure, but the fake does. Why must we let the maker of the originals take advantage of us, setting such a high price for their products? Another example is the microwave oven. It was so expensive in the past. Once we learned how to make it [in fact, it does not require much technology], the price quickly went down. The truth is, the concept of intellectual property is a kind of moral rape, a kind of curse, like that headband Sun Wukong wore which prevented him from flying freely.[3]

Some of my research subjects became defiant when asked how they would respond if someone accused them of counterfeiting. One of them, Chen Jian (H5), a handbag distributor, defended himself as follows:

> Let me ask you this, is the Bible copyrighted? Do I need permission from someone to print the Bible? We are not the same as Westerners; we do not have any concept of trademarks and copyrights. When I see something I like, it is only natural for me to copy it. The so-called trademarks and copyrights are something Western capitalists made up to protect their interests. Of course, they did invest a lot of energy in developing and designing a product, and they spent many hours and money to produce it.

Among my research subjects, Xiao Guan (G13) was a particularly patriotic young man who sings only nationalistic Chinese songs when he visits karaoke clubs. In contemporary China, it is unusual for young people to sing traditional patriotic songs in karaoke clubs, as most of them are keen to perform romantic songs. For Xiao Guan, people in China became involved in counterfeiting because people from overseas wanted what they produced. His narrative reflected the extreme position of some counterfeiters who think Westerners should be the ones to blame for the emergence of the counterfeiting industry in China:

> I do not think the West should blame us for this. It is their demand that fuels this business. Besides, they taught us how to do it.
> The counterfeiting industry in China was established to meet overseas demand. If a market for copies did not exist, there wouldn't

be a supply. When you go to a restaurant and see a menu with a long list of delicious dishes but no customers, what good is that restaurant? That is why I say foreigners were the ones who stimulated the emergence of the counterfeiting industry in China. The local market then was very small because locals did not know anything about brands like Armani or Burberry.

It was not only demand from foreigners that energized counterfeiting here, foreigners were also responsible for coming to China and teaching us how to produce the goods. Otherwise, how would we know how to do it? We did not understand English, or international brands. Sure, people from Hong Kong and Taiwan did play a role, but it was mainly foreigners who taught us counterfeiting skills.

In sum, foreigners have a good deal and yet they complain. They came to China and taught us how to copy, then bought the fakes from us cheap, transported them back to their home countries, and sold them at a good price. They made all the money; we earned a little money to survive. I do not understand why they are screaming that we forge their products and infringe on their intellectual property rights.

Others supported Xiao Guan's points. According to Mr. Zhou (H17), a handbag manufacturer: "Counterfeiting is something foreigners [brand owners] wanted us to do. They knew that if we copied their goods, it would help them make their brands well-known. Once they achieved their goal, they began to suppress us, saying we stole their customers. Those who can afford to buy authentic goods are not going to buy fakes."

In sum, people in the counterfeiting business generally see themselves as good and industrious entrepreneurs trying to make a living in a gray area of society. Laoban (G2) concluded: "None of us feel any guilt because we are not selling drugs or killing people. We are simply responding to market demand. We are just businesspeople walking a fine line between legality and illegality within a gray area. It has nothing to do with morality. You can say this business is a means for powerless people from the bottom of society to rapidly change their economic status." Jane (G1) summed up the self-perception of counterfeiters as follows: "We are not bad people; we do not steal, rob, or harm people. We are all hard-working businesspeople. It's just that we are operating in a gray area."

Everyday Life

According to Lin Jun (G17), owner of a men's T-shirt factory, he spends almost all of his waking hours working: "I come to my factory around seven or eight in the morning every day, work nonstop, and return home around ten or eleven at night." He needs to work hard to make money because he has two children to support: "I have two kids; one is in the fifth grade, and the other is in the first grade. Both of them are attending a private school. The elder son lives in the school's dorm. It costs me about $22,000 a year for schooling for the two of them. For me, this is a heavy burden." Mrs. Jia (G11), the owner of a fashion-ornament store at Guangzhou Zhongda Garment City, became distraught when she described her daily routine: "This is not an easy business. I have to be here from nine in the morning to eight in the evening every day. I work seven days a week; my store is open all year round. I do not want to be stuck here every day, but I have no choice."

Even though these business owners have to work hard, they can reward themselves with the nice things in life. Some of my research subjects, especially the men, spent their money on expensive cars. Xiao Guan (G13), the patriotic clothing merchant, has two cars, a Volvo XC90 he bought for about $118,000 and an Audi A4 that cost about $70,000. Lao Zhu, the husband of Xiao Xin (G15, a garment factory owner), paid $162,000 for a Mercedes Benz imported from Germany. Xiao Qin (H16), a leather handbag merchant, bought a Land Rover for $206,000. Due to high import taxes, foreign cars in China cost substantially more than they do in the United States. For many entrepreneurs in China, as for people elsewhere, a car is one of the most visible reflections of a person's economic status. For rural people operating a business in Guangzhou, returning home in a new imported car is perhaps the best way to let neighbors know that they have made it in a big city. Many drive for days to get home. Only someone who is a salaried worker returns home using public transportation.

Compared to the human smugglers (K. Chin 1999; S. Zhang and Chin 2002) and drug traffickers (K. Chin 2009; K. Chin and Zhang 2015) I have interviewed in the past, the counterfeiters in Guangzhou appeared to be less likely to have indulged in women, alcohol, drugs, and gambling.

Before I examine the profiles of several counterfeiters, I would like to briefly explore the monetary aspects of counterfeiting. This may shed some light on how ordinary migrant workers in Guangzhou transformed themselves from making less than several hundred dollars a month to earning tens of thousands of dollars every month, as business owners, and driving luxury cars. Table 5.4 addresses some of the financial questions such as start-up money, profit margin, rent, monthly salary (for workers) or income (for business owners), and success stories. It provides the ranges and examples to the answers of these questions. As with the legitimate business sector in China, the counterfeiting industry is diversified, with large and small firms trying to survive in a fiercely competitive business environment. Many people became rich as counterfeit business owners, but more people went

Item	Range	Examples
TABLE 5.4. THE MONETARY ASPECTS OF COUNTERFEITING		
Start-up money	From a few thousand to tens of thousands of dollars	Ah Hua (H6) invested between $3,000 and $4,000 in her retail store; Mimi (F7) said she started her shoe manufacturing workshop with $7,200 from her mother; Ah Min (G5) opened a clothing retail store with $12,000 from her father and relatives; and Xiao Zhen (H13) put $64,000 into his leather handbag factory.
Profit margin	From 22% to 194%	Ah Hua (H6), a retailer, purchased a handbag for $41 and sold it for $50 (22% profit); Li Bing (H1) said it cost her $200 to produce a Celine bag, and her retail price was $250 (25% profit margin); Mimi (F7) said her cost for a pair of Chanel sandals was $15, and her retail price was $21 (40% profit); Ah San (F13), a workshop owner, said it cost him $17 to make a pair of sandals that traded for $25 (47% profit); Wendy (G4) spent $1.95 to produce a fake Japanese T-shirt and offered it for sale for $3 (54% profit); Xiao Yuen (G12) said an online vendor bought Diesel men's T-shirts from him for $4.40 and sold them for $8.80 on WeChat (100% profit); Zheng Hua's (G19) cost for a men's T-shirt was $2.80 and his selling price was $6 (115% profit); Xiao Qin (H16), a Celine bag maker, said his cost was $43 per bag, and he traded it for $115 (168% profit); Leslie (H9) purchased a Daniel Wellington watch for $30 and sold it for $73 to $88 on WeChat (144% to 194% profit).
Monthly rent	Dangkou: $1,500–$11,500 Xiezilou: $3,000–$12,000 Gongsi: $1,100–$4,300	Mimi (F7) paid $290 for her workshop; Ah Min's (G5) rent for a store in Kinbo Market was $5,800; Mrs. Jia (G11) rented two stores in a fabric market, one for $4,300 and another for $11,500; and Zheng Hua (G19) paid $4,300 for his gongsi.
Monthly salary or income	n/a	Mrs. Jia (G11) paid her workers $435 a month as base salary; a Baiyun Leather City saleswoman made $580 a month; Xiao Jen (H11) was paid $700 a month as a warehouse worker; Leslie (H9) made $442 a day selling fake watches on WeChat while working full-time for a chip company; Mr. Jin (F14), a shoe counterfeiter, earned $44,000 a month at one point.
Success stories of people who became very rich	n/a	A handbag counterfeiter made $29 million; a WeChat vendor earned more than $1.47 million in just three months; when a Louis Vuitton counterfeiter with a $150,000 daily revenue was arrested, his wife proposed to pay the authorities $15 million for his release.

broke after they entered this business. As stated by Laoban (G2), this is a business where an ordinary person in China (with no connection or education) becomes rich very quickly if he or she develops a "hot" or high demand counterfeit product.

Profiles

To provide a more nuanced understanding of counterfeiters in Guangzhou, I present in this section five individuals from the apparel and leatherwear businesses. I quote them extensively to let them explain themselves in their own words.

Ah Min (Clothing Distributor)

Ah Min (G5) is in charge of a distribution outlet in the Kinbo Market on Zhanxi Road. According to another research subject who knows her well, Ah Min is an excellent salesperson and is well known and well respected in Guangzhou's garment industry. She, her elder brother, and her sister-in-law work together to operate a well-integrated firm that designs, produces, and distributes casual menswear. Ah Min is in charge of sales, her brother takes care of production, and her sister-in-law, Lau Fang (G21), focuses on design and management. Before Ah Min's divorce, her husband, Zhao Zong (G14), was also engaged in her family business.

Ah Min, a fashionable tall woman in her thirties with two young children, explained why she and her brothers left school at a young age:

> I am from Taizhou, Zhejiang. I come from a wealthy family, so when I was a child, I lived like a little princess. I have two brothers. Unfortunately, my dad was a gambler, and he lost all our fortune at the gaming tables. Soon, debt collectors were knocking on our door. That's why after attending middle school for only one year, I quit, so that I could make money and make our family rich again.
>
> After our family went broke, even though my two elder brothers were tall and handsome, nobody would come to us with marriage proposals. In contrast, a young man who lived next door to us who looked very ordinary was approached by large numbers of people with marriage proposals simply because his family was rich. That was what motivated me and my two brothers to leave school and work hard to get rich.[4]

Ah Min recalled how she became involved in sewing and clothing, even though she was interested in doing something else:

Initially, I was interested in hairdressing. Ever since I was very young, I liked to look pretty. However, my parents were against this; they thought good girls should not be involved in this line of work.[5] As a result, I switched my interest to sewing and found a job in a garment factory. Once I began to learn to sew, I became interested in fabrics, embroidery, and other fashion-related things. When I was a seamstress, I was extremely frugal. I made $75 a month, but I saved more than $600 a year.

While I was still a teenager, I told my father I wanted to open a clothing store. He said no because he thought it was risky. He worried that if the business failed, we would lose lots of money. I told him not to worry; if I failed, I would simply marry a man and use the bride price to repay him. When he saw how determined and confident I was, he borrowed $4,400 for me. He had to pay 3.5 percent monthly interest on the loan, which was very high. My relatives also chipped in, from $740 to $1,480 per person. With the loan, I was able to come up with about $10,320 to $11,800 of start-up money.

My clothing store was in Taizhou. I had to pay a lump sum of more than $4,400 as a down payment for rent, plus I had to spend additional money to renovate the place. After that, I did not have much money to buy goods. In the beginning, I was selling men's suits. I bought my garments from Hangzhou, Wenzhou, and Guangzhou, but mainly Hangzhou. Because I did not have enough capital, I was not able to display a full collection of men's suits. Often, I ordered one suit only after I had sold one. I had to regularly visit my suppliers, and it was gruesome. Later, an uncle helped me out by using his connections to find customers to visit my store, and to persuade my suppliers to provide me with good business terms.

She went on to explain how she shifted from men's suits to casual wear and from retail to wholesale:

After more than a year, I realized that the business for men's suits was not as good as for men's casual wear. Even though I was already selling other types of men's fashions and accessories such as jackets, shoes, belts, hats, etc., once I switched to men's casual wear, my business took off, and I began to accumulate some wealth. However, I was not content. I thought to myself: although the profit margins for retail were high, the sales volume was low. By then, one of my brothers was already involved in the hardware business, and the other brother was working with me.

I began to contemplate the idea of wholesaling men's casual wear. There was someone in Hangzhou who was the distributor for all of Zhejiang Province, and he offered me the opportunity to become the sole distributor for Taizhou. All retail stores in Taizhou would have to come to me if they wanted to sell the goods I was carrying. Under such circumstances, my reputation grew rapidly, and everyone in the fashion industry in Taizhou came to know me and my brother. At that point, I had made a certain amount of money, and I could start a wholesale business with $29,500 to $44,000 of start-up money. During that time, not many businesspeople could come up with that kind of capital. I was engaged in retailing men's casual wear for only a year before I became a wholesaler.

After becoming a wholesaler for casual menswear, she was married, and her husband (Zhao Zong, G14) later joined her in her clothing business. Moreover, the couple moved to Guangzhou from Taizhou after their business began to decline:

I got married after I became a wholesaler. My husband was a police officer in our jurisdiction. He continued to work as a cop after the marriage. He did not join me in my business; only my brother and I were involved. After marketing other people's goods for a while, I opened a small factory with about twenty workers and began to produce my own goods. At that point, my husband quit his job and became a buyer for our company. It is best to use one of your own family members as a buyer because he or she can ask for kickbacks from suppliers.

After we were in wholesaling for a few years, our business hit a bottleneck. Our products were not popular anymore, and it was getting tough to make money. So we decided to move our business to Guangzhou. We did not sell our business in Taizhou and moved to Guangzhou abruptly; we took the time to move bit by bit. In Guangzhou, we opened a store at the old Kinbo Market, not long before it was completely renovated.

After moving to Guangzhou, the family business made a big turnaround; however, her marriage began to fall apart when her husband began to fool around. Ah Min looked sad when she talked about her personal life and her lack of English proficiency:

I am now divorced. I have two sons; one is attending middle school in Guangzhou, and the other, an elementary school in Taizhou. They both live in their schools' dormitories. I do not know how to control my sons, so they should be under the care of other people. I spoil them by letting them do whatever they want. I am not a good mother. Besides, my English is very poor; I cannot understand even the most basic English words.

According to Laoban (G2), Ah Min and her brother and sister-in-law were engaged in the production and distribution of high-quality men's casual wear, especially T-shirts and polo shirts. The three worked together very well, and they were all experienced and savvy entrepreneurs. Ah Min's sister-in-law (Lau Fang, G21), in particular, was a professionally trained fashion designer. Thus, it was not surprising that they were doing relatively well. However, according to Laoban, their business got into trouble recently due to rapid expansion and overproduction. Last year, their goods did not sell well, and they ended up with millions of dollar worth of inventory. Regardless, with a new spacious gongsi, a dangkou on Zhanxi Road, and a factory on the outskirts of Guangzhou, Ah Min's family business can be considered "well-established" among the countless small businesses engaged in counterfeiting. According to one source, Ah Min likes to buy apartments as an investment when she has money, and she owns eight of them.

Zheng Hua (Clothing Manufacturer)

Zheng Hua (G19) is the brother-in-law of Lin Jun (G17), also a clothing manufacturer. Both Zheng Hua and Lin Jun are former employees of Laoban, as is Lin Jun's younger sister, who later married Zheng Hua. Lin Jun's father, at one point, was a business associate of Laoban's. I discuss Laoban's network in the next chapter when I explore the social organization of the counterfeiting industry in Guangzhou. Zheng Hua, age thirty-three, introduced himself as follows:

I am from Hubei Province. I was born in 1986, arrived in Dongguan in 2004, and worked as a stitcher for a clothing factory. I had worked as an apprentice for a tailor in my hometown, so I was already somewhat familiar with fashion before I went to Dongguan. The factory in Dongguan was a contract manufacturer for a name brand. My monthly salary at the factory was $72. I left after working for two months.

Zheng Hua recalled how he came to Guangzhou by chance and how his salary increased substantially after the move:

At that point, Xiao Cai was working for Laoban in Guangzhou. Incidentally, a friend of mine was dating a friend of his, and that was how he and I came to know each other. When Xiao Cai invited me to work for Laoban as a sample room stitcher, I agreed because I thought it would be better than the job I had in Dongguan, where I had to sew from morning to dark. It was hard work. Once I arrived in Guangzhou to work for Laoban, my monthly salary shot up to $145. One of the reasons for the dramatic increase was that it coincided with pay raises across the board in China.

Zheng Hua explained how he and Xiao Cai started their own business after their boss moved to another town:

Xiao Cai was a sample designer, but there was also another sample designer, who was actually in charge of the sample room. That's why Xiao Cai could also help me with sewing sample pieces. By May 2006, Laoban and his business partner split, and Laoban moved to Panyu [a district of Guangzhou] to start his own business. In the process, he let go of me and Xiao Cai because he did not need that many workers in Panyu.

That's why Xiao Cai and I decided to start our own business. We did not have much money, only a few thousand dollars given to us by Laoban as severance pay. At any rate, we did not need that much start-up money to begin with because we did not need a store, a factory, or an office. We asked a factory to produce our goods and stored the goods in our homes.

He revealed how he was able to take advantage of large counterfeiting firms by copying their products and selling them at a cheaper price:

We copied the copies of other well-established firms; we produced cheap point-by-point fakes. We focused on the clothing of five or six brand names, including Dolce & Gabbana, Fendi, Y-3, and Diesel. We shopped for the materials and then asked a factory to replicate the samples we provided for them. We then sold the goods to various wholesale and retail outlets. This type of business operation [duplicating other firms' copies and outsourcing manufacturing and distribution] had an 80 percent success rate.

At that time, we only did men's T-shirts. They cost us about $2.80 apiece to produce, and we sold them to wholesalers and retailers for $6.00 each, making a profit of $3.20 per piece. To survive, we relied on our ability to produce and distribute large volumes of ordinary point-by-point replicas. Big counterfeiting firms have more expenses than we did, and that's why their profit margin needs to be $4.70 per shirt, to cover their expenditures. That's why we were much more competitive than they were when it came to pricing.

Zheng Hua suggested that business was much easier to conduct then, even though it was hard work:

> In the beginning, we had to work very hard, and we were stressed all the time. We worked from dawn till dark, and we had to do everything ourselves. We did only men's T-shirts; we did not produce men's polo shirts. It was a lot easier to do business at that time. After our goods were manufactured, we did not have to worry that we wouldn't be able to sell them. Even if we put an item on sale at a bargain price, we would still make a small profit.

Zheng Hua said his wife was operating a store with the help of two young female workers. He was paying $4,300 a month in rent for his new gongsi. Of all the business premises I visited during my two stints in Guangzhou, including dangkou, xiezilou, gongsi, factories, and workshops, Zheng Hua's gongsi was the most impressive. It was located in a relatively new and well-maintained commercial building and had a spacious office with a huge tea table at which he could entertain guests, a waiting area, a big showroom, a design room, a second office, and a sample room on the first floor. Upstairs, on the second floor, there was another big office, a salesroom, an accountant's office, and a large conference room. He had moved into this space only three months earlier, anticipating that he was going to expand his business by establishing his own brands. Unfortunately, his firm was targeted by the authorities, and two close relatives who were working for him were arrested and convicted. I discuss this incident when I explore how the Chinese authorities crack down on counterfeiting in Chapter 8.

Xiao Ma (Leather Supplier)

Xiao Ma (H4), forty-six years old, was born in Chenghai, a district of Shantou City. With a population of close to a million, Chenghai is a toy manufacturing center. The district was listed as a notorious market by the USTR in 2015, 2016, 2021, and 2022. I met Xiao Ma for the first time when he was eating breakfast with his assistant Ah Bao (F12) and a leather supplier from Bangladesh at the hotel where I was staying. After that encounter, I came to know him well; we met often for lunch or dinner and on many other occasions. I also met his wife and their children, a seven-year-old daughter and a five-year-old son.

Xiao Ma migrated to Hong Kong at the age of twelve but moved back to Guangzhou at twenty-seven. His father had passed away. His mother, a former domestic helper, and his brother, a legal aid, still live in Hong Kong. He recalled how he once worked for a leather supplier in Hong Kong:

> When I was in Hong Kong, I worked for a leather supplier. I was the leader of a group of six workers, and we took care of everything for the business owner. Our monthly revenue was more than HK$10 million ($1.3 million), and my monthly salary was over HK$10,000 ($1,300). My boss also gave me a HK$270,000 ($35,000) bonus every year. Business was good, not solely because of me; it was also because we offered quality leather. If you have what buyers want, they come to you.
>
> When I was working for the Hong Kong firm, I did not do anything to exploit my boss. Someone else in my position might have run away with the company's funds, sold the leather in the warehouse and pocketed the money, or fulfilled customers' orders in private and not let the firm get involved. At any rate, I could have done many things to enrich myself, but I did not.

Xiao Ma was determined to start his own business, so he quit, even though his boss offered him a big bonus. Once he became a business owner, he never looked back:

> I quit after working for him for more than four years. He did not want me to go and promised to give me HK$2 million ($260,000) if I would stay for another three years. I told him my ship had been moored in his seaport for more than four years and it was time for me to set sail. I remained for another three months to take care of all the pending transactions, including collecting a HK$150,000 ($19,500) payment from a client. I begged the reluctant client to make the payment so that I could leave the company.
>
> Once I started my own business, it took off right away. At its peak, my monthly revenue was more than HK$10 million ($1.3 million), and my monthly profits were between HK$600,000 and HK$700,000 ($78,000 to $90,000). In general, a company with a revenue of HK$10 million should be able to make a profit of more than a million, but I was not greedy; I wanted to offer my clients a reasonable price. That's why I was making less than others.

While he was riding high, he was arrested and jailed for three years. He recalled what happened:

> I was arrested a little over three years ago. To pay less tax, my customs broker submitted a false claim to the Chinese customs author-

ities for the leather I was importing from Bangladesh. My customs broker did not tell the customs authorities the actual type of leather I was importing. When the leather arrived in Jiangmen and the authorities discovered it was not as described by my customs broker, I was arrested and locked up. I was detained in a detention center in Jiangmen for three years and released only two months ago. My customs broker was also the owner of a large leather factory, and I purchased most of my leather from him. He was sentenced to ten years and is still serving his sentence.

Xiao Ma said he was locked up in a small cell with dozens of inmates. He and the inmates worked every day in a factory from dawn until dusk. They had to meet a daily quota, and, if they did not, they would have to work until the next morning. They were not paid for their work. When he was in custody, his wife took over his leather business, but it soon began to decline.

Xiao Ma said he had been a good leather supplier for many years. He made sure his warehouses were well stocked and ready to fulfill customers' orders promptly: "At any given time, I had more than $1.6 million worth of leather in my warehouses. When you do wholesale, you must have the leather in your warehouse, and you must have a very diverse collection of it. When buyers come to you for leather and you say they have to wait for two to three days, they are not going to wait." He also was proud of his ability to predict what kinds of leather would become popular and to be proactive in making all the preparations to meet the demand: "I was very good at anticipating what type of leather would sell, researching which handbags were popular, and predicting which of these handbags would be counterfeited. Then I made sure I had the right types of leather when counterfeiters came to me. I knew the different types of leather that were needed to copy Hermès, Prada, and Fendi, and then I found a leather factory to produce this leather. I stocked the leather in my warehouses and waited for buyers to come."

Xiao Ma recalled how he at one point was very much into the distribution of leathers ideal for making fake Hermès, Prada, and Chanel handbags: "I once developed a type of leather specifically for making Hermès handbags. I traveled to Hong Kong and Europe and bought a few Hermès handbags, which cost me thousands of dollars each. After I got back, I took apart the handbags to inspect the leather. Sometimes, I could learn about the leather without destroying a Hermès handbag. That's why my wife had quite a few authentic handbags, but she always complained about how much she disliked these bags. I told her the bags were bought not for her, but for my business. Besides Hermès, I also developed leather for Prada and Chanel handbags."

Xiao Ma also disclosed one of the business tricks he used to expand his leather supply firm into one of the key players in the Guangzhou leather goods industry: "I was a smart businessman. For instance, if I knew you were a contract manufacturer for an international fashion house, I would offer you a piece of leather at cost, hoping that you would buy it. I was willing to do that because I knew once your handbags were out, there would be people rushing to copy your products, and that meant they would have to come to me for the leather. I would make my money then. That happened when a contract manufacturer for Bally once approached me for leather and I sold it to him at cost, for $2.90 per foot. When counterfeiters came to me later, I sold the leather to them for $3.10 or $3.50 per foot, and at one point, even $4.20. Can you estimate how much money I made?"

Xiao Ma began to venture into the restaurant business before his arrest and after his release from prison. He opened four restaurants, but, unfortunately, none of them was able to survive, and he lost more than a million dollars.

Xiao Zhen (Handbag Manufacturer)

Xiao Zhen (H13) is a thirty-five-year-old male born in Guangzhou. He came from a poor family, graduated from a vocational high school, and was hired by a state-owned transportation company at the age of nineteen. Soon thereafter, he was married, but the marriage did not last for long:

> I married someone from my village whose last name was the same as mine. Most people in my village share the same last name. It all started with my parents joking with their neighbors about becoming relatives one day. Only after marriage did I realize my wife wanted to have fun and a career, but not children, and that was a problem for me and my family. We divorced in 2012.

One of his classmates, a Chaoshanese, opened a handbag store in Sanyuanli, and this led another classmate, Li Yung, to follow suit. Initially, Li was a leather goods distributor; he asked a contract manufacturer to produce counterfeit bags for him. After being a distributor for some time, Li began to produce his own goods by operating a factory, and he hired Xiao Zhen to work as a purchasing agent in his new manufacturing facility. There were fifty to sixty workers in the factory. After working as purchasing agent for a while, Xiao Zhen became a plant manager. The business, which was mainly engaged in the copying of Chloé handbags, expanded quickly. At one point, Li Yung had six stores in Baiyun Leather City alone; he owned two and rented four. However, after the demand for cheap Chloé fakes declined due to a dramatic decrease in buyers from the Middle East, Li Yung began to imitate other designer brands. Xiao Zhen recalled what happened after he quit working for Li Yung:

> A year after I became a plant manager, I quit. It all started with Li Yung hiring one of our classmates. Not long after that classmate came, he began to criticize how I managed the factory, and I began to suspect that Li Yung had hired him intending to eventually replace me. So I left, and it was a big blow to me.
>
> Once I left Li Yung, I quickly decided to open a handbag factory. I recruited a leather craftsman as a business partner; I would invest money, and he would contribute his skills. I provided more than $64,000 as start-up money to convert a warehouse into a factory and buy new machines. My factory produced mainly Fendi and Dior handbags. I also married for the second time, to a Chaoshanese woman who was a colleague when I was working for Li Yung.

Xiao Zhen's second wife opened a store at Baiyun Leather City, marketing not only her husband's counterfeit Fendi and Dior handbags but also fake handbags of other name brands produced by other manufacturers. Between 2014 and 2016, Xiao Zhen was subject to three unfortunate incidents: (1) a customer returned a large number of finished goods, claiming that they did not meet his standards, and this cost Xiao Zhen more than $48,000; (2) his factory was investigated by the authorities for counterfeiting, but he used his connection to quell the investigation [his mother works for the judiciary]; and (3) his warehouse was raided by the police, and he and his brother were arrested. He was jailed for a month and released on probation for one year. This incident cost him more than $300,000.

After the third incident, Xiao Zhen and his brother quit counterfeiting and his wife shut down her store in Baiyun Leather City. She became a weishang, selling goods on WeChat. He went back to work for the transportation company he was once affiliated with, but he was not happy with his work and was thinking about becoming a Didi [China's Uber] driver or opening a bakery.

Li Bing (Handbag Distributor)

Li Bing (H1) is a forty-five-year-old married woman born in Wenzhou, Zhejiang Province. She recalled how she and her husband moved from Wenzhou to Guangzhou:

> Many years ago, my husband and I were involved in the fake handbag business in Wenzhou. My husband traveled to Guangzhou,

bought handbags, and sent them back to Wenzhou, where I sold them. We did that for six years. He spent a lot of time in Guangzhou during that period. We made money, but after a few years, I began to worry about letting my husband stay all alone in Guangzhou. To protect my marriage, I moved to Guangzhou, and we opened a counterfeit handbag store. At the beginning, I rented a store on the third floor of Baiyun Leather City. Later, I moved to the second floor of the building. The first year, I lost about $100,000; the second year, the store broke even; but from the third year on, I was making tens of thousands of dollars every year, or even every month. Our business took off.

Li Bing explained how she and her husband conducted their business, buying and dismantling genuine handbags, finding materials, and producing replicas. She also recalled the challenges:

During that time, I went to Hong Kong to buy genuine handbags. A handbag could cost up to $3,500, but I would take it apart to see how it was made. Otherwise, how else could you produce point-to-point copies? You have to know exactly how the leather was cut, how it was stitched, and the exact size of the various pieces of the leather.

After I took the bag apart, I would contact people who could help me find the leather, the metal fittings, the zippers, the thread, the lining material, and other components. If a leather supplier said he or she could find the leather, I would give that person the leather pieces from the genuine handbag, and three to five days to source it. The person would have to pay me $3,500 as insurance [to cover the cost of the genuine handbag] plus $800 for the pieces of leather. I would do the same with the suppliers of other materials.

After I got all the materials, I would provide them to a factory for jiagong [production, or contract manufacturing]. This is a critical step because if you deal with a subpar factory, you are going to lose money. The factory has to come up with good quality products, otherwise, you will have to sell the bags at a very cheap price later on.

When the factory started to produce the sample bag, I had to be there until late into the night to make sure they got it right. It was a grueling process, spending many aggravating hours in the factory. The sample bag was produced by one person by hand, not by machines.

After that, there would be mass production. I might order a hundred bags in each color, and the same style of handbag might be produced in eight different colors. Normally, when you are selling a hundred different kinds of bags, only twenty of them will be a success; the other bags will have to be sold for a cheap price. However, as long as there are twenty successful types of bags among the hundred, you are going to make money.

She recalled why she and her husband quit the business after making a substantial amount of money:

Our business was a success, and we made a lot of money. However, we lived a stressful life; we worked long hours, and we worried about our safety. We knew we could be arrested anytime and could lose all our money and property overnight. This happened to many people in this business. Some were imprisoned. That was why we decided it was time to quit, and we did. You need to have a strong will to be able to quit. Many business owners, after making millions of dollars, continue to be involved and eventually pay a huge price. When you are told that there are people from the gongshangju [AIC] in your store, your heart drops. It happened to us once. My husband and I were on our way to our outlet. Once we were inside the market, my husband asked me to hand over all my credit cards, bank cards, and cash, anticipating that I could be arrested, detained, and even sent to prison. This was what happened when a couple was in crisis. What an irony! I walked in, answered their questions with a big smile, and put some money in their pockets, and they left. Whew!

She explained why she only distributed replicas that she produced, with the help of a contract manufacturer, and her cost and selling price for a counterfeit handbag: "I only sell my own products. If I were to sell other people's goods, I couldn't make money. Normally, it would cost me about $200 to manufacture a bag, and I would sell it for $250. The contract factory charged about $45 a bag to produce it. [The rest of the cost was for materials.] Most of the time, store owners like me buy all the materials because it is more cost-effective. If I asked the contract factory to buy the materials, my cost would increase." Li Bing and her husband were mainly involved in copying Celine handbags (see Figure 5.1).

Li Bing was proud of her accomplishments in the counterfeit trade, considering how little education she and her husband had: "I had only two years of elementary school and my husband only six. Neither one of us had much education. However, even though my IQ is not high, my EQ is high. I know how to deal with people, including my husband [laughing]. I also can anticipate my next five moves, not just the next move. I leap when I think the time is right." When she talked about how many residential properties she owns and her children and godchildren, her face brightened up: "I now own

Figure 5.1 A copy of a Celine Clasp handbag.

six apartments in and around Guangzhou. I live in one, in Foshan [a booming city adjacent to Guangzhou, with a population of close to ten million], and rent out the other five. My son is a college student in Australia. We sent him there six years ago as a high school student. It cost us a lot of money. My daughter graduated from college and is now teaching music at a prominent university in Guangzhou. I also have one godson and two goddaughters. They are in their twenties. One of the goddaughters, a twenty-four-year-old college graduate, is in insurance sales."

She also said that she and her husband were devout Christians and spent a lot of time in church activities. Her husband said: "We are Christians, and Christians are not interested in the counterfeiting business. Now that we are out of this trade, we are full of joy every day. It's like after defecating; it is very comforting."

Summary

According to the criminologist R. V. Gundur, author of *Trying to Make It: The Enterprises, Gangs, and People of the American Drug Trade* (2022, 12), people who engaged in the drug trade in the United States, including in El Paso, Texas, Phoenix, Arizona, and Chicago, Illinois, were mostly "ordinary folks just trying to make it from one day to the next." Similarly, there is nothing unique about the people who are involved in counterfeiting in Guangzhou. They are similar to the hundreds of millions of other young men and women from rural areas who leave their hometowns searching for a better future in urban centers and trying to make it (Chang 2009; Gaetano 2016; Ngai 2005). Many of them start as migrant workers in Shenzhen, Guangzhou, Shanghai, and Beijing, waiting patiently for their turn to become small business owners. Those migrant workers who dream of becoming entrepreneurs work extremely hard, learn everything they can about their trade, save as much money as possible, and establish a network they can rely on when they start their businesses.

I received very different answers from my research subjects when I asked them to generalize about the people who are involved in the counterfeiting trade. One of the most often mentioned traits was how motivated the counterfeiters are. Lau Fang (G21), a successful clothing entrepreneur, had this to say about herself: "I came to Guangzhou alone and worked for Laoban for more than a year. At that time, he was making point-by-point counterfeit garments. Even though I was a designer in his firm, I learned everything about his business. I am a go-getter; that is why I am not going to work for others my entire life. This personality was cultivated by my father, who was a builder. He had high hopes for his children." Laoban echoed her point by explaining the historical context of why there was such a strong desire to get rich quickly in China:

There are many individuals in this business with different skills and qualities, so it is hard to generalize about them as a group. Having said that, as an ethnic group, Chinese people want to be business owners, regardless of whether they are qualified or not. That is why commercial property rental rates in China only go up, and rarely come down. Distributors simply move to another market after they have failed in one market and are not bothered by the experience. That is because they have one wish—to get rich quickly and then flaunt it. One of my employees quit and established his own business, and he did not do well in the very beginning. However, he earned $160,000 one season and promptly bought a $70,000 Audi A4. In my view, [the reason for this mentality is] because China was poor for about two centuries and people went through the Cultural Revolution [1966–1976] after the PRC was established; these experiences cultivated in them a strong wish for rapid wealth. That is why family members devote all their time and energy working together from dawn to dark, and do not care about the risks involved. They just want to get out of poverty and become rich, so that the family will be able to bask in glory.

Mr. Wang, a special prosecutor for counterfeiting, characterized people who are involved in counterfeiting this way: "They are ordinary, hard-working people trying to make a modest income. They are the same as legitimate businesspeople."

According to Yu Hua, a writer of contemporary fiction and the author of *China in Ten Words*, large numbers of Chinese strove to become rich after China adopted the economic reform and opening up policy. From his viewpoint (H. Yu 2011, 168–169), these ordinary but risk-taking individuals who were willing to take shortcuts were the engine of China's economic miracle:

China's economic miracle of the past thirty years, it's fair to say, is an agglomeration of countless individual miracles created at the grassroots level. China's grassroots dare to think and dare to act: in the tide of economic development they will adopt any method that suits their purposes, and they are bold enough to try things that are illegal or even criminal. At the same time, China's legal system has developed only slowly, leaving plenty of loopholes for the grassroots to exploit and putting all kinds of profits within their reach. Add to that their dauntless courage, which comes from their having nothing to lose, since they began with nothing at all.

In Yu Hua's book, an incisive appraisal of twenty-first-century China, three of the ten most often used words are "disparity," "grassroots," and "copycat." Yu might be saying that extreme inequality in China in the aftermath of economic reform led many grassroots people to become copycats in order to obtain something that had been denied to them. The underlying force was simple, according to Yu (2011, 25), because: "[In today's China, so] intense is the competition and so unbearable the pressure that, for many Chinese, survival is like war itself. In this social environment the strong prey on the weak, people enrich themselves through brute force and deception, and the meek and the humble suffer while the bold and unscrupulous flourish." The counterfeiters and their facilitators are no doubt the strong, the bold, and the unscrupulous in contemporary China.

6

GROUP CHARACTERISTICS

After having examined the individual characteristics of luxury goods counterfeiters and their associates in the preceding chapter, I explore their group characteristics in this chapter. I focus on the size, scope, and structure of their enterprises and probe how these enterprises compete and cooperate in the market for knockoff fashions and accessories. I also examine the role of corruption, violence, and organized crime in the counterfeiting business.

Size

In a study on organized crime in New York City, the criminologist Peter Reuter (1983, 109) found that most firms engaging in the production and distribution of illegal products tend to be small, and for good reasons:

> The illegality of a product has consequences for the ways in which various participants (entrepreneurs, agents, customers) seek to structure their relationships. The threat of police intervention, either to seize assets or to imprison participants, and the lack of court-enforceable contracts are likely to lead to the formation of small and relatively ephemeral enterprises.

R. V. Gundur (2022) also claimed that the drug trade in the United States was dominated by small businesses, not large illicit corporations. The social organization of counterfeiting in Guangzhou supports the two criminologists' assessments. Even though the counterfeiting industry in China is reported to be a multibillion-dollar business, most enterprises in this industry are small. They could be one-person operations, like Ah Hua's (H6). As mentioned earlier, she opened a small store near the entrance of a food bazaar selling cheap replicas of global brand handbags. They could be businesses run by husband and wife teams like Xiao Wen (G6) and his wife, who sell knockoff men's T-shirts to foreign buyers that they design but have produced by a contract manufacturer. The couple's business has no employees nor any physical operation units such as a store. They could also be family businesses in which several family members work together with a clear division of labor, and no outsiders are involved. If a firm is too big for a family to run, the owner will invite relatives to join. Some businesses may recruit people from their hometowns to work for them in Guangzhou.

According to my research subjects, because counterfeiting is illegal, enterprises involved in it have no choice but to remain small. One of the reasons is to prevent unhappy workers from reporting the businesses to the authorities. Danny (H3), a handbag manufacturer in Dongguan, said: "Fake handbag factories are mostly very small, with about eight to nine workers who are family members or relatives. If you hire an outsider and the person becomes upset, he or she will report you to the authorities."

Many counterfeiting businesses are composed of husbands and wives, with or without employees. In general, if a couple is involved in both production and distribution, the wife is in charge of distribution and the husband, in production. If a couple is only engaged in either distribution or production, then it is very likely that the wife will play the key role.

If a husband and wife team operating a business needs extra help, the couple is most likely to invite family members from their hometown to join them in Guangzhou. They will often start with their brothers and sisters, followed by cousins, aunts, and uncles. Their children will also join them after they grow up. Take Xiao Xin (G15), for example. She and her husband, Lao Zhu, own a garment factory in Guangzhou, and her brother and his wife, and her sister and her husband all worked for her. When Xiao Xiao and Xiao Guan (G13), a couple in the men's T-shirt and polo shirt business, needed someone they could trust to manage their warehouses, they brought Xiao Xiao's sister and her husband from their hometown in Sichuan to Guangzhou.

Instead of seeing these counterfeit firms as small independent businesses operating on their own, it is more accurate to view them as clusters of family businesses based on kinship. In other words, members from the same family or kinship may engage in a particular type of business independently, but they are well connected and work closely with one another. To make it all work, different family members will be involved in different components of the design, production, and distribution of a particular product so that there will be no direct competition among them. According to a report in the *China Daily*, the counterfeiters processed by the authorities in Beijing between 2002 and 2010 suggested that the most prominent form of organization was kinship ties.

Besides having family and kinship as a foundation, the counterfeiting business also relies on people from the same area who speak the same dialect. This way, it is a lot easier to communicate and build trust. According to a travel agency owner from Henan: "The idea is called baotuan qunuan: people sticking together to get warm when it is cold [outsiders' method of survival in an unfamiliar environment]. When people leave home to work or do business in major urban centers, they stick together based on family or place of origin. The whole Chinese economy is one big family business."

There are also relatively large counterfeiting businesses in China. I am not sure how my research subjects determined whether a business was a "large" counterfeiting enterprise, but some of them thought Laoban's business qualified as such. Laoban (G2), the Taiwanese entrepreneur who owned an apparel firm that specialized in men's T-shirts or polo shirts, had about thirty employees at one point. He had a company, outlet stores, and warehouses, but not an office or a factory.

In sum, the counterfeiters I interviewed in Guangzhou all suggested that the majority of the counterfeiting businesses are relatively small, mainly because they are illegal and do not have brands of their own that they can promote and grow. However, when a large number of small businesses are engaged in a particular activity in unison with one another, the results can be formidable. Xiao Lai (H15), the owner of a leather handbag office inside Baiyun Leather City, came up with an interesting comparison between the counterfeiting and drug production businesses:

There is a CCTV [China Central Television] series called *The Thunder*. It is about how a village in China has been transformed into a major hub for drug production. According to the series, drug production in the village is not controlled by one large organization. Instead, the drug business there comprises a network of many small drug laboratories. In other words, the large amount of drugs is the result of the accumulation of small amounts of drugs. The counterfeiting business is the same. We do not have one large organization that plays a dominant role. The counterfeiting industry's enormous size is made possible by the combination of many small factories that are spread all over the landscape.

In sum, the small size of these firms does not prevent them from working in sync with one another to respond to a sudden surge in market demand because all these firms belong to one or more networks. As long as there is a profit to be made, they are willing to cooperate in any way they can so that everyone involved will make money.

Scope

The scope of a business's operations can be examined from two angles: the breadth of its products and services (horizontal scope) and the range of activities (vertical scope).

Horizontal Scope

A business's product mix, or product assortment, refers to the variety of products it offers to its customers. The product mix can be very narrow or can consist of hundreds of products. The product mix or horizontal scope of most of my research subjects' businesses can be considered to be limited. Very few of them were simultaneously involved in counterfeiting more than one category of product. In other words, a research subject in the handbag business did not also engage in the clothing or footwear business. Moreover, he or she limited the copying of handbags to just a few brands and styles. That is, the product line was relatively shallow. In sum, counterfeiters in my study were small business owners who had neither the capability nor the willingness to operate a business with a broad horizontal scope. The breadth and depth of their product mix were small and lean.

Vertical Scope

The vertical scope of a counterfeiting enterprise can be divided into five categories: retail only, wholesale only, both retail and wholesale, manufacturing only, and both distribution and manufacturing. Unlike horizontal scope, vertical scope allows more room for counterfeiters to maneuver.

Retail Only
Some of the shops selling counterfeit goods are involved in retail only. These are microbusinesses owned and operated by a single person who sources goods from wholesalers and sells them to consumers at retail prices. Ah Hua (H6), discussed in Chapter 4, is an example. She purchases a small number of shoes and handbags from wholesalers in Guangzhou and Dongguan, keeps them in her store, and sells them to individual consumers, one pair of shoes or one

handbag at a time. In general, these retail-only businesses are operated by business proprietors with very little money invested in them. The owner takes care of all aspects of the business, and there is no need to rent a warehouse because the owner keeps only a small inventory. Retail-only stores are usually located near residential areas, not in the major markets discussed in Chapter 4. All the stores in the major markets are involved in both retail and wholesale business.

Wholesale Only

But for the one exception described later, I did not encounter any counterfeiters who were involved in wholesale only. All the other wholesalers I met were also engaged in retail through their stores or e-commerce platforms. As business owners, they were reluctant to give up the opportunity to sell even one piece of merchandise, regardless of the size of their businesses. The one couple I interviewed who did wholesale only were solely engaged in export. At the time of the interview, the husband and wife team, Ah Mei and Xiao Wen (G6), did not have a store, an office, or a company. They also did not have their own factory. (They had an office at one time but closed it because business was slow.) They designed men's and women's casual wear, found a contract manufacturer to produce the garments they designed, and then sold the goods to buyers from overseas, mostly from Russia. They had a list of regular overseas buyers. According to Xiao Wen, a clean-cut thirty-nine-year-old man, who said his wife, Ah Mei, was in charge of their business and he was only responsible for design: "Our foreign buyers all have their own offices in Guangzhou, and these offices have Chinese-speaking employees.[1] All we have to do is to deliver the goods to the warehouses they want us to. We are not involved in shipping the goods to their home countries." When I asked them about their production costs and profit margins, Ah Mei replied:

> The cost to produce a T-shirt for a foreign buyer includes the following: $1.10 to $1.70 for fabric, $1 for the factory owner, 70 cents for embroidery, and $1.40 for printing. The total production cost for a T-shirt is around $5. Our profit margin for one T-shirt is $1.40 to $1.70, approximately one-third of the production cost. Besides, our profit margin also depends on the size of an order. For us, an order that is more than ten thousand pieces of clothing is considered a big order, and if the order is that big, we are willing to reduce our profit margin, even down to 72 cents to $1.1 per garment. If a T-shirt is a copy of a name brand, its profit margin is twice as much as for noncounterfeits.

According to Laoban, wholesalers are the ones who make the most money:

> Those who are in wholesale distribution make the most money. Peo-
> ple in production can only earn manufacturing fees. Fortunately, I
> dealt with large quantities of goods. When my business was boom-
> ing, I produced more than 20,000 copies of some garments. Regard-
> less, the regional distributors have the highest profits, especially
> those in Beijing. These regional distributors can buy from many dif-
> ferent types of firms, including those that produce shirts, pants, and
> other fashion accessories. The distributors in Beijing can sell to their
> clients in neighboring provinces like Hebei and Shanxi, and in the
> Northeastern provinces [Liaoning, Jilin, and Heilongjiang]. They also
> have overseas clients in Russia and Eastern Europe.

Both Retail and Wholesale

Most counterfeiters are involved in both retail and wholesale, but the focus is
on wholesale rather than retail. As mentioned earlier, for these businesspeople,
maintaining a store where they can conduct retail as well as wholesale is an
effective way to attract new customers, some of whom might include major
retailers from other parts of China or around the world.

Manufacturing Only

Some counterfeiters are engaged in manufacturing only and have no desire
to enter distribution, even though they know they are making less money
than those who sell the finished goods they produce. Manufacturers can only
charge their customers a manufacturing fee, and as Ah Mei said earlier, it is
only about one-fifth of the cost of a finished product ($1 out of $5). The manufacturers I talked to often expressed their envy of those doing both production and distribution, insinuating the latter were making serious money.
However, these manufacturers also knew that their businesses were less risky,
mainly because they were less likely to be impacted by market uncertainty
or targeted by anti-counterfeiting officials.

Both Distribution and Manufacturing

Some of my research subjects were involved in the design, production, and
distribution of their own goods. For some counterfeiters, the ability to handle all of these different areas by themselves was a sign that they were successful and fully in control of their businesses. However, they still had to rely
on other people for materials, packaging, and other services.

Changing Vertical Scope

Counterfeiters often change their business scope to expand or contract their businesses. Some counterfeiters start as distributors and then broaden their scope of operation to include manufacturing after their distribution businesses begin to grow and they want to assure themselves of a reliable supply of high-quality products. Some are initially involved in manufacturing only but later venture into distribution to increase their profit margin.

Xiao Qin (H16), a leather handbag business owner, explained how he had changed the scope of his business, over the previous several years, from outsourcing manufacturing to owning production facilities and increasing the number of distribution outlets:

> At the very beginning, I opened a store at Baiyun Leather City and relied on several factories on an ad hoc basis to produce my handbags. When my business took off, I turned to contract factories; I signed a contract with one or two factories to make handbags for me exclusively. They would not take orders from other handbag distributors. Profits for the manufacturing end are always the lowest, plus there is always a conflict of interest between them [manufacturers] and us [designers/organizers]. That is why when my contract factories wanted to expand and I was not able to give them more work, it became a problem. Eventually, I bought the contract factories and hired the original owners to run the factories for me. I also increased the number of outlet stores from one to three, and they were all in Baiyun Leather City.

If a firm is involved in both distribution and production, it will have to sell all of its goods and cannot rely on other distributors to market them. Mrs. Jia (G11), an entrepreneur who produces and distributes embroidered patches, explained why:

> Our factory only produces merchandise that we sell in our three distribution outlets. We will not manufacture goods for other outlets because our stores can sell all the goods we produce. At any rate, even if we were willing to produce goods for other stores, they would not accept them because they know we have our own distribution outlets. If they were to let us produce for them, they would have to let us know what they are planning on designing or selling. They would not let one of their competitors like us find out what they are preparing for the next season.

For some of my research subjects, expanding the vertical scope of their business operation was a mistake. Lin Jun (G17) is a case in point. He and his father owned a factory that produced fake name-brand T-shirts and decided at one point to do the printing themselves to reduce costs: "Around 2010, we opened a printing factory. We thought that by doing so we would reduce our production cost. We invested about $59,000 in the factory and asked my wife's elder brother to run it. In the end, we operated it for only two years. We sold the factory for only $3,100 because we were losing money. That's what happens. When you buy machines, they are costly; when you sell them, they are worthless."

If a distributor also engages in production, he or she will have to show up at the production site every day after working long hours in distribution activities. For entrepreneurs engaged in selling goods, the thought of going to a factory after dark daily is daunting. In the words of a handbag store owner, "I do not have my own factory; I buy my goods from other factories. Even though I must spend long hours in my stall, at least I do not have to go to my factory at night."

Mr. Liang (F9), a Skechers shoes counterfeiter, said that people in counterfeiting are normally only involved in distribution or manufacturing but not both. He said: "Most people only do manufacturing; distribution is something that a different group of people do. Manufacturers are passive participants; they are not going to go around and find out what the market wants. That is something distributors do. Manufacturers normally wait for distributors to tell them what they want and show them the samples, and then they copy them."

When a business is expanding, a distributor may consider venturing into manufacturing to control the pace of production in response to market demand, improve the quality of merchandise, and maximize profits. Lau Fang (G21) explained why she, her husband, and her sister-in-law (Ah Min, G5) entered manufacturing after years of successfully distributing men's T-shirts and polo shirts:

> For a long time, our garments were produced by contract manufacturers. Because they could not meet our standards for quality, we decided to manufacture our own goods. We started our factory a few years ago. Initially, we managed the factory ourselves, but now we let a subcontractor operate it. The plant and the machines are ours, but someone else manages the facility, produces the amount of merchandise we want, and meets our quality standards. The subcontractor finds the workers and manages them. Nevertheless, after we had the factory, we learned that it is very time-consuming to run it.

On the other hand, someone who is thriving as a manufacturer may become a distributor because there is a belief among entrepreneurs that distributors make the maximum profits. However, it can be a disaster for some manufacturers who venture into distribution. Lin Jun (G17), the research subject quoted earlier who ventured into the printing business and failed, experienced another failure when he got involved in distribution while continuing with his manufacturing business. His distribution business began to crumple not long after he started it, and he reoriented his business to manufacturing only.

In sum, there are advantages and disadvantages to operating one's own factory. Mrs. Jia (G11), an embroidery patches business owner, who was in charge of sales and spent most of her time in a distribution outlet, while her husband (in production) devoted all his time to their factory, explained why:

> There are pros and cons to operating a factory. Having a factory means you can control the level of production. You do not have to worry if one of your products becomes very popular because you can increase your production to meet the demand. If you do not have your own factory, you must rely on one or more contract factories. They have business with many other distributors, not just you. Very often, these factories will not or cannot meet your request. However, if you own a factory, you have the pressure to take care of your workers. The workers want you to offer them baodi [guaranteed minimum wage], which means regardless of whether there is work or not, they want you to pay them a fixed monthly wage, excluding overtime pay. We pay our factory workers more than $435 a month as baodi. Also, there are many other issues you have to deal with when you own a factory, for example, environmental protection and fire prevention. You are more at ease if you do not own a factory.

Laoban agreed with Mrs. Jia. However, he did not think that a person had to operate a factory to thrive in the counterfeiting industry:

> There are advantages and disadvantages. The major advantage is that you are in control of the production level and can adjust in response to the demand. The major disadvantage is that you have to pay for all the expenses of maintaining a factory during the slow season when there are no orders. The wage for workers is a major expense for a factory owner. During the slow season, you must keep the same workforce even if there is no work. Nowadays, you must pay workers a basic salary if you want to keep them. Moreover, to manage a factory, you must have a good system and a capable management team. Otherwise, when demand surges, you will not be able to meet it. Owning a factory is not a critical factor in predicting whether your business will be a success. The three most important factors are the ability to

design, sell, and manage a business. If a person has these abilities, he or she can easily find a factory willing to cooperate in the long term.

Regardless, many research subjects agree that the major players in the counterfeiting trade are most likely to be those who produce their own goods. An entrepreneur who distributes goods from a contract factory is not likely to be a key player. This point was stressed by John (F3), an expatriate from Taiwan who managed a large factory for a major contract manufacturer in Houjie: "Big-time players in this business are most likely to be engaged in production and distribution and have strong investment capital. If they see something they think will sell, they gamble by producing a large quantity of the item all at once and trying to sell it. If it sells, they get crazy rich; if not, they lose money. Counterfeiting is like gambling; sometimes you win, and sometimes you lose."

Structure

My interview and fieldwork data suggest that most counterfeiting enterprises in Guangzhou have a loose structure. Many are operated by an individual or a husband and wife team. Some of them are family businesses owned by a family member and supported by other family members. If a business needs extra help, the owner will hire relatives or neighbors from his or her home village. There is little division of labor in these small businesses, as employers and employees work together in almost all aspects of the business.

A few counterfeiting businesses exist that have a certain level of organization and a division of labor. Like other well-established legitimate businesses, these counterfeiting enterprises are composed of several departments, including design, purchasing, production, sales, accounting, and storage. Owners of these large firms are called CEOs and are in charge of all facets of their businesses. In this section, I examine three positions in the counterfeiting business: saleswoman, designer (or artisan), and warehouse worker.

Saleswoman

Saleswomen play a vital role in the retail and wholesale distribution of counterfeit fashions and accessories in China. They are also the most visible participants in this business and the most likely point of contact with law enforcement authorities. I rarely saw any male salespeople during my visits to the many retail and wholesale markets. Men are hired mainly for packaging and delivery.

For many poorly educated young women from rural areas looking for a job in an urban center like Guangzhou, sales is one of the main opportunities for employment, besides manufacturing and adult entertainment (Chang 2009; M. Liu 2011; Ngai 2005; K. Zhang 2006; T. Zheng 2009).

Most saleswomen said they work seven days a week and receive one or two days off every month. According to a young woman selling counterfeit handbags in Baiyun: "I am from the Chaoshan area. I work seven days a week and get just a few days off a year. I work from eight to six every day and eat lunch in the store. We make a call, and lunch is delivered to us. I make about $580 a month. I speak a little bit of English, so if an English-speaking buyer walks in, I can communicate with him or her somewhat." Ah Ting (G22), a thirty-five-year-old apparel business owner, said his saleswoman made more than $1,150 a month: "I hired a young woman to look after my other store. I pay her more than $720 a month as a base salary. With sales commissions, she makes more than $1,150 a month."

Not only do these young women have to work long hours every day, seven days a week, for a limited salary but they also have to endure the risk of being arrested. As a result, they are supposed to know what to do when there is word that anti-counterfeiting government officials are coming. A saleswoman at Baiyun Leather City said: "You have to be very brave to do this; if government investigators are coming, you need to react quickly by closing the store and fleeing. If you do not, they will bring you to the police station and ask you questions. There is also the possibility that they might lock you up." Ah Bao (F12), a shoe leather supplier, marveled: "These girls know how to do business; they are not naive by any means."

In sum, many saleswomen I met in Guangzhou can be characterized as intelligent and capable young women who speak one or more foreign languages, even though they did not have much formal schooling. They learn English and other foreign languages, such as French, Portuguese, and Spanish, when negotiating prices with foreign buyers. They are also quick in responding to others. They know how to deal with difficult customers when they run into them.

I also had a chance to talk to Mrs. Lin (H12), a forty-nine-year-old saleswoman from Henan Province. She was working alone at a store inside Yisen Market, a leather goods mall across Baiyun Leather City. As can be seen from her story, it is highly probable that when a person is involved in counterfeiting, it is likely that many of his or her family members are also engaged in it. There is a good chance that these family members will all be working hard to transform themselves from workers to owners one day (see Figure 6.1 for a Hermès wallet from her store):

This store belongs to my younger sister; I am only helping her. She comes to the store occasionally. When I began working after quitting school, I worked for a couple of electrical appliance stores for more than ten years. After that, I opened my own clothing store, and after it failed, I started a retail handbag store. It also lasted for only two

Figure 6.1 A fake Hermès Kelly wallet.

years. At that point, my sister was looking for a saleswoman, so I told
her I could do that. I arrived in Guangzhou only six months ago. Of
course, I am doing this not only to help her but also to help me to open
my own store. I want to open a store in this building, and it will be
a handbag store for both retail and wholesale. All I need to do is to
buy handbags from my sister; this way, I will need only a little start-
up money. I need to learn many things about leather, metal fittings,
and so on. There is so much to learn in this business. When I was in
the retail handbag business on my own, I could survive without knowing much about the leather business, but now that I am into wholesale, I need to know everything about this business.

Designer (or Artisan)

Having a good designer in the apparel business, or a capable artisan in the
handbag trade, is critical for the success of a counterfeiting enterprise. In the
fashion business, most of the owners are themselves experienced and professional designers. Laoban, Lau Fang, and Jane are good examples. Xiao Meng
(G16), one of Laoban's designers, explained what she did as a designer in Laoban's business as it shifted from point-by-point counterfeiting to edge-ball
infringement (see Figure 6.2):

When I design, I pay attention to fashion designs by global brands.
Sometimes, I buy name-brand garments in Hong Kong and bring them
back to Guangzhou. Alternatively, I check fashion magazines for inspi-

Figure 6.2 Fake Gucci garments.

ration. I also look at what's posted on the official websites of those brands. After that, I design a collection of garments by imitating the styles of those brands. Some of the styles I design are not the same as those in the brands' collections. As a designer, I use computer software to select colors, to decide where to place logos, and what size the logos should be, and sometimes I intentionally misspell the name of the brand I am copying. I may add or delete a letter of the alphabet from the brand's name. This is what designers nowadays are doing. In the past, it was mostly point-by-point copying; that is, the copy was an exact replica of the original. Collar labels and hangtags were the same as the originals. When I began working, we were copying Armani, Versace, Dolce & Gabbana, and Gucci garments.

Lau Fang (G21) is the chief designer for her firm, and she and her husband, along with Ah Min (G5), her sister-in-law, are the three owners and partners of the business. Three other designers work for Lau Fang, and Ah Lan (G18) is one of them. Ah Lan, a sister of Xiao Meng (G16), said each designer specializes in particular sorts of garments: "In our company, I am mainly responsible for designing colorful garments, another designer takes care of drawing plain clothing, and another focuses on the construction of clothing made of black fabric with different symbols on it."

I did not have a chance to interview an artisan in the leather handbag counterfeiting business. However, some of the people I talked to suggested that these artisans are skillful and may even be better than the artisans working for international brands. Mr. Bo, an official with the Guangzhou city government, said: "When it comes to making counterfeit handbags, the most important person is the artisan. Everyone in this business is looking for a good artisan; if someone is offering an artisan a $3,000 to $4,000 monthly salary, a pay considered very good here in Guangzhou, another person is going to give the artisan $5,800 to $7,200, so that he can lure the artisan away."

Warehouse Worker

Most counterfeit business owners must keep one or more warehouses for storing their finished products. There are many reasons for this, but among the most important is avoiding the risk of being targeted by the authorities. Contract manufacturers who produce counterfeits demand that the goods must leave their factories promptly, and business owners who have their own manufacturing facilities are eager to move the finished goods to a warehouse to protect their factories from being targeted by the authorities. Branded counterfeit goods are the best evidence the authorities can collect to charge a person with counterfeiting.

I interviewed a former warehouse worker named Xiao Jen (H11). I came to know him because he was one of the lobby attendants at my hotel. He came to Guangzhou from Zhanjiang, but unlike Mimi, Ah San, and Ah Yun, Xiao Jen's original hometown is Leizhou, also in Guangdong Province. Xiao Jen came to Guangzhou in 2014 to work as a security guard at the same hotel where he is now working. After a year, he left and started a small business with a relative. When that business failed, he went back home to Leizhou for a short period. Xiao Jen explained why he returned to Guangzhou:

> Three years ago, in 2016, a friend who had a store at Baiyun Leather City introduced me to a couple who were looking for a warehouse boy. Like my friend, the couple owned a store at Baiyun Leather City. My friend lied to the couple and said that I was his relative; otherwise, the couple would not hire me. They were producing and distributing crocodile leather goods such as handbags and belts. They had all kinds of name-brand handbags, but I didn't know what those name brands were. The handbags all had English labels, but the only brand I recognized was LV.

Xiao Jen was outgoing and talkative, and he spoke Mandarin with a strong accent. Fortunately, I had no problem understanding him because I had been talking with him every day since I checked into that hotel. He recalled his responsibilities as a warehouse boy:

> I usually went to work at six in the evening and worked until eleven o'clock or midnight. Sometimes, I toiled until one or two in the morning. The busiest time was between eight and ten in the evening. I did not work during the daytime because there was nothing to do. We waited until it was dark to restock or deliver goods. My main task was to inspect the goods once they arrived at the warehouse. The boss and one of his relatives who worked for him picked up the goods at the factory. I never went to the factory and didn't know where it was. Every time the two of them went to pick up the goods, they came back with about eighty to ninety handbags. Occasionally, as many as two hundred.
>
> When the goods arrived, they were all nicely packed. I carefully removed the packing paper to check for any defects in the bags—any chips on the leather, or any problems with the opening and closing of the zipper. If a bag had any defects, I put it aside. For those bags with no problems, I polished the zippers to make them run more smoothly and repacked them as before. Most of the bags were in good shape; in each consignment, I found maybe one or two bags that needed to

be fixed. The most common problems were that the stitches were not straight or the zippers did not run smoothly. After the inspection, the warehouse girl would make a record of the inventory. When the bags arrived at the warehouse, they were each affixed with trademarks and any other accompanying materials, so that they looked just like the originals.

The other main task for me was transporting the goods from the warehouse to the store or to the customer's place. I relied on an electric motorbike for delivering a few bags, but I used a car if there were more. I put the handbags in a black plastic bag, and if the authorities stopped my motorbike on my way to the store or the customer's place, my boss told me to tell the authorities that I had just bought the bags from a street vendor, and I did not know where to find the vendor anymore. The boss stressed that if the authorities could not locate the warehouse, everything would be fine.

Xiao Jen revealed that the warehouse was an ordinary apartment unit in a residential area: "Our warehouse was in an apartment complex behind Baiyun Leather City. To enter the complex, one had to go through two security checkpoints. It was a three-bedroom apartment, and every bedroom was more than four hundred square feet. One room was used to store bags that could not be sold, including those with defects. The other two rooms were used to store the good bags that were currently selling. We categorized the bags by their brands."

As far as he knew, the firm he was working for had seven employees besides the couple who owned the business. There was a male relative of the couple whom they trusted, the daughter of the relative and her former classmate who worked as salespeople in the store, another two young men who worked as warehouse boys, and a young woman who worked as a warehouse girl and was responsible for keeping a record of the inventory. Except for Xiao Jen, all of them were Chaoshanese. He said he did not know where the owners lived, and they would not let him know much about them or their business.

Xiao Jen said the owners provided him and the other two warehouse boys free accommodations and meals: "We three warehouse boys lived in a place provided by the boss. It was a small place. The boss also offered us free meals. He gave each of us a card that was issued by a nearby restaurant. Whenever we went in, the card would be swiped once. It was like a monthly meal card. The restaurant was a self-serve place." To cultivate a good relationship with their workers, the owners occasionally took them out for dinner and gave them fake handbags and belts from the warehouse as gifts.

Xiao Jen was paid $700 a month without any bonus. He said he was not fearful because of what he was doing but left after working there for six months:

"I was not scared when I was working as a warehouse boy, and that's because I did not think it was illegal or could lead to my arrest. I quit after six months and returned to this hotel to work, this time as a lobby attendant. I went to work at Baiyun Leather City because I wanted to learn about the leather handbag business so that I could sell handbags on Taobao one day. When I found out that my boss would not teach me anything about his business, I left, thinking it did not make much sense for me to keep working for him."

The Structure of Two Apparel Firms

In this section, I provide a brief illustration of the structure of two apparel firms. One is the business of Lau Fang (G21), her husband, and her husband's sister, Ah Min (G5). The trio's business is divided into three spheres: a gong-si in a village of Baiyun District, a dangkou in Kinbo Market on Zhanxi Road, and a factory in Foshan, a prefecture-level city located twelve miles north of Guangzhou. Lau Fang is in charge of design at the gongsi, Ah Min is responsible for distribution at Kinbo, and Ah Min's brother (Lau Fang's husband) is devoted to production in Foshan. I visited the gongsi and the dangkou and was impressed because they both appeared to be well organized and well managed.

Another apparel firm is owned by Xiao Xiao and Xiao Guan (G13), a married couple. They had a relatively splendid gongsi in an urban village with a sizable showroom and nice-looking business offices. They had a reliable contract manufacturer to produce their goods, a dangkou they operated themselves at Kinbo Market, a contract dangkou at Jinxiang (or Jinshan) Market, and a warehouse near the company. The contract dangkou belonged to a former colleague of Xiao Xiao's and mainly distributed the couple's goods. The couple hired a cousin and her husband to care for the warehouse.

A Case Study of a Network

Individual counterfeiters in Guangzhou all belong to one or more networks. Take Laoban (G2), for example. He arrived in Guangzhou from Taiwan and started an apparel firm. After Laoban sold his business and returned to Taiwan, his employees continued counterfeiting as business owners or workers. Xiao Peng (G8), a sales manager for Laoban, bought Laoban's business and became the owner. Before Laoban's exit from the counterfeiting trade, Lau Fang (G21), a designer for Laoban, opened a business with her husband and sister-in-law, Ah Min (G5). Likewise, Zheng Hua (G19) and Xiao Cai, sample room workers for Laoban, started their own apparel firm. Lin Jun (G17), a truck driver for Laoban, left to join his father, a clothing factory owner. Like Laoban, Lau Fang, Zheng Hua, and Lin Jun all continued to specialize in producing and distributing men's T-shirts and polo shirts. Lin Jun's sister, another one of Laoban's employees, married Zheng Hua and became a store operator. Fan Bing, a young and talented designer for Laoban, also started his own clothing business. Xiao Wen (G6) and Ah Mei, also employees of Laoban, remained in the fashion business, catering to overseas buyers, especially Russians.

Former Laoban employees Xiao Meng (G16), Ah Lan (G18), and Ah Dong, three siblings who were cousins of Xiao Wen, started their own printing business, but it did not last long, and they returned to work for other apparel business owners as designers. Lao Su (G24), who worked for the new owner of Laoban's business, Xiao Peng, for a short period, left and became the manager of a clothing factory. Ah Xia became a life insurance agent after she stopped working for Laoban. She jokingly said that she was the biggest loser among all the former employees of Laoban. Ah Long, a utility man for Laoban, started his own business after leaving Laoban. When the business failed, he became a truck driver. Other former employees of Laoban include Bingbing and Ah Quan, who are running a packaging business for counterfeit cosmetics. Ah Yun (F13) became the owner of a small business that provides dust bags to counterfeit shoe producers. Mimi (F7) is operating a workshop that manufactures fake Chanel sandals. Ah Jun owns a store in Jinxiang Market, selling mainly men's T-shirts and polo shirts produced by Xiao Xiao and Xiao Guan. Xiao Xiao was one of Laoban's best employees, smart and hard working. She and her husband, Xiao Guan, are owners of a thriving men's casual wear business.

Among Laoban's former employees, only Ah Xia and Ah Long were no longer engaged in counterfeiting. Ah Yun and Mimi left the garment industry but switched to counterfeiting footwear. People in this group are also close to Zhang Yan and his wife, Zhao Zong (G14, Ah Min's former husband); Xiao Xin (G15) and her husband Lao Zhu, who own a garment factory; Boss Cao and his wife, who also own a clothing factory; Ah Mi and her husband, who own a store in Baiyun Leather City selling counterfeit children's clothes; and Lao Lin (Lin Jun's father and a garment factory owner who had a business relationship with Laoban for many years). This is a partial list of the people in this network. It includes only the people who I had the opportunity to meet when I was with Laoban in Guangzhou.

Cooperation, Competition, and Violence

According to my research participants, cooperation among businesspeople in the counterfeiting industry is the norm, but it is engaged in only on an ad hoc basis. Continued cooperation happens only if a previous collaboration has succeeded, meaning all parties involved made money. According to Laoban (G2):

> The counterfeiting industry is very fluid; apparel designers and business owners like me look for manufacturers and [regional] distributors [outside of Guangzhou] they can work with. If a business venture flourishes, trust among the three parties will be established, and the partnership will continue; if it is a failure, the partnership will be terminated, and a new partnership will be formed with other parties. That is why the alliance among all parties involved is fragile, depending on what kind of sales volume the partnership can achieve.

Businesspeople are after money, and if there is an opportunity to make a good profit, they are willing to cooperate so that everyone involved will be financially rewarded. The entrepreneurs I encountered were constantly in touch with one another, either through WeChat or in person over lunch or dinner. Those who are close meet at the business premises of one of their associates and talk for hours while sipping tea. In the process, they share information about moneymaking opportunities, including activities unrelated to their counterfeiting businesses. Some are involved in the wine trade, as wine drinking has become popular among "cultured" consumers in China (A. Shen 2018). When they meet, they also ask for specific goods or materials their customers need. When I was visiting Ah Bao (F12) in his shoe leather supply shop, Mr. Chan—one of his friends, a shoe leather supplier from the same area as Ah Bao—was checking a calf leather roll from Bangladesh that Ah Bao had sold him. One roll contains forty-eight hides, each about fifteen square feet. This means a roll has a total of seven hundred square feet of leather. Mr. Chan had a buyer in Hebei Province, a shoemaker. When Mr. Chan realized he did not have the leather, he turned to Ah Bao because he knew Ah Bao had good connections with calf leather suppliers in Bangladesh. That morning, his friend came by to pick up the leather and delivered it to his buyer in Hebei. Ah Bao told me there would be more leather rolls to follow if the shoemaker in Hebei is satisfied with the quality of the leather. In the process, Ah Bao, Mr. Chan, Mr. Chan's buyer, and the buyer's clients, either shoe distributors or consumers, all benefited from this ad hoc cooperation.

One type of cooperation among counterfeiters is zhuanbao (subcontracting). When counterfeiters cannot fulfill a large order, they look for help from others in their network. According to John (F3): "Zhuanbao is very normal in this business. If a manufacturer receives a huge order, he or she will not enlarge his or her factory's production capacity to fulfill the order. What if there will not be any such large orders in the future? That is why there is no choice but to outsource."

Sonny (H10), another handbag business owner, discussed how his peers in the same industry could work together to maximize their access to a wide variety of goods they could market. He talked about the possibility of cooperation among different counterfeiters who specialize in different brands: "Sometimes, five businesspeople will work together, and everyone involved will be responsible for the production of a particular brand, like I do Louis Vuitton, you do Gucci, and him, Chanel. The five of us will find a factory and ask the factory to produce only our goods for a certain period. Under this type of alliance among the five of us, if I want to sell your products, you will accommodate me and allow me to make some money as a middleman. This way, the five participants do not have to worry that they will not be able to sell the products of brands they do not produce."

There is a certain level of cooperation among counterfeiters in conducting their businesses. However, in general, they are unwilling to get too close to their counterparts, especially if they are in direct competition because they are all involved in the imitation of the same type of goods, or worse, the same brand. Xiao Qin (H16), a leather goods counterfeiter, said he interacted only with leather and materials suppliers because they were not his competitors: "People in this business rarely socialize with one another, especially businesspeople who are involved in copying the products of a particular brand. Even if they are not duplicating the same brand, as long as they are all engaged in the counterfeiting of leather handbags, they are unlikely to be associated. However, it is possible that leather handbag distributors like me will wine and dine suppliers of leather and other materials."

Violence is associated with a wide range of illegal businesses, especially drug trafficking, even though frequency and visibility may differ depending on the cohesion of the state security apparatus (if the state is cohesive, the less visible) and the amount of competition in illegal drug markets (if the market is monopolistic, the less frequent) (Duran-Martinez 2018). Because counterfeiting is a crime in China, and competition is high among those who participate in it, one would assume that counterfeiters would not be hesitant to use violence when there are conflicts. However, according to the counterfeiters I interviewed, violence is rare in their business world. One of the most often mentioned reasons for conflict was debt. The most likely scenario was a buyer not paying a seller after receiving goods. According to Xiao Yuen (G12), this was common, and one had to take it in stride: "There is no physical assault among the competitors in this business, let alone murder. In the business world, owing money is normal, and if someone cannot or will not pay, how can you force him to? If he cannot come up with the money, that means he does not have the money, and his business is going downhill. If his business is doing well, he will pay."

Wendy (G4), a young woman who was involved in the counterfeiting of Japanese fashions, also said it was common in her business that buyers reneged on their payments, but this would not lead to violence: "When I was in the counterfeiting business, the most likely source of conflict was that my buyers would disappear with my goods. There were many of these types of buyers, including one from Taiwan. However, it was not a big deal. I lost thousands of dollars, but treated it as a business loss."

Mrs. Lin (H12), a saleswoman, recalled how her sister, a leather goods entrepreneur in Guangzhou, used an "extreme" measure to force a client in Beijing to pay a large debt; even in this incident, violence was not involved:

> Many people owed money to my sister. They were her clients who did not pay after purchasing goods from her. Once, a client in Beijing owed $75,000, and his refusal to pay dragged on for a long time. My sister and I even flew to Beijing and urged him to pay. He promised to wire the money once we returned to Guangzhou, but he did not. Later, my sister went to Beijing again, and he used the same tactic to try to get rid of her. When he was not watching, my sister took his car key, which was on his desk, and left. She drove his BMW to the Beijing airport, parked it there, and flew back to Guangzhou. That guy panicked. My sister told him that his car would be promptly returned once he paid up. Finally, he wired the money. My sister sent the car key to him by express delivery and told him where to find his car.

Law enforcement authorities I interviewed also confirmed that violence is not one of their concerns when they are going after counterfeiting suspects. The economic crime officer Tang said that when he and his colleagues are looking for counterfeit goods in a warehouse, they do not expect any resistance from the people in the warehouse: "When we go to check warehouses, we never encounter any resistance, not to mention any physical assault on us. That is because resisting arrest is a more serious crime than counterfeiting."

In a study on loan-sharking in New York City, the criminologist Peter Reuter (1983, xi) notes: "I observed that much illegal commerce occurs without violence or intimidation. Even loansharking, in which instrumental violence is putatively such a central factor, was curiously peaceful." In my study on the smuggling of Chinese nationals to the United States (K. Chin 1999), the production and trafficking of heroin and methamphetamine in Southeast Asia (K. Chin 2009; K. Chin and Zhang 2015), and the transnational sex trade involving women from China (K. Chin 2014; K. Chin and

Finckenauer 2012), my colleagues and I also find violence was rarely used by the actors in these businesses.

In his study on the drug trade in America, R. V. Gundur (2022, 166, 242) suggested that drug dealers often used a strategy called "smokescreening," for self-protection and to avoid having to use actual violence:

> This strategy creates a smoke screen, an opaque barrier of *paisa* sub-contractors, that both obfuscates the identities of the actors and logistics further up the supply chain and conjures up an illusion that "the cartel" is present and ready to act. This smoke screen, which mid- to high-level drug entrepreneurs deliberately and carefully deploy, causes others—subordinates, retail customers, and even law enforcement—to misidentify the higher-ups. . . . Through smoke screening, criminal actors protect their organizations, activities, and customer base from police and competition with implicit but largely illusive threats of violence, rather than with explicit displays of force. Smoke screening becomes more effective when coupled with the blind compartmentalization that midlevel actors employ to ensure that their customers, if caught by the police, cannot identify them.

Luxury goods counterfeiters in Guangzhou did try to use smokescreening to hide their identities from law enforcement, even though it is not clear how effective it is. However, this strategy is not adopted by counterfeiters as a means of preventing the use of actual violence, since the reputation for violence is a nonfactor in their business.

Counterfeiting and Organized Crime

After examining counterfeiters' individual and group characteristics, I now explore the relationship between counterfeiting and organized crime. I focus on two questions associated with this issue: (1) Are traditional, or well-established, organized crime groups such as the Italian Mafia (Dickie 2004; Lupo 2011; Paoli 2003), Japanese yakuza (Hill 2006), and Chinese triads (Chu 2000; Lo 2010) engaged in the production, distribution, and transportation of counterfeit goods?[2] (2) If these powerful crime groups are not directly involved in counterfeiting, are they victimizing or protecting people who are involved; in other words, do organized crime groups function as quasi-governmental entities in the illegal market for counterfeit goods (von Lampe 2016)?

Over the past several decades, many books, articles, and reports have been written about the role of organized crime in activities such as extortion, protection, gambling, prostitution, loan-sharking, debt collection, and other crimes that are local and territory based (K. Chin 1996; Paoli 2014; Reuter 1983). The use of actual violence or the threat of violence has also been examined in the literature on organized crime (Duran-Martinez 2018; Gambetta 1996; Gundur 2022). The focus is on how mobsters were mainly involved in local crime, not cross-border crime. This changed with the end of the Cold War, in the 1990s, and the subsequent rapid advancement of globalization (Woodiwiss and Bewley-Taylor 2005). As people, goods, and information moved freely across national borders, transnational criminal activities, such as human smuggling, human trafficking, drug trafficking, money laundering, and counterfeiting, became more widespread and easier to carry out (Naim 2005). The rapid development of e-commerce in the twenty-first century no doubt enabled many more people to engage in transnational (and local) illegal activities without being exposed to law enforcement authorities (Smith, Zhang, and Barberet 2011).

Because of the dramatic increase in cross-border crime, some criminologists have argued that there was an emergence of nontraditional crime groups that specialize in transnational criminal activities such as human smuggling and drug trafficking. These newly formed groups differ from traditional organized crime groups such as the Mafia, yakuza, and triads in that they do not have a group name, turf, structure, membership, or longevity, or a reputation for violence. Sheldon Zhang and I (2003) proposed that "structural deficiency" was one of the main reasons that traditional organized crime groups were not able to expand their criminal activities from the local to the international sphere. From our point of view, the shift from local to transnational criminality, or the transplantation of organized crime from a home country to overseas was easier said than done, at least for Chinese triads. The criminologist Federico Varese (2011) has found that the success or failure of the transplantation of the Italian or Russian Mafia abroad depends on various factors. He found that, of the crime groups in Italy and Russia that tried to move their operations overseas, some succeeded, and some failed.

Another group of criminologists suggests that there is no need to differentiate between traditional and nontraditional crime groups, between local and transnational crime, nor among the many forms of cross-border criminal activities (Naim 2005). According to Jay Albanese (2012, 1, 3):

> Over the last twenty years, traditional depictions of organized crime as an ethnic, neighborhood phenomenon have given way to discovery of emerging transnational criminal enterprises involving trafficking, fraud, and corruption in an international scale. The available evidence suggests that these are not two distinct types of criminal conduct. Instead they are overlapping in nature in terms of the crimes committed, the offenders involved, and in how criminal opportunities are exploited for profit. . . . Therefore, transnational

crime is a form of organized crime given its multinational aims and the extent of organization required for success. Transnational organized crime (TOC) can be considered the modern extension of organized crime in the globalized era.

Are organized crime groups such as the Italian Mafia, the Japanese yakuza, and the Chinese triads involved in counterfeiting? Some believe they are and some suggest they are not. The media, government agencies, and law enforcement are more likely to assume that there is a connection between organized crime and counterfeiting. For example, in a 1981 *New York Times Magazine* article on the counterfeiting of fashion goods, Susan Heller Anderson claimed that there was some evidence to suggest the counterfeiting business had attracted organized crime, even though she did not provide any evidence. In Europe, a former secretary-general of the Italian anti-counterfeiting agency suggested that "organized crime is getting involved in all areas of counterfeiting because it is such a lucrative activity with much lower risk than other areas, such as drugs" (Galbraith 2006). Interpol (the International Criminal Police Organization) has suggested that "the high returns that are inherent in the counterfeit goods trade have attracted organized crime groups such as the Chinese triad[s] and terrorist groups such as Hezbollah to the business" (Galloni 2006, B1). The IACC has also claimed that there was strong evidence to suggest that organized crime and terrorist groups were increasingly relying on counterfeiting to generate funds (Wall and Large 2010).

The UNODC, a global leader in the fight against illicit drugs, international crime, and terrorism, has claimed that major organized crime groups around the world are active in counterfeiting: "The involvement of organized criminal groups in the production and distribution of counterfeit goods has been documented by both national and international authorities. Groups such as the Mafia and Camorra in Europe and the Americas, and the Triads and Yakuza in Asia have diversified into the illicit trafficking of counterfeit goods, while at the same time being involved in crimes varying from drug and human trafficking, to extortion and money laundering" (UNODC 2014, 1).

The U.S. DHS suggested in a 2020 report that the Italian Mafia and the Japanese yakuza, two of the three most prominent organized crime groups in the world, were engaged in counterfeiting. Citing a study by the Better Business Bureau, the DHS (2020, 19) claimed: "Law enforcement officials have uncovered intricate links between the sale of counterfeit goods and transnational organized crime. A study by the Better Business Bureau notes that the financial operations supporting counterfeit goods typically require central coordination, making these activities attractive for organized crime, with groups such as the Mafia and the Japanese Yakuza heavily involved. Criminal organizations use coerced and child labor to manufacture and sell counterfeit goods. In some cases, the proceeds from counterfeit sales may be supporting terrorism and dictatorships throughout the world."

According to Anqi Shen (2018, 17), research has also suggested links between IP theft and organized crime. Danny Chow (2003, 474–475), a legal scholar who has written extensively on counterfeiting in China, has claimed that criminal organizations in Hong Kong and Taiwan were the financiers of the counterfeit industry in Guangdong and Fujian provinces: "Criminal organizations based in Hong Kong and Taiwan who have maintained connections with their ancestral homelands often provide the financing for the underground factories that manufacture illegal counterfeits in Guangdong and Fujian provinces. Anecdotal evidence indicates that these are the same criminal organizations that are involved in smuggling products into China, narcotics, prostitution, and pornography." In another article, Chow (2011, 807–808) suggests that the counterfeiting of cigarettes and the worldwide distribution of counterfeit cigarettes could only be carried out by a well-organized and violent crime group similar to a drug cartel: "Only a highly efficient criminal organization has the resources to conduct this kind of trade (cigarette counterfeiting and trafficking), and reports indicate that these criminal organizations are as violent and ruthless as any of the organizations involved in drug trafficking." Moreover, Chow asserts that luxury goods counterfeiting requires the same type of organized operations as cigarette counterfeiting and that cigarette counterfeiters are also involved in counterfeiting consumer goods such as clothing, shoes, handbags, auto parts, and electronics.

Like Danny Chow, Jana Chong (2008, 1158), an IP lawyer in California, in an article published in *Fordham Law Review*, claims that there is an overlapping of counterfeiting with a variety of other transnational crimes, including human trafficking and terrorism: "Counterfeiting of luxury goods continues to be linked to numerous illicit activities, including prostitution, drug trafficking, money laundering, and terrorism. The manufacture of counterfeits in China also relates to human trafficking—since reports indicate that many of the workers making the goods are children who were sold into slavery."

David Wall and Joanna Large (2010, 1110), two British criminology professors, are more nuanced in their analysis of the connection between organized crime and counterfeiting. They argue that organized crime's involvement in the counterfeiting business is limited to retail only: "The counterfeit fashion goods industry has different contributory components and it is unlikely that the commissioning, manufacture, transportation and sale functions will be carried out by the same people. . . . The strongest relationships between organized crime and counterfeiting fashion goods tended to exist at a local level and mainly revolved around retail rather [than] their commission or manufacture." Likewise, Cocks (2006, 510) has argued that organized crime groups are only engaged in the trafficking of counterfeits into the United States and their distribution: "No doubt owing to China's dominance in the manufacturing of counterfeit wares, Chinese organized crime groups, known colloquially as triads or tongs, are responsible for the importation of a considerable portion of the counterfeit trademarked goods that enter the United States, and for the distribution of such merchandise once it reaches American shores."

Anqi Shen, a law professor in the United Kingdom, studied wine counterfeiting in China based on published materials and open sources. As far as organized crime involvement in wine counterfeiting is concerned, Shen (2018, 26–27) concluded: "No evidence suggests the involvement of organized crime rings in the wine counterfeiting trade, and the illicit economic sector in China appears to be made up of individuals and small and medium enterprises."

Like Shen, the British criminologist Georgios Antonopoulos and his colleagues (2018, 27) claim that "criminal entrepreneurs involved in counterfeit markets in the UK are by no means a homogeneous group and many do not meet the archetypal 'criminal entrepreneur' stereotype." They conclude that "the findings from this research do not seem to support the image of the counterfeiting business as a threatening manifestation of 'organized crime'" (69).

From the earlier discussion, it is clear that the media, the authorities, and academics have different understandings of the relationship between counterfeiting and organized crime. Before I present my interview data on the issue, I would like to clarify the term "Chinese organized crime" as it applies to China, Hong Kong, Taiwan, and the United States. Many observers lump groups from these different areas together and label them the "Chinese Mafia" (Bresler 1981; Posner 1988), even though there are many different types of groups, and they have very different traditions, sizes, structures, subcultures, and levels of criminality (K. Chin 2014).

Organized Crime in China

According to Chinese authorities, the most potent and best-organized criminal organizations in China have not yet reached the status of underworld organizations like the Italian Mafia, the Japanese yakuza, or the Hong Kong triads (Xia 2006). Thus, Chinese authorities describe the most advanced criminal organizations in China as "organizations with underworld characteristics" or Mafia-like gangs to differentiate them from other loosely knit and less influential criminal organizations such as criminal gangs (which have some form of structure) and crime groups (which have no structure) (K. Chin and Godson 2006). The Standing Committee of the National People's Congress of China, in 2002, stated that an "organization with underworld characteristics" can be identified by the following characteristics: (1) the formation of a relatively stable organization, with a large number of gang members, clearly identified organizers and leaders, and a reliable core group; (2) the pursuit of economic gains through organized crime or other illegal means, with sufficient economic strength to support its activities; (3) the repeated commission of organized crimes through violence, threat, or other means, such as riding roughshod over people's rights or cruelly injuring or killing them; and (4) the committing of illegal or criminal activities, or the harboring of (or protection by) government officials, so that it dominates people in a given area, or has illegal control or imposes a major influence in a certain region or trade, which seriously disrupts both the economic order and people's daily activities (K. Chin and Godson 2006). It is estimated that at the turn of the twenty-first century, there were more than four thousand Mafia-like gangs, with more than a million members (Xia 2006).

Mafia-like gangs in China are relatively small; most of them have twenty-five to one hundred members. They are led by a leader who relies on several core members to carry out his orders. As mentioned earlier, to be considered a Mafia-like gang, the gang has to be sheltered or protected by one or more government officials; it is common for many of these gangs to have police officers as their "protective umbrella" or for police officers to be core members who act as enforcers for their gangs (K. Chin and Godson 2006). High-level political leaders from the executive branch or the party apparatus rarely act as a protective umbrella for underworld figures.

Mafia-like gangs in China are mainly involved in robbery, extortion, gambling, prostitution, and loan-sharking. These gangs at times engage in assault, kidnapping, and murder to achieve their goals. They are also active in the distribution of the so-called newly emerging drugs (i.e., ketamine powder, ecstasy, amphetamines) but not heroin, because they do not want to antagonize the authorities who are protecting them (K. Chin and Godson 2006; K. Chin and Zhang 2015). Like organized crime groups elsewhere, Mafia-style gangs in China are becoming more active in legitimate business sectors (P. Wang 2017).

The Role of Mafia-like Gangs in Counterfeiting

From the discussions in Chapter 5 on the individual characteristics of counterfeiters and in this chapter on the group characteristics of the counterfeiting business, it seems that there is no evidence to suggest that the design, production, and distribution of fake luxury fashion goods are associated with Mafia-like gangs in China. First of all, none of my research subjects was a member of a Mafia-like gang. None of them had ever been arrested for offenses other than counterfeiting, except for Zhao Zong (G14), the clothing merchant from Zhejiang, who was arrested and detained for three months in Yunnan Province for visiting neighboring Myanmar without legal travel documents, and Xiao Ma (H4) who was imprisoned for three years for tax evasion.

Sun Lu (F15) said her ex-husband was a "big brother" (gang leader) who had a few violent young men as followers. Sun Lu and her ex-husband were engaged in the fake shoe business. Regardless, she said that she was in charge of their business and her ex-husband was more interested in having fun with other women and hanging out with his "little brothers." She did not elaborate on how her ex-husband's gang background had anything to do with how they operated their business. Mr. Song, an anti-counterfeiting private investigator, said that he probed into a counterfeiting case that might have been related to criminal groups in Russia and Italy, but he was not sure: "One of our cases involved a bunch of Northeasterners placing orders all over China, especially in Fujian Province, for fake name-brand shoes, including Adidas and Nike. Our investigation found that these Northeasterners worked for a group of Russians. All the shoes they bought were exported overseas. We heard that the Italian Black Hand Society (Mafia) was behind that group of Russians, but we did not know the reality."

Except for Sun Lu and Mr. Song, none of my research subjects mentioned anything about Mafia-like gang involvement in the counterfeiting industry. Even Sun Lu's ex-husband could be just a leader of an ordinary small gang and not a Mafia-like gang as defined by the Chinese authorities. When asked why Mafia-like gangs were not interested in their trade, Xiao Peng (G8), a clothing business owner, came up with three reasons: low profit margins, the large number of participants in the apparel industry, and the Chinese authorities' ability to control organized crime:

> Organized crime groups do not engage in this business because they look down on the apparel market. They are interested in businesses like construction, waste disposal, and other activities, not a low-profit-margin business like ours. They also do not extort money from people in the garment industry. Don't forget, there are so many people in the clothing industry that the population is too large for them to threaten into submission. Besides, the Chinese government will not allow organized crime groups to become too powerful. The authorities often go after these crime groups and treat them harshly.

Lin Jun (G17), the owner of a garment factory, said gangsters are not attracted to the garment business: "Organized crime groups are not going to enter this line of business because it is hard work. They like to be involved in commercial sex, gambling, and drugs. Also, they are not going to come and extort us." Like Lin Jun, Laoban (G2) thought that organized crime groups are mainly interested in making easy money from providing illegal goods and services that they are familiar with: sex, gambling, and drugs. Counterfeiting is hard work, so gangsters do not want to be bothered with it. According to Laoban, counterfeiters and gangsters belong to two different worlds.

Xiao Yuen (G12), a garment business operator, reiterated what Lin Jun and Laoban said about the lack of Mafia-like gangs' engagement in the clothing industry in general and apparel counterfeiting in particular. He also stressed how unlikely it is for gangsters to victimize those in this business: "This industry is not subjected to extortion by gangs. You have to understand that the people who run the wholesale markets have powerful backgrounds and are not people to mess with. Also, gangsters are not going to enter this business. This business is not appealing to them because it requires hard work."

If Mafia-like gangs are not directly involved in the operation of counterfeiting businesses or in exploiting people who are engaged in counterfeiting, what about counterfeiters approaching organized crime groups for help when business debts or disputes are to be settled. Mr. Jin (F14), a shoe business owner from Jiangxu, who at one point was dealing with a staggering amount of bad debts, told me why he did not think it was a good idea to ask for help from Mafia-like gangs: "Later, my business began to decline because I was having a hard time collecting from businesspeople who owed me money. When they flee, there is no way you can get your money back, even if you ask for help from the police. We would not ask a debt-collection company for help, because many of these companies are run by violent gangsters. Besides, their fees are high—normally, half the money they collect. The bottom line is we do not want to be associated with these people."

My research subjects said there is little connection between organized crime groups and counterfeiting. They also argued that calling counterfeiting a form of *transnational* organized crime is a misnomer because counterfeiters in China are not responsible for the movement of counterfeit goods from China to the international market. Xiao Ma (H4), a leather supplier, asked: "How can this be a form of transnational organized crime? There are overseas markets because foreign buyers come to China to buy fake stuff, and after that, transport the stuff to their countries themselves, and work as wholesalers or retailers."

Officer Tang, with the Economic Crime Unit, also suggested that counterfeiters are not Mafia-like gang members, and their enterprises should not be labeled as organized crime groups. He claimed that counterfeiters are unlikely to engage in other illegal activities aside from counterfeiting:

How can this business be considered transnational organized crime? This business is not controlled by one or a few large groups. It is composed of many small businesses operated by ordinary people. They are not making crazy money, only enough for themselves to survive. Since there is no crazy money to be made, there is no need to use violence. Using violence would not be worthwhile. People will not commit a more serious crime (violence) to cover a less severe crime (counterfeiting).

My research subjects were baffled when I asked them about the connection between counterfeiting and organized crime. Mr. Zhou's (H17) wife, who was active in producing and distributing fake leather handbags along with her husband and a couple of family members, was perturbed when I asked her whether there was any resemblance between her business and organized crime. "What is organized crime? Our handbag business is operated by my husband and me, my younger sister, and the husband of one of my cousins. Can you say this is organized crime? Of course, we also have factory workers and salesgirls, but I do not see us as an organized crime group."

In addition to Mafia-like gangs in China, we must also examine the role of Hong Kong–based triads and large organized Taiwan-based gangs as well as its small jiaotou (street corner) groups in counterfeiting.[3] According to Yiu-kong Chu, a criminologist, Hong Kong triads are not dominant in counterfeiting (Chu 2011). In my study on the nexus between organized crime, business, and politics in Taiwan, I did not find that members of organized gangs and jiaotou groups were engaged in counterfeiting (K. Chin 2003).

In the United States, ethnic Chinese have been arrested and charged with the trafficking and distribution of counterfeit goods. In the Patrick Siu case, Mr. Siu of Richardson, Texas, along with thirteen other male and female defendants from Texas and New York, was charged with importing $300 million worth of counterfeit goods into the United States. In the Nin Guo case, Nin Guo and eleven defendants from New York and New Jersey were found guilty of (or were arrested for) smuggling $47 million of knockoff Nike sneakers and designer handbags into the United States. In the case of Le Fu Chan and his wife, Hai Fan Huang, the authorities seized one hundred thirty thousand items of counterfeit merchandise, bearing such brand names as Coach, Michael Kors, and Ray-Ban, from an office in Manhattan, and six storage facilities in Port Washington, New York. Su Ming Ling, a fifty-year-old naturalized U.S. citizen who came from Taiwan and resided in Queens, New York, was charged with the importation of $250 million worth of counterfeit Nike shoes, UGG boots, and True Religion jeans in two hundred forty-foot-long shipping containers. In another case, Miyuki Suen and four other de-

184 / CHAPTER 6

fendants were arrested and charged with importing fake Air Jordan sneakers worth $73 million. Finally, Hai Long Zhou, fifty-three, and three other defendants who lived in Queens and Brooklyn, New York, were charged with smuggling into the United States $130 million worth of fake Nike and Yeezy sneakers, UGG shoes and boots, Timberland boots, and Beats and Apple headphones. None of the defendants mentioned earlier were accused of associating with Chinatown tongs and street gangs in the United States.[4] The selling of counterfeits in New York City's Chinatown along Canal Street and Mott Street is not affiliated with any Chinatown gangs. Of all the gang members active in New York City's Chinatown over the past forty years, only one is known to have been involved in the counterfeiting business. David Thai, a Chinese Vietnamese who was the leader of the Born-to-Kill (BTK) gang, sold counterfeit watches on Canal Street before he became a gang leader (English 1995).

In sum, as noted by the researchers cited earlier, there is no evidence to suggest that the counterfeiting industry is dominated by organized crime groups such as tongs in the United States, Mafia-like gangs in China, or triads in Hong Kong. In my other studies on transnational crime involving ethnic Chinese, I also observed that illegal cross-border activities such as human smuggling (K. Chin 1999; S. Zhang and Chin 2002), sex trafficking (K. Chin and Finckenauer 2012), and drug trafficking (K. Chin and Zhang 2015) were not associated with Chinese organized crime groups.

In his work on the definition of organized crime, my colleague and co-author James O. Finckenauer (2005, 76) suggests that "we should also recognize a distinction, for purposes of clearly defining what is organized crime, between certain crimes that may be extremely complex and highly organized in their commission—but which are not committed by criminal organizations, as we have defined them earlier—and true organized crime. I do not regard such crimes 'that are organized' as being the same thing as organized crime." From his point of view, crimes such as human smuggling, drug trafficking, human trafficking, arms trafficking, and money laundering are certainly "organized," and groups or networks of people are involved in them. But this does not mean these groups or networks are the same as traditional and well-established criminal organizations such as the Italian Mafia, Chinese triads, Japanese yakuza, and the Russian Mafia. The designing, manufacturing, and marketing of counterfeit goods obviously require a level of organization. But what my data suggests is that counterfeiting is more akin to being a crime that is organized than being organized crime. Finckenauer has argued that the distinction between "organized crime" and "crime that is organized" is important because it determines the most effective ways to combat these two different types of groups. In fact, after a careful examination of the development, production, and distribution of counterfeit goods and the individual and group characteristics of the people involved in these activities, it might be more appropriate to say that counterfeiting is a "business that is organized."

Jianghu *versus* Pianmen: *Two Different Subcultures*

In the book *Chinese Subculture and Criminality* (K. Chin 1990), I proposed that one way to understand the nature and relationship of Chinese organized crime groups worldwide is to view these groups as part of a subculture called jianghu (literally, "rivers and lakes." It denotes members' rootlessness). The various groups include the legendary Hung and Qing secret societies,[5] the Hong Kong triads, the Taiwan-based organized gangs and jiaotou groups, the U.S.-based tongs and street gangs, the China-based mafia-like gangs, and other Chinese crime groups in Southeast Asia and Western Europe. Although these organizations are not structurally connected and rarely work together to commit a crime, "These groups share the same norms and values, worship the same god (General Guan as depicted in the novel *The Three Kingdoms*),[6] memorize the same Triad poems and slang, and adopt the same initiating ceremony, using similar Triad paraphernalia. Members of all these organizations view one another as 'brothers' of the same 'Triad Family'" (K. Chin 1990, 143).

In that book, I maintained that "once a person is initiated into the world of jianghu, he has to internalize, cherish, and observe Triad norms. In the romantic world of jianghu, members view themselves as patriotic, heroic, righteous, and loyal. Chinese conventional norms and values such as filial piety, attachment to family and village, and nonradical philosophy are replaced by loyalty to the organization and its members, rootlessness, and radicalism. Within this world, a powerless and detached person can become connected to a legendary and honorable society" (K. Chin 1990, 144–145).

As to what jianghu people do for a living, I claimed that they "are involved in the exploitation and intimidation of the rich and powerful, and in the provision of illegal services. Besides, they have always monopolized extortion and protection rackets, gambling, and prostitution. Members of the subculture believe they are simply making a living in an alternative way—a way that is justifiable because it redistributes wealth in an imperfect society" (K. Chin 1990, 143).

On the other hand, there is a different subculture called pianmen (literally, side door). People in this subculture are primarily involved in pianmen shengyi, a generic term for all kinds of businesses that are either semilegal or outright illegal, including human smuggling, prostitution, money laundering, counterfeiting, drug distribution, etc. Their moneymaking activities are called lao painmen (scoop up side door) or *zuo painmen* (do side door).

More than anything else, they consider themselves businesspeople, not hardcore criminals or gangsters like the jianghu people.

People who make money through illicit enterprises have no prior criminal records, no identifiable organizations, no rigid structure, no norms, and no values. They can conceal their illegal activities through their involvement in lawful business activities. Their engagement in criminal activities is opportunistic and sporadic rather than continuous.

Table 6.1 provides a comparison between the characteristics of jianghu and pianmen subcultures. It indicates that most crime groups in the jianghu

TABLE 6.1. JIANGHU VS. PIANMEN: ORGANIZED CRIME VS. ILLICIT ENTERPRISE

	Jianghu Subculture	Pianmen Subculture
Key groups or networks	Hong Kong triads (14K, Sun Yee On), Taiwan-organized gang and jiaotou groups (United Bamboo, Four Seas), China mafia-like gangs (Liu Yong, Chan Kai), U.S. tongs (On Leong, Hip Sing), and street gangs (Ghosh Shadows, Flying Dragons)	*Snakehead, druglord, chickenhead, zutou, copycat, etc.
Leadership Structure	Hierarchical (associational and illegal governance)	Nonhierarchical (entrepreneurial)
Activity	Extortion (protection), mediation, gambling, prostitution, drug distribution, and a variety of legitimate businesses.	Different networks specialize in one type of activity, such as human smuggling, drug production and trafficking, prostitution, gambling, and counterfeiting. Most of them are also involved in legitimate businesses.
Name	Yes	No
Turf	Yes	No
Visibility	High	Low
Violence	Yes	No
Focal concern	Brotherhood and justice	Money
Strategies used against the state	Corruption and confrontation	Evasion
Rules and regulations	Yes	No
Monopoly	Yes, if possible	No
Social embeddedness	High	High
Justice-involved persons	Many	Few

*Snakehead, "human smuggler"; chickenhead, "pimp"; zutou, "bookie."

subculture have names, turfs, hierarchies, leadership structures, member-ships, norms, and values. They tend to maintain a high-profile lifestyle, have a reputation for violence, and are most likely to use corruption or confron-tation against state authorities. Their core values are brotherhood and righ-teousness, not material gains. Most jianghu individuals have been involved with the criminal justice system as defendants.

In contrast, most groups or networks that are involved in pianmen busi-nesses do not have a name, a turf, or a leadership structure. These groups do not have membership or rules and regulations. People in this subculture prefer low visibility, use evasion tactics to hide from the state authorities, and rare-ly use violence. Their main goal is to make money.

Shanzhai as Pianmen Business

In this study, I examine counterfeiting as a form of transnational organized crime activity that is suppressed by government authorities worldwide be-cause it reportedly victimizes large numbers of multinational firms and consumers. The victimization not only involves financial loss to rights hold-ers and consumers but also may cause harm to the physical well-being of con-sumers. However, numerous scholars consider counterfeiting, as implied in the term "shanzhai," not as an illegal activity but as a cultural phenomenon deeply embedded in the development and success of China's reform and opening up (Bosker 2013; Chubb 2015; Keane 2012; Liao 2020; Pang 2012; Raustiala and Sprigman 2015; Yang 2016; H. Yu 2011).

Yu Hua, an acclaimed Chinese writer who authored the 2011 book *China in Ten Words*, included "shanzhai" as one of the ten words on which he based his essays on modern China, along with the words for people, leader, revolution, grassroots, and bamboozle. According to Yu: "The word here ren-dered as 'copycat' originally denoted a mountain hamlet protected by a stock-ade or other fortifications; later it acquired an extended meaning as a hinter-land area, home to the disadvantaged. It was also a name once given to the lairs of outlaws and bandits; the word has continued to have connotations of freedom from official control" (181). Yu claimed that the concept of shan-zhai started with the copycatting of cell phones in China: "Copycat cell phones began by imitating the functions and designs of such brands as Nokia, Sam-sung, and Sony Ericsson; to muddy the waters further, they gave themselves names like Nokir, Samsing, Suny Ericcsun. By plagiarizing existing brands and thereby skimping on research and development costs, they sold for a fraction of the price of established products; given their technical capabili-ties and trendy appearance, they cornered the low end of the consumer mar-ket" (182). Yu asserted: "Once copycat cell phones had taken China by storm, copycat digital cameras, copycat MP3 players, copycat game consoles, and other such pirated and knockoff products came pouring forth. Copycat brands have rapidly expanded to include instant noodles, sodas, milk, medications, laundry detergent, and sports shoes, and so the word 'copycat' has penetrated deep into every aspect of Chinese people's lives" (185).

For Michael Keane, a professor of Chinese media and cultural studies, shanzhai connotes many things to many people. In one of his articles (2012, 217) on shanzhai, he commented:

> As the word entered into the vernacular it came to represent a blurring of commodity and simulacra: cheap copycats, fakes, pirated goods, local versions of globally branded goods, celebrity impersonators, as well as parodies of mainstream and official culture. Drawing on an association with the popular Ming novel *Outlaws of the Marsh* (Shuihuzhuan) about a brotherhood of renegade bandits, shanzhai conjures up associations of escape from authority, rising up against social injustice, and developing a set of rules parallel to those of the government.[7]

According to Andrew Chubb (2015, 272), "The value and appeal of the shanzhai identity (for the consumers of shanzhai products) include ingenuity and Chineseness, marginality and grassroots independence, playful ambiguity and ambivalence."

Sara Liao (2020, 2) provided her understanding of the *shanzhai* phenomenon in China as follows in her book *Fashioning China: Precarious Creativity and Women Designers in Shanzhai Culture*: "A neologism in Chinese, shanzhai literally means 'mountain strongholds' and evokes images of treks into the wildness, risk-taking, and even a sort of Robin Hood ethos. Shanzhai also carries a strong connotation of subalternity, with the savageness, cruelty, and rebelliousness of the participants serving as symbols of resistance to the dominant group. In Contemporary China, shanzhai is a well-known term for counterfeit goods and copies, having been originally associated with counterfeit cell phones produced by networks of local and regional entrepreneurs."

From Yu's viewpoint, the shanzhai phenomenon results from the imbalance in the development of political and economic reforms. After the events in Tiananmen Square in 1989, political reform halted, but economic reform continued rapidly and massively: "It seems to me that the emergence—and the unstoppable momentum—of the copycat phenomenon is an inevitable consequence of this lopsided development. The ubiquity and sharpness of social contradictions have provoked a confusion in people's value systems and worldview, thus giving birth to the copycat effect, when all kinds of social emotions accumulate over time and find only limited channels of release, transmuted constantly into seemingly farcical acts of rebellion that have certain anti-authoritarian, anti-mainstream, and anti-monopoly elements. The force and scale of copycatting demonstrate that the whole nation has taken to it as a form of performance art" (H. Yu 2011, 189).

After examining the shanzhai phenomenon in China, H. Yu (2011, 193) made a scathing remark: "The moral bankruptcy and confusion of right and wrong in China today, for example, find vivid expression in copycatting. As the copycat concept has gained acceptance, plagiarism, piracy, burlesque, parody, slander, and other actions originally seen as vulgar or illegal have been given a reason to exist; and in social psychology and public opinion they have gradually acquired respectability. No wonder that 'copycat' has become one of the words most commonly used in China today. . . . You may have done something illegal or unconscionable, but as long as you justify yourself with some kind of copycat explanation, your action becomes legitimate and aboveboard in the courtroom of public opinion."

The same argument was made by Raustiala and Sprigman (2015, 10), when they claimed: "Shanzhai is significant for understanding both luxury goods and counterfeits in China because shanzhai culture links the desire for wealth to copying of luxury goods, and makes production and consumption of counterfeits more socially legitimate than they might be otherwise."

In sum, the concept or phenomenon of shanzhai has been transformed from negative connotations such as "mountain fortress," "lawlessness," "banditry," "cheap," and "inferior" to "cleverness," "ingenuity," "functional," and "cultural creativity of the common people" (Bosker 2013, 25; Lin 2011, 13; H. Yu 2011, 181). In her book on the phenomenon of China's architectural mimicry of Western-style structures, Bianca Bosker (2013, 29–30) notes the thin line between real and fake for Chinese people:

> Classical Chinese theory offers evidence that the Chinese have embraced a more "fluid" position on distinctions between the real and fake. In this worldview, duplications and their originals may not be so different since all are connected by energy (*qi*) [气] that merely mutates among different iterations and informs both forms. The Chinese have erased many distinctions between the "authentic" and the "copy," as a result, their perspective allows for the essential *dao* [道], or life force, that informs the original to percolate with like intensity through the simulated copy. The spiritual energy lodged in the replicated facsimile can be as powerful as that embedded in the original.

In line with the scholars and authors cited earlier, my research participants justified the shanzhai business as a lifeline for the poor and the marginalized in a country like China, where urban people with education and connections benefit most from the country's economic reform and opening up. Mr. Cheng (F1), a migrant worker turned footwear manufacturer, was unapologetic when asked how he felt about copying shoes by Ecco and Timberland: "To counterfeit is to resist inequality in the distribution of benefits, and to protest commercial imperialism. Why do I have to work so hard and yet receive so little? I must obtain a substantial reward for my work."

Laoban (G2), an educated and analytical garment business owner, thought the counterfeit trade was a godsend for the powerless in China: "This is a business where the marginalized and the weak can change their economic status rapidly. There are large numbers of them in China, and they want to get rich quickly and be proud of themselves." The handbag businessman Sonny (H10), one of the outspoken research participants, offered a nuanced understanding of how the social and economic systems in China were responsible for the creation of people who were not only clever but also desperate to achieve economic success: "Chinese people are very savvy because they are forced to be like that by our system. Under the current, imperfect system, when everyone is trying to get ahead by any means, to make his or her first bucket of gold, the person has no choice but to operate in a gray area or make a shortcut."

Raustiala and Sprigman (2015, 271), on the other hand, suggest that shanzhai offers poor people a taste of what it is like to be rich and simultaneously calms them down: "A vibrant culture of copying has social value in a highly unequal society such as China's; by allowing the less well-off to access versions of the products that only the wealthy can afford in their original form, the widespread availability of shanzhai products may be useful as a brake on the social unrest that contemporary China's high level of social inequality tends to create."

Besides viewing the shanzhai phenomenon positively as a new form of revolutionary action (Yu Hua), an opportunity for poor people to get rich (Laoban, Sonny), or a factor in preventing social unrest (Raustiala and Sprigman), there are also arguments that it does not have any negative impact on innovation or harm rights holders. For example, Raustiala and Sprigman (2012, 5, emphasis in original) assert: "All this copying has not killed the fashion industry. In fact, fashion not only survives despite copying; *it thrives due to copying.*" Chow (2011, 785) also stresses that "although multinational companies (MNCs) often complain about enormous financial losses from counterfeiting, they are not really harmed by counterfeiting. MNCs cannot substantiate their claims of massive losses through credible evidence; instead, they use methods for calculating losses based upon dubious and spurious assumptions."

Many fashion designers are happy that their products are counterfeited. According to Anderson (1981), "Coco Chanel once said that the fact she was copied meant she was famous. . . . Deep down, some of them even have a certain pride in being good enough to be ripped off." After conducting a study on counterfeit goods buyers, Renee Richardson Gosline (2010), a marketing professor, found that more than half of his 112 research subjects who had bought counterfeit handbags bought a genuine luxury handbag within two and a half years.

Peter (G7), a native Guangzhounese, returned to Guangzhou after graduating from an Australian university. At one point, he was very active, and highly successful, in the copying of the products of an American urban fashion company. Peter has a theory about the positive role of imitation or emulation in China's economic transformation:

> Counterfeiting is one of our grand national strategies. After the Eight-Nation Alliance attacked us [in 1900] and returned home with a massive amount of our treasures, they suddenly transformed themselves into developed countries because of our money. Now, we adopt a three-stage development strategy. First is contract manufacturing, and that is to let them [foreigners] come to China to produce goods, let some of our factories help them manufacture, and learn their technology in the process. The second is emulation or imitation, not counterfeiting, because the word counterfeiting is an ugly word, and it is not correct. We are simply emulating. Third is innovation. We innovate after emulating so that we can surpass them. In sum, regardless of whether you consider counterfeiting as transnational organized crime or crime that is organized, the big boss behind the scenes is the Chinese government. Everything is part of the government's grand strategy: welcoming foreigners to outsource their manufacturing to us, learning their techniques, copying their goods, and finally surpassing them.

If we examine counterfeiting from the lens of shanzhai, it becomes a subcultural phenomenon that is not only beneficial to small business owners and working-class consumers but also a national strategy to transform China from a labor-intensive to a high-tech economy. This may be the reason why so many people I talked to in China could not understand why people in the West consider counterfeiting as a form of transnational organized crime. For them, counterfeiting is simply a *pianmen* business unrelated to the jianghu underworld.

7

Risk Management

For entrepreneurs who own a counterfeit business in China, it is vital that they not be arrested and punished by the Chinese authorities for their involvement in counterfeiting. The thought of being arrested and imprisoned terrifies these business owners because they are not career criminals accustomed to interacting with the criminal justice system. The uncertainty about the extent of loss or possible punishment, if charged with counterfeiting, keeps counterfeiters on edge.

Unlike other types of criminal activities that are hidden from the public, the production and distribution of counterfeit goods is out in the open and deeply integrated into the formal legal economy. In their 2018 book *Fake Goods, Real Money: The Counterfeiting Business and Its Financial Management*, Georgios Antonopoulos and his coauthors note: "An important aspect of counterfeiting that is ignored by official, media and business analyses of the phenomenon is the fact that counterfeiting is embedded in legal production and trade practices in a globalized economy" (29). Because counterfeiters conduct their business in the open, they know that no matter how hard they try, they are unlikely to evade the authorities for long. Xiao Peng (G8), an apparel business owner, responded fatalistically when asked what he did to protect his business from government officials: "If they want to investigate you, you are not going to get away. All they have to do is post a man outside your distribution outlet and follow your store employee when he or she heads to the warehouse to pick up counterfeit goods."

Nevertheless, counterfeiters in China spend much time and energy on risk aversion. Before I examine some of the risk-aversion practices, I explore the issue of informants because most counterfeiters pay particular attention to preventing people around them from becoming informants.

Informants

According to my research participants, Chinese authorities are unlikely to proactively investigate counterfeiting, especially if the counterfeited goods are clothing and accessories, not food or medicine. They believe that if the authorities target them, it must be because someone has blown the whistle on them. This is called jubao (reporting to the authorities). As a result, they are conscientious when dealing with people who can tip off government officials. They are fully aware of the possible sources of conflict between them and potential informers and are ready to take whatever precautionary measures are necessary to prevent the escalation of a conflict. Employees, business rivals, clients, and reward-motivated individuals are the primary potential informants.

Employees

In his book *Disorganized Crime: Illegal Markets and the Mafia*, Peter Reuter (1983, 115) explains why employees in illicit enterprises pose a major risk to their employers: "Employees present a major threat to the entrepreneur, having the most detailed knowledge concerning his participation. Not only do they represent effective witnesses concerning past dealings, but they also can provide to the police information about future dealings that might lead to his arrest and seizure of assets involved in the transaction. The entrepreneur aims then to structure his relationship with employees so as to reduce the amount of information available to them concerning his own participation and to ensure that they have minimal incentive to inform against him." According to Reuter, money, fear, and the recruitment of relatives as employees are some of the measures utilized by entrepreneurs to ensure employees' loyalty.

Likewise, the American criminologists Scott Decker and Margaret Townsend Chapman (2008) studied the social organization of drug smuggling. They interviewed thirty-four drug smugglers incarcerated in the U.S. federal prison system. In their book *Drug Smugglers on Drug Smuggling: Lessons from the Inside*, they recounted how "almost three-quarters of their research subjects were caught through members of their crew, despite the care taken to recruit crew members and limit information sharing" (Decker and Chapman 2008, 127).

For businesspeople in the counterfeit trade, the loyalty of employees is of great concern. Employees who become upset with their employers can provide the authorities with damaging information if they decide to betray them. As a result, employers are very tolerant of their employees as long as the employees do not do something outrageous. According to a clothing business owner not formally interviewed, "I had a store employee who stole my garments repeatedly. People like us who are involved in the counterfeiting business must take this kind of loss in stride because we fear that these employees might inform on us if we upset them."

Employees, especially saleswomen, can take advantage of the regular absence of their employers from the business premises. Some owners stay away from their retail stores as much as possible as a precautionary measure. They will go to their stores only if necessary and will not stay long. As a result, the salespeople are in a position to make extra money if they so desire. One way is to divert an order to another store and receive a kickback from that store's owner. Another way is to lump several retail sales into one wholesale transaction and pocket the price difference. Most distribution outlets are involved in retail and wholesale, but the retail price is slightly higher than the wholesale price. Without the owner there to keep an eye on the transactions, a salesperson can play games after the store is closed.

Besides salespeople, employees in management positions can also divert business to another firm for personal gain. Mr. Fu, a private investigator, revealed how his company investigated high-level employees on behalf of their employers: "We also deal with a variety of corporate investigations. Many of them are prompted by executives in the headquarters suspecting their branch managers are diverting the firm's business to other companies that the branch managers are secretly affiliated with. There are also many cases in which a company suspects that one of its managers is counterfeiting the company's products."

Another possible source of tension between an employer and an employee is the fear that the employee might leave to start his or her own business, copy the employer's fake products, and steal the employer's clients. Because copying is the norm in the counterfeit trade, no one in this business can blame another person for copying, even if that person is a former employee. In her book *Fashioning China: Precarious Creativity and Women Designers in Shanzhai Culture*, Sara Liao (2020) examines the phenomenon of how the copies are often copied in the highly competitive world of counterfeiting. Laoban has this to say about one of his favorite employees who became his competitor:

I promoted Xiao Xiao (who later married Xiao Guan, G13) from a worker to a manager within a short period because she was talented.

She was not only smart but also hardworking. She often worked until midnight to ensure that finished goods were delivered on time. Even though there was no overtime pay, she did not complain. However, after she left my company and started her own business, the first shot she took was at me. Not only did she copy my garments but also she tried to lure away my major clients who were wholesale distributors in Beijing. Luckily, she failed.

Aware of the possible repercussions if he were to do something to Xiao Xiao, Laoban pretended that nothing had happened and maintained a good relationship with her. She and her husband, Xiao Guan (G13), went on to expand their men's clothing business and became relatively successful. Laoban said he could tolerate Xiao Xiao's disloyalty because he thought the market at that time was big enough for everyone. However, Laoban must have also realized that if he reacted strongly, Xiao Xiao might have reported Laoban's engagement in counterfeiting to the authorities. Taiwanese operating counterfeiting businesses in China have no choice but to be extremely careful not to antagonize local people, not to mention their own employees.

Laoban (G2) revealed how another employee, Lin Jun (G17), a young man from Sichuan Province, exploited him:

When Lin Jun was looking for work after he arrived in Guangzhou, I offered him a job in my firm. After working for me for about two years as a truck driver, he knew who my clients were because he delivered our goods to various long-distance bus stations daily. After he quit, he went to work for his father, who was also in the garment business. The two of them then stole my clients by selling similar goods at a lower price. After they made enough money, they opened their own sales outlets.

One way for employers to make sure that they do not upset their employees is to pay them on time. If employees do not receive their salary on payday or on the day they quit, there is a good chance that they will contact the police and inform on their employers. According to Ah Yun (F13), a dust bag manufacturer:

Workers are going to report their employer to the authorities for counterfeiting if they do not receive their wages on time. That is why I do not dare to owe my workers their wages or delay payments. If a worker says he or she is quitting, I pay the person all their wages immediately. I am afraid that if the worker is unhappy with how I handle the payment, he or she might report me to the authorities.

Business Rivals

According to my research subjects, when their business is doing well, but their rivals' is not, their rivals may decide to blow the whistle on them. When the counterfeiting business was expanding in the early 2000s and everyone was making money, this type of whistleblowing was rare. When the business began to shrink and many enterprises were struggling, the owners of counterfeiting firms might betray their competitors to lessen the competition. Some might do it simply out of jealousy.

Chaoban (copying) is one of the most likely sources of conflict for entrepreneurs in the counterfeiting industry. It is ironic that while counterfeiters are busy copying name-brand luxury goods, they are also making sure their copied goods will not be duplicated by their rivals. As discussed in Chapter 4, there is a perception among businesspeople and consumers in Guangzhou that product quality and market location are closely related. For the apparel industry, garments traded in Baima and other markets around Zhanxi Road are considered high end, followed by markets around Shisanhang. Markets in Shahe are viewed as a step below those in Shisanhang. As a result, store owners in Baima and Zhanxi Road are hostile to any customers from Shisanhang and Shahe because they believe that these people come to their stores to steal their ideas and copy their goods.

Clients

Sellers of counterfeit goods have to deal with two types of clients: distributors and consumers. The first type includes wholesalers and retailers. The second type purchases counterfeit goods for their own use. Because most consumers know they are buying fake products, it is unlikely that they will get very upset if they are not satisfied with the quality of the goods they buy. It is unusual for customers to approach the authorities and blow the whistle on a counterfeiter because they are unhappy with a copy. It is the first type of client—the distributors—who may betray a counterfeiter. According to Ah Yun (F13), it is the distributors who approach the authorities out of dissatisfaction with their providers' services: "Most counterfeiters are exposed to the authorities because their clients did not receive the goods they purchased promptly, not because their competitors are jealous of their successes. When a client does not get the goods on time, he or she loses money, and this upsets his or her buyers. This is why the person is so angry."

Reward-Motivated Individuals

The Chinese authorities offer monetary rewards to anyone who can provide crucial information that helps them arrest a counterfeiter. According to Xiao

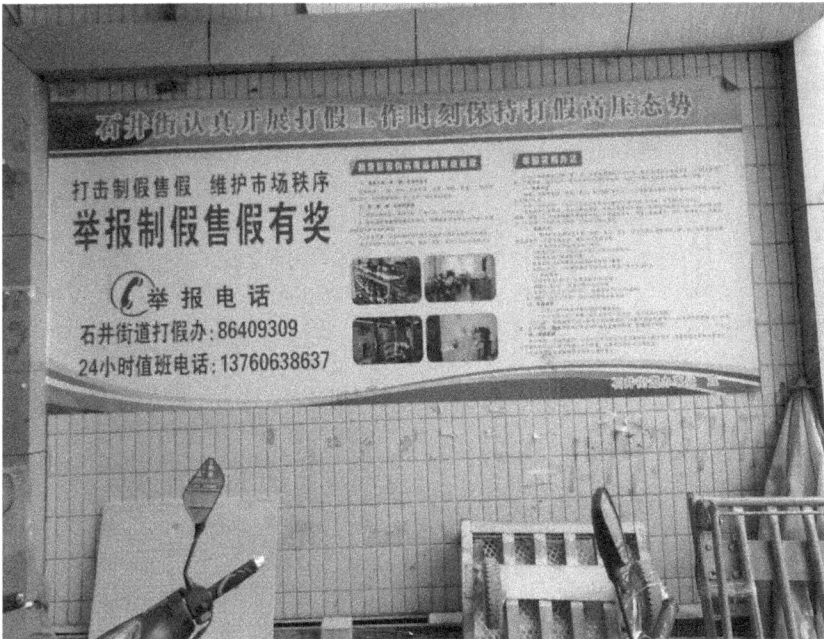

Figure 7.1 A poster urging people to report IPR-infringing activities.

Zhen (H13), a leather handbag business owner: "The policy to give monetary rewards to informers is a savvy one. This incentivizes people to report counterfeiting activities to the authorities." However, of all the markets I visited in Guangzhou and other parts of China, only the Guangda/Guoda Shoe Market in Shijing had a poster urging people to report IPR infringing activities. Unlike other propaganda posters in China, this one was hidden in a small alley. It was four feet by ten feet, small by Chinese standards (see Figure 7.1).[1] It gave the impression that the local authorities did not want to promote an anti-counterfeiting strategy aggressively. It is unclear how many reports are made by strictly reward-motivated individuals and not by those who have other motives while pretending that they are after monetary rewards.

Risk-Avoidance Business Practices

Because counterfeiting is illegal in China and a perpetrator can be subject to arrest, fines, or even imprisonment, participants in this business are compelled to develop various risk-avoidance measures to protect themselves from the authorities. Peter (G7), a clothing business owner, explained the differences in operating a counterfeit versus a legitimate clothing firm: "As far as the apparel industry is concerned, there is not much difference between counterfeiting and running a legitimate business with your own brand. When you are copying, you do not have to design; all you need to do is duplicate goods designed by other people. Copying is easy and less costly because you save all the expenditures of designing, developing, and marketing a new product. Of course, counterfeiting is a lot riskier than having your own brand. This means counterfeiters have to spend a lot of time and money to ensure they will not be investigated, arrested, convicted, and imprisoned." Entrepreneurs from the two types of businesses have very different focuses: legitimate businesspeople operating under their own brands pay attention to their designs and the reputation of their brand, whereas counterfeiters focus on the many ways they can shield themselves from anti-counterfeiting private investigators and government officials. The pressure for self-preservation can be overwhelming. Xiao Peng (G8), a clothing business owner from Zhejiang Province, said: "There is a saying among us: Counterfeiting is like making a vegetable vendor's money but enduring a heroin dealer's stress."

In the following sections, I examine the measures counterfeiters adopt to minimize the risk of being targeted and punished by the authorities. From these courses of action, it is apparent that counterfeiters and law enforcement authorities are playing a cat and mouse game, and many of the tactics used by IP infringers are subtle, intuitive, and remarkable.

Having a Registered Brand

One of the most critical things for self-preservation in the counterfeiting trade is to have a registered brand so that, on the surface, all business activities are legitimate and integrated into the mainstream commercial sector. In a sense, counterfeiters are performing the art of face changing in a Sichuan opera. According to Wikipedia (2023), "Face changing (bian lian) is an ancient Chinese dramatic art that is part of the more general Sichuan opera. Performers wear brightly colored costumes and move to quick, dramatic music. They also wear vividly colored masks, typically depicting well known characters from the opera, which they change from one face to another almost instantaneously with the swipe of a fan, a movement of the head, or wave of the hand." Mr. Song, an agent for a private investigating firm, explained how and why there is a thin line between legal and illegal business practices for fashion entrepreneurs: "There is another world spinning underneath the world you see on the surface. Every store carries goods affixed with its own brand, and if you want to buy these goods, the stores are willing to sell them, regardless of how many or few you want to buy. However, selling goods with their own brands will not sustain them, so they need to rely on counterfeiting. Besides, these stores already have their networks of buyers and distribution channels to market counterfeit goods."

Laoban (G2) agreed with Mr. Song:

> Most counterfeiters will register their own brands with the state. To avoid being investigated, they will affix the logos of their own brands on all the samples on display at their sales outlets or company showrooms. When an order is fulfilled, they will affix the logo of the client, the factory, or the international fashion house, depending on the circumstance. This is the current modus operandi in this industry. Counterfeiting in China has been in existence for more than twenty years; everybody in this trade knows the risk-free modus operandi, and that is why only a few counterfeiting businesses have been investigated.

Besides having their own brand names on the collar labels of the products that are on display in their retail or wholesale outlets, offices, or showrooms, IP infringers also slightly alter the logos, marks, or names of the international fashion houses when there is a need for them to be displayed on their merchandise. For example, many fake Gucci casual wear items have the word "Gucc" across the chest. Mrs. Jia (G11), the owner of an embroidered patch store, has this to say about how she was able to operate an outlet with hundreds of patches with names and marks similar to those of international designer brands:

> All the embroidered patches on display here have misspelled brand names, like Chanee instead of Chanel. If a customer wants us to change the label from Chanee to Chanel, we will do so; it is just that this person has to be a regular customer. If the person is not someone we are familiar with, we dare not agree to meet the request. People from the gongshangju [AIC] often come here asking you to do this or that, and if you are not careful, you get caught.

Compartmentalizing the Business

Counterfeiters compartmentalize their operations to minimize financial loss and legal punishment if government authorities investigate them. There are many ways for them to insulate their operations. First of all, firms keep their dangkou, xiezilou, gongsi, factories, and warehouses separate from one another and, if possible, register these various businesses under other people's names. Jane (G1) rented a place just to keep her computers away from the rest of her business operations.

Counterfeiters said they would not keep their merchandise in their offices or homes. Xiao Zhen (H13), whose mother was an official in the Guangzhou criminal justice system, paid a huge price for storing his leather hand-bags in his home and not moving quickly enough to mitigate the risk:

> I got into trouble in 2016. I used my home as my warehouse because I had a lot of space to store my stuff. Even so, I was worried, so I looked for a place to be my warehouse, and I found one. When I was about to sign a lease with the landlord, my wife, and parents urged me not to sign it, insisting that home was the safest place. That is why I gave up looking for a warehouse. Not long after that, the authorities showed up at my home, and they found 500 Fendi and Dior hand-bags. They estimated that the market value of my handbags amount-ed to more than $1.5 million.

As discussed in Chapters 3 and 4, a counterfeiting operation includes the purchase and "studying" (or dismantling) of an original, the "designing" of a similar product (in the case of non-point-by-point imitation), the acqui-sition of manufacturing materials, the production of the goods, the storage of the goods in a warehouse, and the distribution of the goods. Since it is legal to copy a name-brand product as long as the copy is not affixed with the brand name and logo of the original, counterfeiters are vulnerable only after their merchandise is branded. This was made clear by Mr. Bo, a Guang-zhou city government official: "In the leather handbag counterfeiting busi-ness, the cutting and manufacturing factories are not at risk; even if the au-thorities check them, they are safe because they are not involved in any illegal [branding] activities."

According to Xiao Jen (H11), a warehouse worker, not only were brand-ed handbags not on display in the sales outlets, but they were also handled with care inside the warehouse: "We did not dare to keep any branded hand-bags in the store, only blank handbags. All the branded handbags were stored in the warehouse. Even within the warehouse, we made sure these bags were not visible; we hid them."

For some counterfeiters, the risk of keeping branded merchandise in a storage facility is too high because there is a good chance that the authorities may find out about the existence of such a place. As a result, they further compartmentalize their operations by keeping only blank copies in their warehouses and affixing the label and the logo after a sale is made. Xiao Qin (H16), a leather handbag counterfeiter, recalled how he adopted this practice for a short period and was forced to abandon it due to the increased cost:

> After my warehouse was raided, I kept only logo-free handbags in my warehouse. If someone placed an order, I moved the handbags in my warehouse to a nearby place to affix the labels and logos. It was

safer this way; if the authorities found no-logo handbags, it would not be a problem. However, I increased my costs by doing this. Because I was copying mainly third-tier luxury handbags, my sale prices were already low. I simply could not absorb the increase if my costs went up by an additional $7 to $14 [per bag]. Of course, if I was duplicating Hermès handbags, maybe I could handle the increased cost. So, I changed my strategy. I increased my warehouses from one to more than a dozen and kept only a minimal amount of branded goods in each place.

Leather handbag merchant Sonny (H10) also said that many entrepreneurs in the counterfeiting industry maintain more than one storehouse to minimize the risk: "Factory owners demand zero inventory, so once a batch of handbags is produced, they must be taken away promptly. The owner of these handbags will store them in several warehouses. No businessperson will maintain only one warehouse, mainly to lower the risk of being detected and reduce the amount of fine and length of sentence if arrested and convicted."

To minimize risk, distributors of high-end point-by-point counterfeits, like Kenny and Gigi (G23) in Dongguan, said they were not branding their merchandise anymore. If their clients request branding, they include the labels, logos, hangtags, and all the other items needed to make the products look like point-by-point copies in the bags along with the merchandise and ask the buyers to affix the brands themselves.

Studies on drug trafficking note that drug smugglers often compartmentalize their operations to evade law enforcement authorities and to minimize the impact of interdiction (K. Chin and Zhang 2015; Decker and Chapman 2008; Gundur 2022). The same is true with sex-ring operators in the commercial sex industry in China. Commercial sex venues such as nightclubs, spas, or karaoke hostess clubs are located in buildings adjacent to high-end hotels instead of being in the same building as the hotels (Moore 2010). If one of these sex venues is raided by the police (prostitution is illegal in China), the luxury hotel will claim that it has no affiliation with the sex business.

Keeping the Business Small

There is a saying in Chinese, "Human beings are afraid of getting famous; pigs are afraid of getting fat." Chinese authorities like to stress that "if they [violators of the law] stick their heads out, we strike them," meaning they are not very aggressive toward low-key criminals in a small group; however, if these criminals become high profile, and their group becomes large and powerful, the authorities are going to go after them.

Decker and Chapman (2008, 115) note that "the number one rule for almost all [drug] smugglers is to keep the size of crew small, for both practical and precautionary reasons." After examining research on upper-level drug traffickers in the United States, the United Kingdom, Canada, and the Netherlands, Frederick Desroches (2007, 833) concluded that "the predominant view in the literature is that smaller is safer as far as drug distribution enterprises are concerned." In my research on the smuggling of Chinese nationals to the United States, I also found that Chinese human-smuggling organizations were small, even though these groups were engaged in complex transnational criminal activities (K. Chin 1999). Likewise, sex-ring operators responsible for the cross-border movement of Chinese women for commercial sex belong to small groups (K. Chin and Finckenauer 2012).

When asked what the average size of a counterfeiting business is, garment businessman Laoban said: "When you are involved in counterfeiting, the smaller the size of your business, the safer you are. Plus, it is the best way to increase your profits." Dust bag manufacturer Ah Yun (F13) responded succinctly to the question about the relationship between business size and danger: "You do great, you die first!" Mr. Jin (F14), a footwear entrepreneur who said he was never very successful with his business, said he thought his lack of success was a blessing in disguise: "I never ran into any trouble with the authorities. Those who did were normally successful counterfeiters. If your store is packed with customers all day long, store owners around you will get jealous, and they will report you to the authorities."

For business owners, the best way to keep a minimum number of employees is to rely on themselves to carry out as many tasks as possible or outsource as much as possible. Australian-educated apparel entrepreneur Peter (G7) said: "You'd better do everything yourself, so not very many people will be involved or know what you are doing and how you are doing it." However, for a thriving business, an owner cannot do everything himself. The alternative is to recruit loyal and trustworthy workers and treat them well.

Hiring the Right Workers and Treating Them Well

As mentioned in Chapter 6, operators in the counterfeiting industry prefer to hire family members, relatives, or someone from their hometown to help them. They believe that these workers are more reliable and loyal than outsiders recruited through advertisements. The wife of Mr. Zhou (H17), a handbag manufacturer said: "We had about thirty to forty workers in our factory, so it was a relatively large operation. Most factories had only up to twelve workers. My workers were people I knew well; at least, they were referred to us by our friends. We did not advertise when we were looking for workers.

We did not hire strangers because we feared they might report us to the authorities."

Counterfeiters from Taiwan have no choice but to hire local people in China. However, they will ask the initial group of workers to refer family members or relatives if they find the first group of workers capable and reliable. Xiao Wen (G6) recruited his three cousins from Sichuan Province not long after being hired by Laoban as a designer. Laoban said that, of all the employees, business owners are most afraid of those in the accounting department. That was why when he was looking for a bookkeeper, he hired a then seventeen-year-old girl named Mimi (F7) (who later became a sandal manufacturer) with no experience. Xiao Yuen (G12), who understood why Laoban recruited such a young person who had just arrived in Guangzhou from a rural area, explained why:

> Mimi came to Guangzhou when she was about seventeen and applied for a bookkeeper position at Laoban's company. Laoban was surprised that such a young girl was applying for the job. When Laoban told her she was hired, she was shocked too. Mimi probably only had a vocational high school degree and had just arrived in Guangzhou. Laoban thought Mimi was young and innocent and did not look like a smart aleck, so he decided to hire her. That was precisely the kind of employee he wanted: someone who did not have to be very capable, but was honest, reliable, and not scheming. Later, as Laoban had predicted, he found that Mimi was not a very good bookkeeper, but he thought he had done the right thing in hiring her.

Training workers how to react when the authorities show up unexpectedly is critical for business owners who want to minimize the damage of a raid. According to Chaozhounese handbag merchant Sonny (H10), "We have a high sense of self-preservation. You cannot imagine how well prepared my workers are if and when I were to be arrested. Each of them knows what to tell the authorities; this is the most basic requirement I have for my employees. If we run into trouble, we are not going to panic because we are completely prepared."

For workers to cooperate with an employer and protect him when he is in trouble, the employer needs to treat his employees well. Many business owners pay their employees on time, turn a blind eye when their employees pilfer, give them money when there is a family crisis, and wine and dine them whenever possible. In sum, counterfeiters will go out of their way to do little things to keep their employees happy. Laoban is an excellent astrologer, and he regularly did fortune-telling for his employees free of charge. When he foresaw misfortune, he would help an employee change his name to change his fortune. Likewise, he helped all offspring of his employees come up with names that would bring them good fortune. If an employee becomes indispensable, it pays to make him a business partner by offering him a percentage of the profits. Leather supplier Xiao Ma (H4) offered 20 percent ownership to a manager in his luggage materials business and 10 percent to Ah Bao (F12), his right-hand man in his shoe leather business.

If an employer mistreats his employees, there is a good chance that one of them may blow the whistle on him. Sometimes, a worker may become upset for no reason and report his employer to the police. Handbag producer and distributor Xiao Zhen (H13) was one of these employers. When his home (where he kept his leather goods) was raided by the authorities and he suffered a huge loss, this is how he understood the unfortunate incident:

> I believe someone fingered me to the authorities. I live in a remote area, so who would have known I was using my home as a warehouse? Besides, when the investigators came, they did not go to other houses, just straight to mine. I suspect it was my pattern cutter because he was very unhappy when he quit. First, I hired another pattern cutter, and he thought I was about to get rid of him. I was trying to help him to focus exclusively on running the factory and nothing else. Second, he asked me for a pay raise threateningly, saying if I didn't, he was going to leave. I did not like that, so I asked him to go ahead and leave. He knew where I lived and that I kept goods at my home. Not knowing who reported me to the police still makes me bitter, even though this happened more than three years ago.

Regardless of how well a business owner treats his employees, the latter will not be completely protective of their employer, especially if the workers are not relatives. Leather goods merchant Xiao Qin (H16) recalled an incident in which one of his employees responded to a raid by the authorities: "I was in trouble once; the authorities raided my warehouse. I did not know how that happened, but I came to their attention, so they checked my warehouse. They found over four thousand leather handbags, confiscated the goods, and arrested a male worker. Once the authorities interrogated the worker, he exposed me to the authorities, telling them that I was the boss. However, he said nothing about my factory and outlet store."

Preventing Customers from Becoming Unhappy

Counterfeiters are careful not to upset their customers because, if they do, there is a good chance the customers may contact the police and finger them.

Since none of my research subjects were involved in deceptive counterfeiting, they did not have to be concerned about customers calling the police because of counterfeiting. In other words, buyers know they are buying counterfeit goods. However, as mentioned earlier, there is a possibility that a seller may not deliver the same quality of handbag to a buyer as the blank handbag on which the buyer based his order. In other words, the seller may display a high-quality blank handbag and deliver a low-quality trademarked handbag. Clothing entrepreneur Xiao Yuen (G12), for one, said sellers will refrain from doing this because they do not want their customers to approach the authorities: "I believe the stores in Baiyun (Leather City) match the delivered items with the displayed samples in the store. These are reputable businesses operating in the open that will not cut corners. Besides, they do not dare to cheat their customers because they are afraid that if they do, the customers will tell the authorities they are selling fake goods. These stores don't want this kind of trouble." Warehouse worker Xiao Jen (H11), on the other hand, suggested it depends on whether a buyer is a local person or someone from overseas: "Whether a dangkou will be honest or not depends on who the customer is. If the buyer is a foreigner, the store will not match the sample, thinking that a foreigner will not know the difference between a high-quality and a low-quality fake."

Improvising

Adopting certain business practices is another way for people in the counterfeiting industry to reduce the risk of being targeted by the authorities. There are many risk-avoidance business practices, but one of the more peculiar measures is to operate only after dark. The reason for doing so is apparent: most of the authorities do not work at night, so conducting business then is safer. Three places notorious for counterfeiting activities, Guangda/Guoda Shoe Market in Guangzhou, Liaoxia in Dongguan, and Putian in Fujian Province, offer good examples of how this practice is adopted. According to leather handbag factory owner Danny (H3) in Dongguan: "The factories in Liaoxia do not operate during the daytime. They come alive only at night. The reason for this is to avoid officials from the Administration for Industry and Commerce [AIC]. After these officials leave their offices at night, they do not conduct any raids."

According to Xiao Fei (F11), owner of a small hardware factory that specializes in producing name-brand metal fittings for counterfeiters: "I produce all kinds of shoe hardware. In this business, we have to deal with wastewater. That is why environmental protection officials have become very active lately, forcing us to start work after 9:00 P.M. By that time, none of the officials are working. How the hell are they going to check on us?"

When I visited Guangda/Guoda Shoe Market, almost all of the stores were closed during the daytime. Only a few were open, and there were very few customers. However, the place came to life after six in the evening, and activity peaked after ten. Sometimes, business there continued until two or three in the morning.

There are many reports in the English and Chinese media about how Putian City in Fujian Province, the fake shoe capital of the world, is lifeless during the daytime but, by night, is transformed into one of the busiest places on earth (Pierson 2017; Schmidle 2010).

Even those markets that are bustling with people during the daytime, like Baiyun Leather City, deliver counterfeits to buyers only after the stores are closed and not when the deals are made. According to handbag merchant Sonny (H10), this practice is mainly to protect the sellers from the authorities: "The outlets in Baiyun [Leather City] will deliver the goods to their customers after dark, or they will ask customers to return the following day to pick up the goods. The reason behind this is that they are worried that if they send an employee to pick up the stuff from a warehouse [in the daytime], he or she could be followed by the authorities, and the location of the warehouse might be exposed. This is their number one concern. That is why they do not give customers the goods right away."

Creating moving targets is one of the most frequently adopted risk-aversion strategies—that is, moving manufacturing facilities, distribution outlets, and warehouses as often as possible so that they will be less likely to come to the attention of the authorities. According to leather supplier Xiao Ma (H4): "Fake handbag store owners will not stay in the same location for long. They prefer to move from one place to another constantly. This way, the authorities are less likely to notice them." Guangzhou city government official Mr. Bo, who identified himself as a "researcher" for the city, estimated that factories and warehouses normally operate at a location for six months to a year at the most. Changing phone numbers is another popular tactic counterfeiters use to shield themselves. Handbag distributor Mr. Mu (H8) characterized contract factory owners who worked with him this way: "They never let us visit their factories. If there are new items or samples to review, we find a place away from their business premises. They are very secretive. The factory owners also change their phone numbers all the time, like every three or four months. If they do not tell us their new phone numbers, we will not be able to contact them anymore." My research participants said moving by cars, vans, or trucks is relatively easy for the majority of the small or medium businesses in counterfeiting. One said it would take two days at the most.

To avoid coming to the attention of law enforcement authorities, some counterfeiters move their business operations, especially the manufacturing component, to their hometowns, far away from Guangzhou. Leather supplier Xiao Ma (H4) explained why: "There are many advantages to this. First, workers in the remote hometowns do not know anything about international brands, and therefore they do not know that you are involved in the counterfeiting of name-brand handbags. Second, if you run into trouble with the law there, it is easier to get out of it. After all, it is your hometown, and you have all the connections there. Government officials there can also be easier to bribe. Third, since the workers there are from your village or township, even if they know you are engaged in counterfeiting, it is unlikely that they will report you to the police."

Some entrepreneurs also register some of their businesses under the name of a family member or a relative. For example, when a couple and their relatives are engaged in counterfeiting, and their business begins to expand, the factory will be registered under the name of the husband, the dangkou under the name of the wife, and the gongsi under the name of a cousin who is involved in the business but does not have an ownership interest in it. It is not clear how effective this strategy is in shielding the real owner from being exposed to the authorities. Prosecutor Wang said it is not that effective: "An owner may register the dangkou under a relative's name, but it is not that difficult for us to track down the real owner. Plus, once a saleswoman is arrested, she will not hesitate to tell us who the real owner is."

Another practice adopted by business owners to minimize the impact of an investigation by the authorities is to limit their role in the counterfeiting business by demanding other business partners assume some of the responsibilities if and when authorities knock on their doors. This is in response to how the authorities have changed their investigation tactics. According to garment factory manager Lao Su (G24): "Nowadays, if a retailer or wholesaler is arrested, there is a chance that the authorities might go after the manufacturer. In the past, the focus was on the distribution end. Now, not only factories, but also raw material suppliers are investigated. That is why when a factory makes counterfeits for a distributor, the factory owner will demand that the distributor take responsibility if and when he is arrested, making clear that he is not going to take all the heat. A manufacturer certainly has all the information about his distributor; otherwise, the two parties would not work together."

Keeping a Low Profile

Most business owners I met in Guangzhou keep a low profile, regardless of how rich they are. As stated earlier, some of them own expensive cars, but they rarely drive them in the city and rely on the subway or taxis when they move around the city. Guangzhou city government's researcher Mr. Bo told me the story of a successful counterfeiter:

> I have a friend who became acquainted with a Jiangxi man who owns a store in Baiyun Leather City. That man was originally a poor peasant. After he began to engage in the counterfeiting of handbags in Guangzhou and his business grew, he earned a large amount of money. He bought a brand new Land Rover for more than $98,000. He also purchased a big house. After he became rich, he turned low-key. Now, it is very difficult to ask him out for dinner. He will not agree to meet any strangers. Moreover, he will not allow anyone to send anything to where he lives. He will make sure all packages are delivered to a nearby address, and will go over there to meet the delivery person and pick up the packages. After that, he will walk around the block for a while before heading home. Also, he does not live in the big house he bought. Instead, he lives in a rented apartment to avoid having his house confiscated by the authorities if he is arrested.

Minding one's own business is also a norm for counterfeiters. As mentioned earlier, they do not ask their business associates or clients unnecessary questions; they focus only on the business at hand. Leather trader Xiao Ma (H4) said: "Many buyers showed up at my store with designer-brand handbags and told me they were looking for exactly the same kind of leather as on those authentic bags. However, they were low key and discreet and would not say they were in the counterfeiting business. I did not ask what they were up to."

Risk Management in General

Peter (G7), a fashion business owner, offered a detailed answer to the question of how participants in the counterfeiting industry minimize risk and avoid detection. According to him, risk-management strategies for various stages in the supply chain differ because some of those stages entail no risk at all, while others involve varying degrees of risk. Consequently, business owners develop different strategies for different stages in the supply chain (see Figure 7.2). Because he is most familiar with the apparel industry, his answer pertains to that particular industry. However, he made the point that risk management for counterfeiters in the apparel, leather goods, and shoe businesses is relatively similar. His words are as follows:

> *Sourcing fabric*: There is no risk at this stage because everyone can buy and sell fabric freely, unless the fabric bears the monogram of a name brand like Louis Vuitton. If the authorities catch you with Louis Vuitton–monogrammed fabric, it could be a problem.

Cutting fabric: Also no risk here. Cutting fabric in and of itself is not illegal.

Crafts: When you get to this stage, risk begins. When you do printing or embroidery and need to copy a brand's logo, there is risk even though you have not yet made the finished garment. How are you going to handle this? Well, the best strategy is to do these tasks after dark. By that time, anti-counterfeiting officials have stopped working; they are not going to conduct any investigations at night.

Factory: This is riskier than the first three stages, because you are about to manufacture finished products, and we are talking about mass production. The best way to reduce risk is to keep the factory small, hidden, and mobile, with only a few people involved.

Affixing labels: This is a very high-risk phase in counterfeiting. Even if people in this business do not mind copying styles, design elements, printing, and even logos, they become concerned when they have to put a label on the garments. There are many ways to handle this. Some manufacturers do not mind helping you produce counterfeit garments, but they will not put the labels on the garments and insist that you do this yourself after you pick up the finished garments from them. Alternatively, they will ask you to pick up the garments with the brand labels affixed immediately after production. They will not keep any branded counterfeit garments on their premises.

Packaging: This activity also involves risk because boxes, poly bags, packing papers, "birth certificates" [certificates of authenticity], receipts, and hangtags all bear the labels and logos of name brands.

Warehouse/Delivery: Warehouses are the primary targets for anti-counterfeiting officials and investigators. Protecting warehouses is one of the most important risk-avoidance measures. First, you need to maintain multiple warehouses so that you can diversify your inventory. Second, you need to move your warehouses as often as possible, ideally every three months. Third, you need to set up a small distribution warehouse near your dangkou and keep only a small amount of goods in it. The distribution warehouse should be responsible for the delivery of goods to buyers. Fourth, deliveries should be made only after dark. Fifth, only family members and relatives should work in the warehouses. Sixth, salespersons from the dangkou should not be informed of the locations of the warehouses. They only receive orders from the customers and nothing else. Seventh, when going in and out of the warehouses, you should drive around the premises a few times to make sure that nobody is following you.

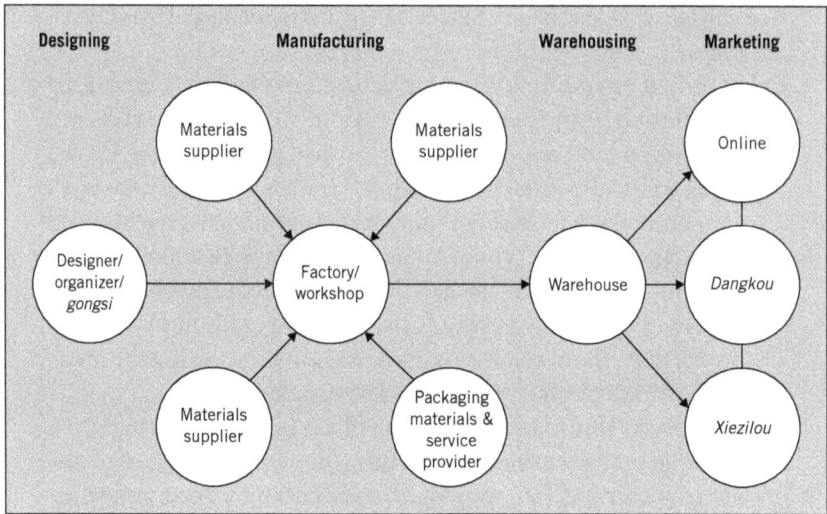

Figure 7.2 The supply chain of counterfeiting. (*Map by Rutgers Cartography*)

Fashion entrepreneur Jane (G1) also revealed what she did to protect her business from the authorities. First, she thought that a counterfeiting business should contain only a xiezilou and a dangkou, not a gongsi or a factory: "It is best not to have a gongsi. Why do you need a gongsi? It is useless, and it only creates trouble. It is OK to have a xiezilou, so you can talk business with important clients. It is also easier to show the clients your goods in a xiezilou. Doing so in a dangkou is hectic because so many people are coming and going. A dangkou is a place to draw in buyers. If you have one, you can attract new buyers. You can do both wholesale and retail from a dangkou. You can also operate more than one dangkou [in one or more markets to achieve a broad reach]. When you are in the counterfeiting business, it is best not to have your own factory. It is not necessary. Although there are some advantages, the disadvantages outweigh the advantages." Jane suggested that the following principles should be followed to minimize risk, and they are similar to the many risk-aversion measures discussed earlier: (1) keep the number of people involved small—the smaller, the better, (2) hire only relatives and people you can trust, (3) compartmentalize each business stage, (4) use a small revolving depository method to fulfill orders, and (5) be extra careful when going to your warehouses.

Most counterfeiters are smart people who know how to avoid being targeted by the authorities. Their risk-aversion measures are innovative, intuitive, comprehensive, and probably as good as or better than some of the strategies developed by the most successful drug cartels (Bunck and Fowler

2012; K. Chin and Zhang 2015; Decker and Chapman 2008). However, some private investigators say that Chinese counterfeiters are not that clever. They think that counterfeiters become astute only after they are caught, pay the price, and learn from their experience. According to private investigator Mr. Song:

> When I began as a private investigator, people did not know what intellectual property was. Counterfeiters conducted their businesses openly. After the authorities repeatedly apprehended them, they developed a heightened alertness and came up with all kinds of tactics to protect themselves from law enforcement.
>
> Counterfeiters in the manufacturing sector mainly adopt the following measures: (1) They divide the manufacturing process into two stages. The first stage is conducted in a factory that has heavy and expensive machines. This stage involves only risk-free activities such as cutting. The piecework or components will then be moved to a second factory, without heavy and costly machinery, where they will be assembled; (2) They operate only at night, lock the factories during the daytime and do nothing; (3) They do not affix any brand labels, logos, or other trademark-infringing materials to the finished goods in the factories; they do this elsewhere.
>
> For counterfeiters in the distribution sector, the main risk-avoidance measure is not keeping any goods with name-brand labels or logos in their dangkou or xiezilou. Take Baiyun Leather City, for example. The dangkou there do not display trademarked leather goods, only generic products. If someone places an order, a nearby warehouse will deliver the trademarked item to the store or the buyer's designated address. That warehouse is located in a residential area not far from the dangkou, and residential areas in China cannot be raided by public security at will, unlike warehouses in commercial districts.

Regardless, many successful counterfeiters are prepared for a worst-case scenario in which they would be arrested and the authorities would seize all their assets. They often make all the necessary arrangements in advance for an escape route. According to Mr. Zhou (H17), a leather handbag businessman:

> When we were operating our dangkou at Baiyun Leather City, the dangkou next door was doing exceptionally well. That dangkou was packed with customers all day long, and its leather handbags were considered the best. If you wanted to buy a copy of a particular brand, you had to buy it from that dangkou. Every evening, the owner left the dangkou with bags of cash. They had to move in a group of three

for safety reasons. Within Baiyun, they had more than ten dangkou. At that time, the boss had already prepared an escape route. He moved his whole family to Canada and bought a house there. He also moved all the money he could to Canada. One day, when he got wind that the authorities were coming to arrest him, he immediately fled to Canada. He left all his dangkou, inventory, and factories behind. His loss was immense, but he did not care because he had already made a lot.

Business Risk

Many counterfeiters said they were concerned not only with legal and compliance risks but also with business or operational risks, which could be equally devastating. Often, they went out of business not because of law enforcement crackdowns but because of market uncertainty, poor product design, inefficient distribution channels, fierce business competition, or unusual weather. While they were confident in dealing with legal and compliance risks, they were less assured when facing business or operational risks. In this section, I examine some of the business or operational risks not related to the illicit nature of counterfeiting.

Poor Product Design and Inefficient Distribution Channels

Many in the apparel industry say product design determines the fate of their merchandise. They believe good design is the critical first step in developing a winning product and ensuring a good season. They also believe that an efficient distribution network is indispensable for guaranteeing that a product reaches large and small markets across China. If a product is good but the distribution network is poor, it will not sell. According to Xiao Yuen (G12), a garment merchant: "In the apparel industry, the most important thing is whether your distribution channel is good. If you have excellent wholesale distributors, they will sell everything you offer them, even if your goods are garbage. If your distributors are incapable, even if you give them very excellent stuff, they cannot sell it."

Fierce Business Competition

As in all legitimate businesses in China, competition in the counterfeiting business is fierce. Since counterfeiting is illegal in China, participants in this industry cannot approach the authorities for help if business rivals copy their counterfeit products and sell them at a lower price. According to Laoban (G2), "It is not easy to come up with a hot item, and even if you are lucky enough to do so, there are many small workshops and factories out there, and they are going to quickly mass produce your hot item and saturate the market with their products."

Garment businesswoman Lau Fang (G21) said she tried her best to prevent adversaries from copying her products: "One thing that gives me the biggest headache in this business is genban (copying). This means that other people follow or copy my sample [or styles or goods] and then sell them at a lower price. That is why our manufacturing principles are first we make sure that our products are not easy to copy, and second, even if our products are copied, the production cost for the people who do the copying will be higher than for us."

Peter (G7) explained the challenges a business owner faces when competitors copy his products: "If one of the fake T-shirts I produce becomes a hot item, I need to have the capability to produce another batch quickly [before my competitors do]; otherwise, the initial success means nothing. To do so, I must have enough fabric for another cycle of manufacturing. I must stockpile a certain amount of fabric to prepare for this. If I do not, and try to look for fabric after my initial success, it will take about two weeks to get the materials. I do not have that amount of time under such circumstances."

Demand Volatility

According to my research subjects, demand volatility is one of their main concerns, and, regardless of what they do to reduce it, they are still vulnerable when it hits them. Xiao Yuen (G12) said: "I suffered a big loss a few years ago. I designed a collection of clothes and invited many distributors from all over China to come to Guangzhou for a private viewing. They all said my garments were excellent and would sell well. As a result, I asked a factory to manufacture a large amount of them. After the garments were delivered to the wholesalers, they found out the goods did not sell, and they returned them to me. Ultimately, I went out of business because I ended up with too many goods that I couldn't sell."

According to Laoban (G2), one of the reasons for demand volatility is that "every season, hot items come from different global brands, and it changes from season to season. They come and go quickly; nobody knows what will be hot tomorrow in this market." Jane (G1), who agreed with Laoban, stated: "Counterfeiting is an ever-changing business, especially regarding which brands we will copy. In the past, Dunhill apparel was heavily counterfeited. Now, that brand is over the hill, and garment counterfeiters have shifted to

Armani. Likewise, Rolex was the most counterfeited watch in the past; now, it is Piaget. As for handbags, it was Louis Vuitton, and now it is Gucci and, especially, Hermès."

Another reason for a dramatic change in demand can be attributed to the weather. Markets for apparel and fashion accessories are seasonal, and the length of a season depends on the weather. Laoban explained how important the weather is in determining the success or failure of a season: "Due to climate change, it is hard to predict the weather for the next season. Autumn and winter are short in China, and if it is hot during these two seasons, then jackets, sweaters, and down coats will not sell. Once these two short seasons are over, there will be no demand, and these garments will become inventory. That is why counterfeiters in Zhanxi Road do not actively copy autumn and winter wear. If the weather is relatively cool until early May, summer garments are not going to sell well. If counterfeiters do not make money in the summer season, they are most likely to lose money for that whole year because summer business is the key."

Production and Inventory Management

For business owners who do not have their own factories but must rely on contract manufacturers, there is also the question of how many contract manufacturers are needed at a given time. Some counterfeiters revealed that it is critical to maintain a working relationship with several contract manufacturers simultaneously. According to Peter (G7): "You need several contract manufacturers for production. You cannot rely on one factory because these factories are very small. If you have enough materials to produce a second or third round [of a popular item] but no factory to help you with the quick turnaround, it will be a problem. Quality is another big issue. If the goods they produce are very different from the original, nobody will buy them."

While it is crucial to be able to manufacture quickly after an initial batch of goods sells very well, business owners have to be careful to avoid overreacting and ending up with a huge inventory. For many, inventory size at the end of a season determines whether they make money. This is especially true since the overseas markets for leftover garments from China have disappeared. According to Xiao Yuen (G12):

> How much you make in a season depends on how much inventory you have in stock at the end of that season. During the season, your sales can be good, and it seems like you are making money, but if you have a large amount of inventory left over at the end of the season, you will find that you have not made that much money after all. In the past, it was not a problem because there were buyers for our

inventory. If our production cost was $2.50 per garment, these buyers would pay us at least $1.50. They would then export these garments overseas. When the Chinese yuan began to appreciate against other currencies, these overseas buyers began to decrease, and they were replaced by local buyers from Shijing in Guangzhou. Buyers from Shijing pay us only 50 to 80 cents per piece, and they do not export the garments. Instead, they dump the goods locally, which profoundly hurts the regional distributors.

What happened to a successful apparel business during the summer of 2018 is an excellent example of the mishandling of second or third purchase orders. According to Ah Lan (G18), a designer with that firm: "Last summer, my employers ended up with a large inventory of T-shirts and polo shirts. At the beginning of the season, their shirts were selling relatively well. However, when their clients [distributors] placed more orders near the end of the season, they could not produce the shirts promptly. When the shirts were made, their clients said they did not want them anymore because the opportunity to sell them had gone. That is why they had so much inventory last year."

Skyrocketing rent is another challenge for counterfeiters' ability to make a profit and remain in business. As mentioned earlier, the rent for commercial space in Guangzhou had risen dramatically over the past three decades; it began to stabilize or even decline after 2015, when the overall business climate in China began to deteriorate. Business owners have also had to deal with rising wages and labor shortages.

Conclusion

In this chapter, I examine the legal and compliance risks of counterfeiting and what businesspeople in the industry do to shield themselves from these risks. I also explore some of the business risks they encounter, and how counterfeiters are equally, if not more, concerned with business risks than with legal and compliance risks. Many firms in counterfeiting have gone out of business not because law enforcement authorities targeted them but because they were not able to overcome the many business risks.

Kellee Tsai, a political scientist, has written a book on the private sector in contemporary China; in it, she examines how private entrepreneurs in an undemocratic China get things done. According to Tsai (2007, 6): "Local economic and state actors have evaded, exploited, and appropriated formal institutions through a variety of informal adaptive strategies" because "formal institutions comprise a myriad of constraints and opportunities, which may motivate everyday actors to devise novel operating arrangements that are not officially sanctioned" (Tsai 2007, 19). Other authors have made similar observations, that "outside the formal regulations of every kind of system in Chinese society, and behind every clear statement, there are unwritten rules that are widely recognized" and that "these kind of unwritten rules determine the rhythms of everyday life" (Keane 2012, 220). Alibaba is one of the world's largest retailers and e-commerce companies. It owns Taobao, the number one online shopping platform in China, which has been accused of being responsible for the rapid expansion of the counterfeiting industry. Alibaba came up with the following conclusion after many years of attempting to curb counterfeiting on Taobao: "The aggressiveness of Chinese authorities in anti-counterfeiting not only did not eliminate the production of counterfeit goods, it actually led counterfeiters to become more diversified in their operations, more intuitive in developing various countermeasures and maintaining their secrecy" (Alibaba 2018, 16). There is a Chinese proverb: If the Buddha grows one foot taller, the demon grows ten. It means that unjust forces always outnumber just ones. This may also explain why, regardless of how hard Chinese authorities try to contain counterfeiting, the participants in this trade can come up with so many countermeasures to evade them.

8

CRACKDOWN

Many people assume that counterfeiting is rampant in China because of weak or nonexistent IPR enforcement (Chow 2000, 2003; Kerns 2016). From their point of view, if Beijing were serious about cracking down on counterfeiting and punishing offenders accordingly, counterfeiting would never have become so pervasive in China. After examining the existing explanations for why IPR enforcement is lax in China, Johannes Lejeune categorized them into three broad frameworks: "lack of political will to implement existing IPR laws (the political framework), lack of a tradition and a culture supportive of IPR (the cultural framework), and structural problems that hamper the implementation of IPR laws (the structural framework)" (Lejeune 2014, 699). As for the structural framework, it is mainly the fragmentation and decentralization of the Chinese political system that explains the persistence of widespread IPR violations despite elaborate legal measures:

> IPR-friendly interest network consists not only of foreign actors and Chinese owners of IPR but also, notably, of the central political level in China—what in the political framework might be referred to as the Chinese leadership. . . . However, although the IPR-friendly interest network is able to formulate policies and laws, it is much less able to control their implementation. This has to be done at the local level, where the second, IPR-adverse interest network is trying to defend the status quo. Quite naturally, those who engage in IPR violations are part of this second network. Crucially, not only can they profit

from other's achievements, but they also face a low risk of being severely sanctioned from the other members of the IPR-adverse interest network: local governments, party branches, administrative agencies and courts. . . . Cadres have few incentives to crack down on factories that produce counterfeits since this would only mean less tax revenues, fewer workplaces, and also fewer possibilities to receive illegal side-payments from those who seek protection. It is sometimes also argued that counterfeit goods keep prices low and thus increase popular satisfaction. (Lejeune 2014, 708)

Lejeune (2014, 710) concluded that "the structural framework provides the most convincing explanation for the discrepancy between the written law and legal practice with regard to IPR in China."

Martin Dimitrov, a political scientist and the author of *Piracy and the State: The Politics of Intellectual Property Rights in China* (2009), concurs with Lejeune, although he emphasizes the lack of coordination among various (local) agencies as the reason for the problem, not the disjunction between Beijing and the local authorities. Contrary to the allegation that the Chinese government is doing nothing about counterfeiting, Dimitrov (2009, 17) asserts that "no country in the world devotes as many resources to IPR enforcement as China does." The question is, Dimitrov (2009, 5) asks, "why, in spite of its high volume, is China's enforcement of IPR laws typically ineffective in resolving the problems of copyright piracy and trademark counterfeiting?" According to him, there is the question of the quality of law enforcement in addition to its volume: "To assess state capacity in a given area, we need to know what agencies are empowered to provide enforcement and how well they do it. This book insists that both the volume and quality of IPR enforcement are relevant for this assessment. It argues that under some conditions the Chinese state can provide high quality enforcement of IPR laws [patents]. Most of the time, nevertheless, there is a high volume of enforcement, which, however, is of a low quality [copyrights and trademarks]. This is characteristic of both campaign-style enforcement and most routine enforcement" (Dimitrov 2009, 5). Patent enforcement is high quality because it is consistent, transparent, and procedurally fair (Dimitrov 2009, 6). Dimitrov concludes (2009, 271): "The key finding is that the presence of multiple bureaucracies with poorly defined and overlapping jurisdictions is a serious obstacle to the emergence of rationalized enforcement. A secondary, related finding is that, although a high volume of IPR enforcement already exists in China, in general this enforcement is uncoordinated, duplicative, inefficient, and unaccountable."

Some observers suggest that IPR enforcement in China is often the result of foreign pressure, especially from the U.S. government, certain European nations, and some of the primary rights holders from the U.S. and Europe (Alford 1995; Chow 2010, 2011, 2022; Young 2016). According to a report by the office of the USTR (2021, 12):

> On January 15, 2020, the United States and China signed a historic and enforceable agreement on a Phase One trade deal that requires structural reforms and other changes to China's economic and trade regime in the areas of intellectual property, technology transfer, agriculture, financial services, and currency and foreign exchange. The IP chapter addresses numerous longstanding concerns, including in the area of enforcement against pirated and counterfeit goods. For example, the IP chapter obligates China to significantly increase the number of enforcement actions against pirated and counterfeit goods at physical markets in China. In addition, it requires China to provide effective and expeditious action against infringement in the online environment, including by requiring expeditious takedowns and by ensuring the validity of notices and counter notices and also requires China to take effective action against e-commerce platforms that fail to take necessary measures against IP infringement.

Andrew Mertha, in his book *The Politics of Piracy: Intellectual Property in Contemporary China* (2005, 3), examines this question: "What has been the impact of external pressure on China's policymaking and implementation processes?" He concludes that there are two types of external pressure, top down and lateral, and each type has a very different impact (Mertha 2005, 230):

> Exogenous pressure can indeed have an effect on the formulation, implementation, and enforcement of policy. The analysis has also shown that the nature and the "location" of that pressure also matters. Top-down pressure in the form of confrontational negotiations with the USTR may have an immediate impact on the formal legislation that frames China's formal IPR regime—but such pressure has been less effective in promoting and facilitating effective and sustained enforcement. Likewise, lateral pressure between foreign actors and local Chinese enforcement agencies may have little, if any, impact on the national legislation of IPR laws and regulations, but it has proven to be absolutely crucial in establishing effective enforcement.

On the other hand, legal scholar Danny Chow argues that local protectionism is the main reason IPR enforcement is weak and ineffective in China. His argument is similar to Lejeune's structural framework explanation. In Chow's opinion, "Local protectionism in China is widespread and poses probably the single most significant problem in enforcement against counterfeiting. The trade in counterfeit goods has now become a vital portion of some local economies, providing employment for otherwise unemployable workers and generating significant revenue for the local economy" (2000, 26–27). Chow suggests that local governments play an important role in the promotion of the counterfeiting trade "by helping to create the distribution channels that serve the vital role of delivering goods to retail markets and consumers" (2000, 4). According to Chow (2000, 28), the AIC, the key agency in IPR enforcement, was complicit in almost all aspects of the distribution phase of the counterfeiting trade:

> In a typical case, the AIC will invest in the construction of buildings, in the refurbishment or construction of outlet stores, booths, stalls, and warehouse space and will charge rent and management fees to private businesses for the use of these facilities. The AIC will then charge management fees in the range of up to 1,000 renminbi (RMB), or $120, for each vendor in a wholesale market. . . . The AIC is empowered also to issue business licenses for all that seek to do business in these wholesale centers and operating a business without a license is illegal under PRC law. Moreover, . . . the AIC is responsible for enforcement against counterfeiting based upon its jurisdiction over trademarks. Overall, the AIC has assumed the roles of investor, manager, regulator, and law enforcer for these markets.

Besides providing a legitimized platform for the distribution of fake goods, local protectionism also hampers law enforcement efforts in various ways. Chow (2000, 30) notes: "Local protectionism can effectively undermine enforcement efforts. For example, in some cases after a complaint is filed, the local AICs and TSBs [SQTSB] may delay enforcement actions for several hours, until the next day, or even for several days. . . . By the time law enforcement officials finally arrive at the suspect premises hours or even days later, the counterfeiter, offending goods, machinery, and equipment have all disappeared. In addition, some local officials have been known to confiscate goods, machinery, and equipment only to return these materials to counterfeiters once enforcement actions have been concluded. Moreover, since local enforcement officials have broad discretion in determining the amount of fines and penalties and are not constrained by any mandatory minimum limits, local enforcement agencies are able to impose low penalties that fail to deter the counterfeiter."

At the time of Chow's writing, in 2000, due to local protectionism, counterfeiting cases were "rarely transformed from administrative authorities to police and prosecutors for criminal prosecution" (33). In a 2010 article, Chow concludes: "In most cases, the current approach—raids and seizures that result in a slap on the wrist—merely disrupts the counterfeiter's operations temporarily but does not shut down the operations permanently. The disruption only incites and provokes counterfeiters to get back into business with a vengeance and to increase production; counterfeiters are angry that their business has been disrupted and react with a furious frenzy of counterfeiting" (765–766). Chow summed up his research on the impact of local protectionism on IPR enforcement: "Enforcement authorities do not wish to shut down counterfeiting because it will seriously damage the local economy. Local government officials, who control the enforcement authorities, often have direct or indirect interests in sustaining the counterfeiting trade. As a result, enforcement authorities will bring actions, but there are few consequences for counterfeiters: finesse are [sic] very low and compensatory damages are negligible. Criminal prosecutions are rare and actual imprisonment even more rare" (759).

Like Chow, Dimitrov (2009, 34) suggests that "under decentralization, the interests of local authorities are aligned with those of the local state, which, far from perceiving fake[s] as a problem, often derives sizable financial benefits from condoning business that engage[s] in the production and sale of pirated and counterfeit goods." Vincent Wenxiong Yao, a business school professor, has examined many nonmarket factors attributable to the widespread sale of counterfeit goods in China, and one of the factors he mentions is regionalism: "The counterfeiting manufacturer is often an important source of revenue for a certain locality, thus the local governments naturally become the umbrella or shield of the infringing enterprises" (2006, 122). Tricia Brauer, a legal scholar, has also concluded that "not only have Chinese courts failed to enforce judgements against infringers, penalties and damages assessed against infringers by Chinese courts have been so low that they fail to act as a deterrent for infringers" (2012, 279).

In this chapter, I examine the history of anti-counterfeiting campaigns in China, the official agencies responsible for anti-counterfeiting enforcement, the role of private investigating firms in anti-counterfeiting activities, the measures adopted by the Chinese authorities to suppress IPR infringement, and the role of corruption in the war against counterfeiting.

Anti-counterfeiting Campaigns in China

According to Mr. Tang, a police officer with the Economic Crime Unit, "We do not arrest people for buying fake goods, only those who produce or sell these goods. A buyer is not guilty, regardless of whether the person is a retailer or a wholesaler (sourcing goods for resale) or a consumer." Thus, the Chinese authorities focus on only the supply side of counterfeiting.

My research subjects recalled that anti-counterfeiting measures emerged not long after China acceded to the WTO, in 2001, and picked up steam before the Beijing Olympics, in 2008. According to clothing manufacturer and distributor Lin Jun (G17), who, at one point, was a store owner at Kinbo Market: "Starting in 2003, the government began to investigate counterfeiting more stringently. As a result, management at Kinbo began to inform us in advance if and when the authorities were coming. In response, we removed certain goods from the shelves or out of the store." Jane (G1), a fashion entrepreneur from Taiwan, said: "When China joined the WTO in 2001, nationwide anti-counterfeiting measures were initiated for the first time. Anti-counterfeiting took off in 2009–2010. However, before the Beijing Olympics, the Chinese government conducted many crackdowns in Beijing and Shanghai for a short period."

When Wang Yang was the party secretary of Guangdong Province (2007–2012), he was active in implementing anti-counterfeiting measures. He was credited for a campaign called sanda liangjian (three strikes and two establishments, meaning to strike hard on commercial fraud and monopolies, counterfeiting, and bribery; and to establish social trust and a market control system) to transform Guangdong into a happy and prosperous province (Irwin and Willis 2013). A lawyer shared his experience in helping a couple who were engaged in infringing activities when Wang Yang was in charge of Guangdong:

> A couple asked me to help them after they were arrested for the first time for manufacturing infringing handbag hardware. They were shocked because they thought that many people were doing what they were doing and yet they were the only ones being targeted by the authorities. I understood why they were arrested; it was because their business was much bigger than others. When the couple contacted me, their case had already been brought before the court and there was not much I could do. Eventually, the husband was sentenced to one and a half years in prison. The wife was not prosecuted. She was released because she needed to care for the couple's children. After the husband came out of prison, he was arrested again for the same type of offense. This time, he did not have to go to prison because he bribed someone when the case was still being investigated by the police. The police reduced their estimate of the amount of the seized goods so that the crime would be considered a minor one. It was possible to do so because by this time Wang Yang had

been promoted and had moved to Beijing. Without Wang, cracking down on counterfeiting was not a priority anymore.

Xiao Yuen (G12), a garment business owner, agreed with the lawyer. According to him: "It is true that after Wang Yang stepped down from the post of party secretary of Guangdong and moved to Beijing, anti-counterfeiting campaigns in the province slowed down."

After Xi Jinping assumed power in 2012, counterfeit goods vendors became much more discreet in conducting business. During my trip to China in 2012, I observed that, from the Louhu Market in Shenzhen in the south to the Wu Ai Market in Shenyang in the north, shop owners stopped displaying brand-name copies and were reluctant to admit to first-time customers that they were selling counterfeit goods. They all said the Chinese authorities were becoming more aggressive in cracking down on the counterfeit trade. As China's economy continued to grow and became the world's second-largest economy after the United States in 2010, Beijing concluded that China had no choice but to establish its own brands if the country wanted to compete with advanced countries.

Official Anti-counterfeiting Agencies

In this section, I examine some of the Chinese government agencies responsible for curbing the production and distribution of counterfeit goods.

State Administration for Industry and Commerce (SAIC)

The SAIC[1] was the key government agency in the war against counterfeiting in China before it was replaced by the State Administration for Market Regulation (SAMR) in 2018. SAIC was established in 1952 under the State Council, the chief administrative authority, chaired by the premier. In Mertha's book *The Politics of Piracy* (2005, 175–176), he explains the many duties of SAIC as follows:

The SAIC's responsibilities include supervising the growing local market economies and ensuring that pricing and other related behaviors remain legal and above board; managing all administrative aspects of enterprise and business registration; supervising contracts and mediating contract disputes; registering and protecting trademarks; managing advertising; supervising individual/self-employed economic undertakings (*getihu*); striking out against speculation;

and inspecting groups, units, enterprises, undertaking units (*shiye danwei*) to ensure production by legitimate means.

According to Mertha (2005, 187), SAIC was inefficient in curbing counterfeiting in China because it "is both enormous in scope and fragmented in nature, providing the worst of both worlds to a unit charged with anti-counterfeit enforcement." An official of SAIC in Guangzhou, who was interviewed right before her organization was restructured, admitted that the SAIC's power was limited in the enforcement of anti-counterfeiting measures. Moreover, its poor relationship with Ministry of Public Security and the dramatic increase in e-commerce activities posed a major challenge to it. She also expressed her frustration in dealing with the businesses in Baiyun Leather City and why:

> We could only seize the counterfeit goods or fine the counterfeiters; we could not arrest or detain them or bring them to court. Only the Public Security's Economic Crime Unit could do that. We did not have a good relationship with Public Aecurity, and the development of e-commerce made our job a lot more difficult because we could not do anything about business transactions involving foreign buyers or people from outside of Guangzhou. Many stores in Baiyun do not affix name-brand trademarks to their products, so there was nothing we could do.

State Quality Technical Supervision Bureau (SQTSB)

Besides the SAIC, the most important state agency in anti-counterfeiting enforcement in China was the SQTSB, which was primarily responsible for maintaining product quality and overall standardization. According to Mertha (2005), the emergence of SQTSB was why trademark enforcement in China improved from the late 1990s to the early 2000s. The SAIC patrolled the markets, and the SQTSB inspected the factories and warehouses. SQTSB was later renamed the General Administration of Quality Supervision, Inspection, and Quarantine (AQSIQ).

Economic Crime Investigation Bureau, Ministry of Public Security (MPS)

The MPS is a nationwide police force that oversees more than 1.9 million of China's law enforcement officers. Within the ministry are twenty-three bureaus, including the bureaus of Domestic Security Protection, Public Security Management, Criminal Crimes Investigation, Border Entry and Exit Affairs, Jails Management, Foreign Affairs, Anti-Narcotics, Smuggling Crime Investigation, and Economic Crime Investigation. The Economic Crime Investigation Bureau was originally under the AIC (Mertha 2005).

The economic crime officer Tang explained how his unit differed from the AIC regarding IPR enforcement:

> Generally, those government authorities who show up at the distribution outlets are mostly from the AIC. We only get involved if a case is a crime, meaning it involves a large amount, or a high value, of counterfeit goods. Usually, you will not find a large amount of goods in a store or a factory, unless a store is about to make a big delivery or a factory has just finished producing a large batch of goods. That is why counterfeiters are very careful in protecting their warehouses, where you are more likely to find a large amount of counterfeits.

Officer Tang also revealed why his unit was not very active in investigating counterfeiting: "One of the reasons we are very passive in the fight against counterfeiting is that we do not have the authority to decide whether a product is genuine or fake. We do not have any say in this matter. How can we know if a branded item is fake? We must rely on an expert from that brand to come and decide. Many experts work for private anti-counterfeiting firms hired by designer brands." He admitted that, although his unit is one of the two government agencies (along with AIC) tasked with combating counterfeiting, this particular crime is not his department's priority: "The manufacturing and distribution of counterfeits is not our department's main concern. Our number one priority is financial crimes involving the public, that is economic crimes that pose a great risk to the general public, including telecommunication fraud, illegal loans, Ponzi schemes, and illegal investment schemes."

Mertha (2005, 187) also pointed out in his book that, for the Chinese police forces, anti-counterfeiting work was not as "attractive" as other types of police work:

> Apart from the difficulty and the potential physical danger of challenging government- or military-sponsored "local protectionism" and the near impossibility of cauterizing a distribution network for counterfeit goods for any reasonable period of time, the attractiveness of trademark enforcement and the laurels bestowed upon successful enforcers traditionally tended to be less prized than those associated with cracking down on "gray market" goods or ambitious enforcement actions that could become a "big and important case"

(*zhongda anjian*). Anti-counterfeiting enforcement tended to be piecemeal and labor-intensive—requiring almost constant follow-up, which as one veteran investigator noted is particularly neglected in China—and often does not carry the cachet of enforcement actions directed at other economic or commercial criminal activities.

State Administration for Market Regulation (SAMR)

Among those who study counterfeiting in China, the lack of cooperation among various government agencies is often mentioned as one of the reasons for the ineffectiveness of anti-counterfeiting enforcement (Chow 2022; Mertha 2005). Mr. Bo, a Guangzhou city government official, made the following remarks about this problem: "The State Quality Technical Supervision Bureau is responsible for the investigation of factories that are engaged in counterfeiting. This bureau used to belong to the SAIC. The SAIC is in charge of investigating distribution. If a particular case is serious or the counterfeiter under investigation resists violently, Public Security might also get involved. Coordination among these three units is not ideal. We are also now examining how we can put the three units together as one." Not long after the interview with that official in 2018, the State Administration for Market Regulation (SAMR) was formed to consolidate in one ministry the market regulation functions previously shared by three separate ministries, the General Administration of Quality Supervision, Inspection and Quarantine (AQSIQ), the China Food and Drug Administration (CFDA), and the SAIC. According to one source (K. Wang 2018), "With the change, the Chinese leadership has tapped the SAMR as the single most powerful market regulator to address the public's ever-mounting concerns, including drug and food safety, protection of IP and product quality issues in general. As such, the SAMR will have a broad mandate, overseeing everything from drug safety supervision, quality inspection, fair competition and commercial bribery, issuance of business registrations, certifications and accreditations, management of IPR and comprehensive supervision and management of the market order." There is little information on how this consolidation is working.

Private Anti-counterfeiting Agencies

Besides the various government institutions mentioned earlier, international and local private anti-counterfeiting agencies also play a crucial role in the fight against IPR violations in China (Chow 2010, 2022; Mertha 2005). According to Moises Naim, the author of *Illicit: How Smugglers, Traffickers, and Copycats Are Hijacking the Global Economy*, "Security consultants like

Kroll and Pinkerton, along with local subcontractors in targeted countries, do a brisk business in intellectual property protection. At the very least, the fight against counterfeits has spawned its own thriving industry" (Naim 2005, 129). My research subjects claimed that Chinese authorities are not proactive when investigating counterfeiting, especially when the items being counterfeited do not pose a risk to public health or security. They believed that Chinese officials act only if someone reports to them in-progress counterfeiting activity or if they are asked by international brand owners to conduct an investigation because they have evidence to show that their products have been counterfeited. Since it is unlikely for designer brands to collect information on the ground in China themselves, they have to rely on international and local private agencies to conduct the initial inquiry and then ask Chinese law enforcement authorities to act and dismantle the counterfeiting operations. According to the legal scholar Chow (2010, 763): "Tracking down counterfeiters involves weeks or months of investigative work and often requires the use of operatives who assume false identities to gain the trust of counterfeiters and infiltrate counterfeiting rings. PRC enforcement authorities do not have the resources to conduct these investigations, and as a result, a large number of investigation companies have been established to complete this work."

In his article on the anti-counterfeiting strategies of MNCs, Chow (2010, 760–761) explains how MNCs attack the counterfeiting problem in China:

Many MNCs have established their own dedicated brand protection units that specialize in the enforcement of intellectual property rights. MNCs that have set up internal brand protection units usually establish the unit under the corporate security department and not the legal department because anti-counterfeiting is viewed as a type of investigative and enforcement activity that is similar to police work. . . . MNCs use their brand protection units, sometimes with the help of private investigation companies, to support PRC government enforcement entities in locating and identifying the counterfeiter. Armed with the appropriate intelligence, the MNC's representatives (accompanied by private investigators or outside lawyers) go directly to the PRC authorities and ask for a raid. . . . The MNC's representatives are usually allowed to accompany PRC authorities. The MNC's representatives sit in the vans or trucks used by the enforcement authorities and give directions to the counterfeiter's location (the location is not revealed until the raid is in motion to avoid tip offs). Representatives of the MNC are usually present at the raid to identify the counterfeit products for PRC officials.

The essence of the working relationship between the MNCs and the Chinese authorities, as observed by Mertha (2005, 166), is that "the former lay the groundwork and absorb the costs, the latter provide the official authority (i.e., legitimacy and legality) and take the credit."

According to Mertha (2005), the private investigative agencies can be categorized into three types: (1) law firms, like Rouse and Co.; (2) Chinese-owned IRP investigation firms, such as Eastern Consultants Limited (ECL) and China United Intellectual Property Protection Center (CUIPPC); and (3) foreign-owned "consulting" firms specializing in IRP enforcement, such as Factfinders, Kroll Associates, Pinkerton, Hill and Associates, and Markvess. Mertha (2005, 198) remarked, "These firms have no legal authority but rather assist (and aggressively recruit) clients by identifying counterfeits in the marketplace, gathering evidence, and working together with the relevant law enforcement agencies to undertake law enforcement actions on behalf of their clients."

Some private investigation firms in Guangzhou provide anti-counterfeiting services to global brands. Mr. Fu, a private investigator, explained how his company works with nationwide firms in Beijing or Shanghai:

> Our work can be categorized into two types. The first type is work outsourced to us by large China-based investigation firms hired by international brands. The second type is the work we initiate. For the second type of work, after we collect the intelligence, we contact name brands to see whether they are interested in buying it. Generally, these brands are interested in what we have to provide and are willing to pay from $3,000 to $30,000 for the information. Of course, when they pay us for intelligence, they use local wage standards, not the wage standards of their own country, and that is why we are paid very little. These deals are made between us and their representative agencies in China.

Mr. Fu went on to describe how his colleagues investigated counterfeiting activities by working in the factories suspected of producing counterfeit goods:

> After we decide to conduct an investigation, we send our young Hunanese or Hubeinese colleagues to the urban villages to collect evidence. I am not able to do this because once the people in these urban villages see me (I'm from Enping, Guangdong), they will know I am not one of them. This will immediately raise the alarm. Our Hunanese and Hubeinese colleagues can pose as migrant workers looking for work and find a way to get into these factories because

many of the factory workers are from Hunan or Hubei provinces. Once they are hired, they try to understand the modus operandi of these establishments, take pictures, and, if they can, steal some manufacturing materials or finished products. This way, we will have concrete evidence that a particular factory is engaged in counterfeiting. After we have collected the evidence, we can ask the SQTSB to go to the factory to arrest the people involved and shut it down. Typically, we contact the AIC only if the suspects are engaged in sales. AIC is not concerned with manufacturing. International brands pay less attention to distribution; they are more concerned with factories.

However, as counterfeiters began to change their modus operandi to evade law enforcement authorities, private investigators also shifted their targets—from factories to warehouses. Mr. Fu remarked:

Nowadays, many factories are only willing to produce generic handbags. They will not affix any logos or trademarks of name brands. This way, even if the authorities raid their businesses, they cannot be charged with infringement of intellectual property. That is why now our attention has shifted to warehouses—that is the place where counterfeiters keep their branded handbags. Many warehouses are located in Huadu District, not Baiyun District. There is also the possibility that handbags in the warehouses in Huadu have no trademarks. After customers place their orders, the handbags are moved from Huadu to a workshop near the stores, and logos and trademarks will be affixed there. Once they are affixed, the branded fake handbags are delivered to customers promptly. This way, their risk of being detected for counterfeiting is minimized.

Besides factories and warehouses, private investigators may also look for traces of counterfeiting in Guangzhou's wholesale markets, including famous markets such as Kinbo (apparel) or Baiyun (leather handbags). Clothing merchant Zheng Hua (G19), who suffered a big loss after his warehouse was raided, recalled how his workers came to the attention of private investigators:

One day in March of this year [2019], we delivered goods to our two stores at Kinbo, and investigators from a private detective agency spotted our car. We did not drop our merchandise in front of Kinbo. We delivered the goods to a place near Kinbo. Regardless, they and the authorities tracked us down to our warehouse and arrested my younger brother and my business partner's brother-in-law. They found more than 40,000 garments with different branded names such as Fila, Gucci, and Prada.

Not all private investigation companies operate professionally. In the words of Chow (2010, 764), "In China, observers refer to the uncertain status of the private investigation industry as falling in a 'gray' area, a euphemism describing an industry that is unregulated, unlicensed, and in which abuses, such as giving bribes to government officials and extorting money from counterfeiters, are commonplace." Leather handbag businessman Sonny (H10) recalled how a counterfeiter was victimized by employees of a private investigation firm:

Anti-counterfeiting operations conducted by private agencies are very sinister. I have a friend who is also in the counterfeiting business. When he was looking for workers, his business was infiltrated by two men from a private investigation company. After working for a few weeks, the two walked into my friend's office and immediately sat down without being asked. They shouted: "We have collected all the evidence, and at this moment, our people are outside, ready to storm in at any time to make arrests. You have the opportunity to solve this crisis. Just give us a sum of money, and we will be gone. Otherwise, you are not going to get away."

Guangzhou city government official Mr. Bo explained why there was a dramatic decrease in the number of private investigating firms in Guangzhou. He also stressed that some trustworthy private detective agencies still provide quality anti-counterfeiting services to rights holders via their representatives in China:

There were many private investigation firms in Guangzhou, but they did not specialize in intellectual property investigation. They also conducted marriage investigations, like following a husband to see whether he was having an affair. Some of these firms came to the public's attention after they were accused of violating people's privacy. As a result, many firms were forced to shut down [in 2013]. A few are still in operation, but they keep a low profile. Foreign brand owners are not going to deal with these local private firms directly. However, the big companies they hire to represent them in China might enter into a contract with local private investigation firms, asking them to investigate the factories and stores that are involved in counterfeiting. After all, some private investigation firms have established a good reputation, and the big companies are willing to ask these small but reputable firms for help.

According to Mr. Song, a private detective, the relationship between private investigation firms and the Chinese authorities has improved significantly over the past several years because the latter is under pressure from higher-ups for an enhanced crackdown on counterfeiting. He said: "When we reported a counterfeiting activity to Public Security in the past, they might or might not pay any attention. Now it is a different story. If we report to them, they will respond because they are under pressure to process a certain number of counterfeiting cases yearly. It is like they are begging us to file a complaint."

Anti-counterfeiting Measures

In this section, I examine some Chinese authorities' anti-counterfeiting measures and the punishments for counterfeiting, including propaganda campaigns, patrols, investigations, forfeitures, fines, detentions and arrests, and imprisonment.

Propaganda Campaigns

Whenever there is a severe social problem, Chinese authorities are accustomed to using propaganda to communicate to the public that the central government recognizes the problem and is doing something about it (Oi 1989). Propaganda is also utilized to urge the general public to join the government in the "people's war" against a specific problem (see Figure 8.1). Regardless of the effectiveness of propaganda in the fight against complicated social problems in a rapidly changing Chinese society, there has been excessive use of propaganda in the many "people's wars" against social evils, including drug use (K. Chin and Zhang 2015; C. Ting 2004; S. Zhang and Chin 2018), irregular immigration (K. Chin 1999; S. Zhang 2008), prostitution (Ling 2018; M. Liu 2011), and organized crime (K. Chin and Godson 2006; Irwin and Willis 2013; P. Wang 2017).

One of the most popular propaganda campaign tactics is to saturate a "hot spot" with many eye-catching red banners and colorful posters. During the early 1990s, when illegal immigration from Fujian Province to the United States was rampant, local authorities in the sending communities put up red banners at village entrances and other public places to discourage people from immigrating unlawfully. Among the slogans in Chinese were: "Attack the snakeheads [human smugglers], destroy the snake pits, punish the illegal immigrants"; "Anyone participating in illegal immigration must be stringently punished according to law"; and "Be aware of the risks of unlawful immigration" (K. Chin 1999, 134). Although signs and banners denouncing illegal immigration are prominently displayed on the walls of major thoroughfares in the sending communities near Fuzhou City, it is doubtful that their

Figure 8.1 An anti-counterfeiting billboard at the entrance of a leather goods market.

messages have been widely heeded; like other political slogans of the past, they may be viewed as routine government propaganda.

Several years ago, I conducted a study with Sheldon Zhang on drug trafficking, its use and control in China. In a book we coauthored (K. Chin and Zhang 2015, 233), we stated that:

> Much in line with political tradition of the Communist Party, propaganda campaigns are regularly launched in China as the main venue to indoctrinate and mobilize the masses to combat illicit drugs. The government has always portrayed its fight against illicit drugs as a people's war, stirring up public sentiment and enlisting participation from the masses. . . . The Chinese government launches these campaigns on national scales, particularly around June 26 each year, the International Day against Drug Abuse and Illicit Trafficking, to showcase the government's resolve to combat this growing social problem. On these occasions, mass events are held across the country, featuring visits by high-level government officials to drug treatment facilities and drug enforcement police units, public display and destruction of seized drugs, public gatherings, a media blitz of major drug raids, presentations by former addicts, and public trials of drug traffickers.

When I visited the markets in Guangzhou, I noticed the spectacular anti-counterfeiting red banners hanging across the markets' main entrances. A giant red banner prominently displayed above the main entrance of Huimei (an apparel market in Zhanxi Road) declared: "Strike hard on the illegal acts of exporting fake/shoddy and IP-infringed products to Africa." Like all other propaganda campaign materials, the banner was in Chinese, so it was obvious that the intended audience was local people and not foreign buyers. It was baffling because it specifically mentioned Africa as the destination for the counterfeit goods. It is not clear why the banner in Huimei focused on Africa, especially since that market was not one of the more popular destinations for buyers from Africa.

There are also a large number of small red acrylic banners hanging beneath the ceiling in the hallways of Kindo Market. In this market, many stores sell fake sunglasses, clothing, shoes, and other fashion accessories. There were banners every few feet, and they repeated the same messages in Chinese. The messages were:

"Strictly forbid the distribution of fake/shoddy products."
"Strike down hard on fake/shoddy products."
"Protect the lawful rights of consumers."
"Be a trustworthy business entity."
"Strengthen our legal concepts."

Inside the markets along Zhanxi Road, especially near the elevators and restrooms, there were notices posted by the buildings' management urging the public to be aware of counterfeiting and explaining what they do to alleviate the problem. A notice in Chinese was posted near an elevator in Kinme, a market adjacent to Kindo and a popular shopping destination for African buyers. The following is my translation of the notice:

NOTICE REGARDING HOW TO
CONDUCT A LAWFUL BUSINESS

Respectable Business Owners:
In order to create a good business atmosphere, vendors in this market must obey the national laws, display their business certificates, and conduct their businesses legally.

1. You are not allowed to operate a business without a certificate, or to distribute or stockpile shoddy goods, counterfeit products, or other merchandise that infringes intellectual property rights.

2. Our management office has the right to confiscate or destroy on the spot fake and/or shoddy goods belonging to a vendor and to order the vendor to cease operating until the business is reorganized.

3. If a vendor does not pay attention to repeated warnings from the management office and continues to engage in counterfeiting or dealing in shoddy goods, the management team will, as per the lease, evict the vendor.

4. If a vendor is engaged in illegal activities and is being reported to the authorities and investigated, the vendor should not flee, deny involvement, or put the blame on others, but should actively cooperate with relevant government agencies and the management office. The vendor should also assume all responsibility.

Kinme (Foreign Trade) Apparel City

When I stepped into the elevator, I saw an eye-catching anti-counterfeiting poster affixed to the elevator's mirror. There were four female cartoon characters (each one in the form of a package) with similar names, all pronounced mingpai but written with different Chinese characters. One of the names means "Name Brand"; the others can be translated as Magic Brand, Inscribed Brand, and Drunken Brand. In the poster, Name Brand yells at the other three: "You all are infringers!" After leaving Kinme, I walked over to an adjacent market, Kinbo, and saw the same just presented Notice Regarding How to Conduct a Lawful Business, except that instead of Kinme, the signature was that of Kinbo (Foreign Trade) Apparel City.

Even though Baiyun Leather City is the best-known market for fake designer leather goods, there are not many anti-counterfeiting banners or notices on display inside or outside the market. Most of the notices on the walls are related to the risk of interacting with solicitors, warning customers not to be victimized by them. For example, an aluminum-framed notice board (in Chinese and English) read:

IMPORTANT NOTICE

Dear Customers,

Please pay more attention to the following events:

Recently there are many people who don't work in The Center come here to send business cards to the passerby. Usually standing in the lobby, near the entrance or on the overpass they sell products in a low price to reach the purpose of fraud. We have received many reports of customers being deceived. So we here to remind you not to get business cards and buy products from these people. Please call the police at 110 or 86565410 once you detect the fraud.

The Chinese version of the notice was on top of the English version. It said the notice was issued by Guangzhou Baiyun World Leather Goods Trading Center on November 4, 2011. There was another notice a few steps away from the first; this one was more to the point and in English only:

WARNING NOTICE

Dear customers,
Be careful about the soliciting guy's misguiding for the fake and inferior goods outside the shopping mall.
It had come up many cases like extortion, blackmail, robbery, etc. illegal and criminal behavior.
Alarm Call: 110

As discussed in Chapter 4, the Guoda footwear market was once a hot spot for the trading of counterfeit shoes. The authorities conducted a series of crackdowns when the market became well known as a distribution hub for fake shoes. The market is still in operation, but the merchants keep a low profile. To convince the public that the authorities are keeping a tight grip on business activities in the market, they ask every store owner to post a "No Fakes Pledge" (in Chinese) on the store window. The following is my translation of the pledge:

A PLEDGE NOT TO SELL FAKE/SHODDY AND IP-INFRINGING PRODUCTS

To establish a trustworthy social system and a comprehensive market regulation system, to protect the legal rights of customers, and to crack down on the production and distribution of fake and IP-infringing goods, and based on Contract Law, Trademark Law, Customers' Rights Protection Law, Product Quality Law, and Guangdong Provincial Law on the Investigation of the Manufacturing and Distribution of Fake/Shoddy Products, this store has signed a pledge with the management of this market. This store solemnly pledges to:

1. Abide by the laws and regulations of the Government. It is registered, civilized, operates its business in good faith, and actively participates in Government or market management sponsored public awareness and education activities.
2. Actively cooperate with investigations by the Government and law enforcement units.

3. Ensure that the products it sells meet the Government's quality requirements.
4. Refrain from selling fake and/or shoddy products and trademark-infringing merchandise.
5. Remove IP-infringing goods from the store's shelves, cooperate with Government units in their investigations, and voluntarily seal up and destroy IP-infringing goods.
6. Earnestly implement a system for quality inspections, business registrations, documenting transactions, and proper accounting.
7. Voluntarily accept monitoring and inspection by law enforcement units and market management. If there is any violation of this pledge, the store will voluntarily accept the outcome of the investigation by law enforcement units and the decisions made by market management, as stipulated in the lease.

There are two copies of this pledge, one for market management and one for the store owners. The pledge becomes effective after the two parties sign it.

Guangzhou City
Guoda Shoe City Management (Seal)   Store Owner: (Signature)

_____

Patrols

In the war against counterfeiting, constant and high-profile patrolling of markets where counterfeit goods are traded is another way for the Chinese government to let their people (and the world) know that it is not ignoring the problem. However, like the propaganda campaigns discussed earlier, the policing of markets is superficial and often merely symbolic.

Some markets in Guangzhou are heavily patrolled by teams of from four to eight people. The teams are often made up of guards who work for the building management; however, authorities from the AIC, Public Security, and the State Taxation Administration participate in some patrols.

Whenever I visited Baiyun Leather City, I saw a team of uniformed security guards wearing armbands patrolling the corridors (see Figure 8.2). Vendors and customers ignored them. The security guards rarely stopped to say or do anything, as if they were merely on their daily rounds. However, if anyone soliciting business sees these guards, he or she will walk away. If the solicitor does not, there is a good chance the guards will ask the person to leave the building. The guards may ask store employees to remove goods or stools blocking passageways.

Figure 8.2 A regular patrol in Baiyun Leather City.

Investigations

Chinese authorities occasionally conduct proactive investigations. One way for an investigator to build a case against a counterfeiter is to engage in several small legal transactions with the suspect in order to gain his or her trust. After that, the investigator will ask the target to produce a large amount of high-price IP-infringing commodities. Garment businesswoman Wendy (G4) shared this story with me:

> I know a person who is involved in the production of embroideries. One day, a buyer asked my friend to produce 2,000 pieces of [non-infringing] embroideries for 15 cents per piece. My friend did as he asked, and the man returned later to ask for another [non-infringing] 2,000 pieces, also at 15 cents per piece. After my friend completed the second order, that man returned and asked my friend to produce 5,000 pieces of Nike embroidery for 75 cents per piece. After my friend produced the items and notified the man to pick up the merchandise, the police arrested my friend.

More often than not, Chinese authorities will act against counterfeiting only after they are pressured to do so (Alford 1995). This is especially true when the pressure comes from a well-established law firm or an investigation agency in China or Hong Kong that is representing a foreign fashion house (Mertha 2005). In an article on how MNCs attack the counterfeiting problem in China, Danny Chow (2010, 765) observed, "Some MNCs directly hire law firms and the law firms then hire private investigation companies. Other law firms have established their own private investigation companies that function essentially as a department of the law firm."

According to Mr. Wang, a prosecutor who has handled many counterfeiting cases in Zengcheng, a district of Guangzhou known as the capital of blue jeans, "Of all the IP-infringing cases that we prosecuted, more than 50 percent were launched because local investigators working for foreign companies approached us. Foreign companies hire law firms in Beijing or Hong Kong who recruit local investigators in Guangzhou to go around and look for counterfeit goods. After they find out who is doing what, they contact us, and we react."

Mr. Tang, an officer with the Economic Crime Unit of Public Security in Guangzhou, echoed the prosecutor Wang:

> Our anti-counterfeiting efforts are reactive because we act only when someone reports suspicious activity to us. Most reports by ordinary people are not valid reports because they can only say that [name-brand] copies are either sold or produced somewhere. This kind of information is not very useful to us because it means we have to collect more information. Valid reports are mostly prepared by private investigators. Before they submit their reports, they have already collected abundant information and know a lot of stuff. This makes our work much easier. These private investigators are a mixed

bag, hired by China-based law firms or investigation firms. These well-established firms do not want to do the work themselves, so they find local, small investigation firms to do the dirty work.

In brief, the international fashion houses, the Hong Kong– or China-based law firms, the well-established Beijing- or Shanghai-based investigation agencies, and the Chinese Public Security Bureau are not interested in doing the dirty work. They all rely on private investigation agencies in Guangzhou to collect the evidence in the field. According to Chow, this is a short-term approach that emphasizes enforcement: raids of counterfeiters, seizures of products, and destruction of machinery and equipment, and it is not working because it ignores the role of local protectionism in supporting the trade in counterfeit goods. Chow (2010, 749) concludes: "In China today, there is plenty of enforcement but little or no deterrence."

The prosecutor Wang also provided a candid answer as to why his office was not very forceful in going after IP infringers:

> We are not very aggressive in going after counterfeiters because counterfeiting is a business that does not harm the vital interests of luxury brands. It may somewhat hurt the reputation of a genuine brand, but those who are buying the genuine and the fake products are two different groups of consumers; they do not overlap. The fake product buyers are not buying the genuine products, and the genuine product buyers are not buying the fake products.

The prosecutor further revealed the intricate relationship between street-level local authorities and infringers and explained how powerful enforcement institutions need to defer to local authorities regarding IPR enforcement:

> If you want to know what is happening on the ground, you have to talk to the lowest level of authorities: members of the street/block committees (jiedaoban). They are the ones who are most familiar with what is going on in their jurisdictions and decide what to do, or what not to do, about counterfeiting. Even though there is a gongshangju [AIC] and a gonganju [PSB] to monitor illegal activities in the commercial sector, they are not going to do anything [about counterfeiting] without the tacit approval of the street/block committees.

According to garment factory owner Xiao Xin (G15), designers and organizers are more likely to come under the scrutiny of law enforcement authorities than are manufacturers: "In general, if the authorities discover counterfeits in our factory, they will investigate the designer/developer who asked us to produce the goods. That is because the designer/developer is the one who started this. On the other hand, if government officials come across counterfeits in the business premises of a designer/developer, they will not bother to find out who the manufacturer is."

Forfeitures

If the Chinese authorities discover any copies, their most likely action will be to confiscate them. It is not clear how the authorities dispose of these confiscated goods. In the past, they occasionally conducted public ceremonies where bulldozers would destroy large hauls of pirated CDs, DVDs, and counterfeited items such as watches (Mertha 2005). Unlike the high-profile public destruction of confiscated illicit drugs on June 26, World Drug Day, every year (C. Ting 2004), the destruction of counterfeit goods is much more restrained and irregular.

Whenever law enforcement authorities seize counterfeit merchandise, they announce the value of the forfeited goods to the media. According to the prosecutor Wang, the standard practice for them (as it is for the authorities in the United States and many other countries) is to estimate the value of the confiscated fakes based on what their retail prices would be if they were genuine. He also revealed how this practice had the unintended consequence of forcing counterfeiters to provide the authorities with the actual cost of producing the forfeited goods:

> The most prominent case we prosecuted involved the counterfeiting of handbags. We confiscated over $12 million worth of fake handbags. The estimated worth was based on what the retail value of these bags would have been if they were genuine. The fake handbags were worth only about $300,000. The funny thing is that when we arrest someone for counterfeiting, they will not tell us anything about their financial records. However, once we begin to assess the value of the confiscated goods as if they are genuine, they will come up with documents to show that these fake items are quite cheap to produce.

For most of my research participants, the confiscation of their goods was no doubt a major financial blow. However, it was not something they were exceedingly concerned about because they were confident that they could recover the loss as long as they remained in business.

Fines

In addition to confiscating fake merchandise, Chinese authorities may impose fines on the perpetrators of counterfeiting, regardless of whether the defendants are eventually imprisoned. Although fines may have a significant impact on their financial well-being, counterfeiters are willing to pay the fines as long as they do not have to go to prison. Also, even though the fines can be hefty (they can run into tens of thousands of dollars), they do not necessarily bankrupt a counterfeiter.

Detentions and Arrests

In China, when a person is suspected of having committed a serious crime, the authorities may detain (juliu) the suspect for up to thirty-seven days. During this time, law enforcement authorities will investigate to decide whether the suspect should be formally arrested (daibu). According to my research subjects, this period of detention is the best time for them to do something to avoid being arrested or to, at least, lessen the severity of their crime. Leather handbag businessman Xiao Qin (H16) revealed how he saved his warehouse worker from being arrested after the authorities raided his warehouse and found over four thousand fake designer handbags:

> I rescued my worker and got him out. If he had been arrested, we would have had to go through the whole judicial procedure, which would have been much more troublesome. At any rate, my worker was detained for a while and then placed on probation for a year. When he was detained, I gave his family double the amount of his salary. I also gave him thousands of dollars after his release. I lost over $320,000 when the authorities confiscated my goods. I also spent more than $160,000 paying a fine and establishing the guanxi [connections]. In sum, this incident cost me about $650,000.

If a suspect is formally arrested after detention, his case will be transferred from the police to the court, and he will be prosecuted, convicted, and punished. This is why when the authorities raid a counterfeiter's business, seize a substantial amount of fake merchandise, and detain one or more workers, the business owner will frantically look for help from a person who is powerful or well connected. The counterfeiter would like this person to use his power or connections to reduce the estimate of the worth of the goods seized (so that the case would be considered less severe, and any resulting fine or punishment would be less) and to prevent the detained workers(s) from being formally arrested (so that there would be no prosecution). However, the search for help is not only hectic but also costly and, in the end, probably futile. The story of clothier Zheng Hua (G19) is a good example. When the authorities stormed into his warehouse, they discovered more than twenty thousand counterfeit men's T-shirts and detained two

employees—one Zheng Hua's brother and the other a brother-in-law of
Zheng's business partner. Zheng Hua recalled how he and his partner reacted:

> When that happened, we promptly looked for guanxi. One man said
> he could get my brother and my business partner's brother-in-law
> out, but it would cost $40,000 per person. After a long wait, nothing
> materialized, so we found another person who promised to free both
> of them for only $45,000. That person was of no use either. Then my
> employees were formally arrested. Once a suspect is arrested, that
> person must go through the entire legal process. At that point, we
> located another person who claimed he still could help, but it would
> cost $240,000. We said fine and paid him half the fee, $120,000. But
> it turned out that he could not help, and eventually he returned the
> money. However, he only returned $60,000 at first, and we had to
> wait for a long while to get the rest of the money back. The first two
> people who said they could help also returned some of their fees;
> they did not "eat" the whole amount. When we met these people, we
> were accompanied by our lawyer.

Because the two arrested workers were not just employees but also family members, they took all the responsibility and admitted to the authorities
that they were in charge of the counterfeiting business. The two were sentenced to eighteen months in prison. Neither Zheng Hua nor his business
partner was ever investigated or punished. Zheng Hua believes that someone
reported his business to the authorities in order to obtain a reward.

Xiao Zhen (H13), a leather handbag producer and distributor, avoided
imprisonment after a raid because of his connections. His mother works for
the judicial system, and he graduated from a criminal justice academy:

> After I was arrested and interrogated, I tried not to reveal much to
> the authorities, but my younger brother did the opposite and con-
> fessed everything. Luckily, I knew a lawyer who was close to some-
> one in the court system, and that person knew the Economic Crime
> Investigation officer who was in charge of my case. [The subject's
> mother works for the court, and it is not clear what role his mother
> played.] The landlord of my factory also helped me. I need not get
> into the details of this. [The subject smiled and continued.] In sum,
> because of my connections, the authorities ultimately took my word
> instead of my brother's. Eventually, I was detained for only one
> month, and put on probation for one year. The fine was only about
> $4,500. I was fortunate; usually, the sentence for this type of crime

is three years, and the fine would be a lot more than $4,500. My younger brother was let off too.

Imprisonment

Most IP infringers investigated by the authorities do not move through the court system. Even for those convicted for counterfeiting, very few are imprisoned. According to a report by Alibaba (2018, 21), "The number of detected cases that ended in a criminal court was not even one percent of the total cases. Of those who were convicted in a criminal court, about 79 percent received a suspended sentence." In their examination of fifty-seven civil and criminal court cases related to the counterfeiting of automotive components, A. Shen, Turner, and Antonopoulos (2022) found that, in nearly two-thirds of them, the counterfeiters were not sentenced to prison.

Of all the possible punishments, imprisonment is the number one concern for most participants in the counterfeiting business. In the opinion of Sonny (H10), a leather handbag business owner, "When people get into trouble with the law for copying luxury handbags, they must spend money to solve the problem. If the authorities confiscate their goods, it is not that bad because they know they can earn their money back. Some people not only have their goods seized but also have to pay a fine. The worst outcome is imprisonment. Once a person is incarcerated, what can he or she do?"

The dust bag producer Ah Yun (F13) was confident that it was unlikely that someone like him would be sentenced to prison for his role in the supply chain of counterfeit shoes. He emphasized that imprisonment is for those producing fake shoes only on a large scale: "Normally, the authorities go after shoe manufacturers, not those who produce shoeboxes, dust bags, and other accessories. If someone is found to be involved in the production of shoe accessories, the government will most likely ask the person to move the business somewhere else."

Corruption

As detailed in the existing literature cited here, corruption is a serious problem in China, especially after the country adopted the economic reform and opening up policy in the late 1970s (Ang 2020; Irwin and Willis 2013; Shum 2021; P. Wang 2017; Q. Zhou 2016). As the economy of China grew exponentially, the scope and scale of corruption expanded rapidly (Dikotter 2022; Pei 2016; Shum 2021; Vogel 2013). However, it is important to differentiate between the two major forms of corruption in China: the political-criminal nexus and official corruption (K. Chin and Godson 2006). The political-criminal nexus is primarily the connection between gangsters and low- and midlevel government officials from the criminal justice system, including police officers, prosecutors, and judges. Political leaders from the executive branches and party apparatuses rarely act as protective umbrellas for underworld figures. High-ranking administrators and party officials are more likely to be affiliated with and corrupted by seemingly legitimate businesspeople. In China, the public, the media, and the authorities usually do not see these issues as the same. For the nation's leaders in Beijing, official corruption is a more serious issue than the political-criminal nexus because it involves higher-level government officials and greater economic losses.

As a southern province far away from the central government in Beijing and home to a booming and freewheeling economy, Guangdong has long been viewed as one of the most corrupt provinces in China. According to a magazine article on corruption in Guangdong, the number of provincial-level officials investigated and punished in the province increased from 38 in 2013 to 170 in 2015 (Q. Zhou 2016). One of the officials convicted of corruption was Zhu Zejun, the director of the provincial SAIC, the primary anti-counterfeiting agency in Guangdong. It was alleged that Zhu has been involved in a power struggle with the deputy mayor of Guangzhou and the party secretary of Meizhou, and the three blew the whistle on one another. Not long after that, Wan Qingliang, the party secretary of Guangzhou, and Li Jia, the party secretary of Zhuhai, were investigated for corruption, in 2014 and 2016, respectively. In addition, Chen Yingqun, deputy mayor of Shenzhen, died two days after Zhu Zejun was investigated, after mysteriously falling from a high-rise building. The article also exposed three major networks for corruption in Guangdong: the Eastern Yue Network (the Chinese word Yue is an abbreviation for Guangdong Province),which is centered in Maoming and is primarily known for corruption involving the illegal selling of government land; the Western Yue Network, which is based in Meizhou and Jieyang and is notorious for the buying and selling of government posts; and the Pearl River Delta Network, with a sphere of influence that includes Shenzhen, Zhuhai, and Guangzhou, which is active in collusion between political and business interests. These three networks are mainly concerned with economic growth, and they would be quick to dash through a red light to achieve their goals. In the process, they also find opportunities to enrich themselves through their cronies (Q. Zhou 2016). Xiao Ping, a professor at the Management School of Politics and Public Affairs at Sun Yat-sen University (also known as Zhongshan University) in Guangzhou, has suggested that corruption in Guangdong is not new. It is deeply rooted and hidden and has developed into a strong collusive network (Q. Zhou 2016).

How rampant is corruption in the counterfeiting industry in China? Western media and law enforcement authorities have alleged, without much evidence, that corruption must be widespread in the production and distribution of counterfeit goods because corruption is rampant in other areas of the Chinese economy. They also allege that for so many people to be involved in an illegal activity, on such a large scale, the Chinese authorities must be protecting, or at least tolerating, counterfeiting in exchange for bribes.

On the question of how pervasive corruption is in the counterfeiting business, my research participants can be categorized into two groups. Those in the first group say there is little bribery in their business because they want to stay away from government officials and law enforcement authorities as much as possible. If they were to offer bribes, they would be exposing themselves to the authorities. According to Jane (G1): "Most of us do not wine and dine, or willingly associate with, government authorities because we are afraid that doing so would make the authorities come after us. We can only manufacture fake goods secretly; it is impossible to operate a factory producing counterfeit goods and be protected by corrupt government officials." The clothier Xiao Peng (G8) agreed with Jane, although he had a different reason for not engaging in bribery. He said: "We do not have to go out of our way to bribe government officials. Unlike in other cities in China, the business environment in Guangzhou is well regulated, so you need not have to offer bribes in order to get things done. The problem lies with the businesspeople themselves because, during certain festivals, they try to get close to officials with gifts and money. Regardless of what these businesspeople do, there is no guarantee that the authorities will protect them."

Although most IP infringers are unlikely to proactively bribe the authorities, those in the second group said they would not hesitate to use bribery if law enforcement officials were to detain them or their employees for counterfeiting. According to Laoban (G2), "There is not much corruption in this business. The only time corruption may happen is when a counterfeiter is detained and he or she has the connections and the money to make a serious case become a minor case, or a minor case become a dropped case." Lin Jun (G17), a clothing factory owner, agreed: "We do not take the initiative to aggressively try to get close to government officials by offering them money and gifts. Normally, we keep a distance from them. We seek them out only when we are in trouble with the law, to see whether they can help us make the trouble disappear." As discussed earlier, this can be achieved only when the case is still under the control of the police. As I found in my studies of heroin trafficking in China (K. Chin 2009; K. Chin and Zhang 2015), many detained drug traffickers also try to bribe officials so that the seriousness of their crimes can be lowered.

Besides corruption, there is also the allegation that some officials steal the counterfeit goods they seize. It is unclear how the officials dispose of the fakes they misappropriated. Xiao Qin (H16), the owner of a leather handbag company, recalled how more than four thousand of his handbags were confiscated but that number did not match the number in the official report. He also revealed that he took that in stride: "In their report, they said they seized more than a thousand handbags. Then where did the other three thousand handbags go? They 'ate' them! I did not say a word. Some people in this business would not do that. Their mindset is that if they are going to 'die,' they will drag a whole bunch of people with them. They will lay it all out when they are in court." The handbag merchant Sonny (H10) was convinced that the police and private investigators work together to sell the confiscated counterfeits.

Corruption was believed to be especially rampant in China when Jiang Zemin (1992–2002) and Hu Jintao (2002–2012) were in power. After Xi Jinping took over in 2012, he began to crack down on corruption (Gong and Tu 2022; Jin 2023). Many high- and low-level government officials were arrested for taking bribes and were sentenced to long prison terms (Wong 2023). The opportunities to use official funds to indulge in overseas travel, lavish dining, and entertainment were drastically reduced. The business in the so-called decadent streets (streets lined with fancy restaurants and entertainment venues that officials blatantly frequented), in most Chinese cities, also began to decline (Pei 2016). Many research participants agreed that, as a result, trying to bribe government officials to keep them from investigating IP infringements is more challenging than it was before. According to Ah Bao (F12), a shoe leather supplier: "It was possible several years ago to make this type of problem [being investigated for counterfeiting] go away using guanxi. At that time, you could wine and dine and bribe officials. Now, finding someone who dares to intercede is hard. Even if an official agrees to help, he or she will tell you the price, and you pay. Wining and dining are out of the question because the official would be afraid to be seen in public."

In sum, the data I collected from the interviews and fieldwork suggest that the relationship between counterfeiters and government officials is not as close as what has been reported in the media, popular books, and Western government reports. Unlike operators in other illicit activities, such as gambling and commercial sex, counterfeiters are not aggressive in establishing close affiliations with government authorities and prefer to stay under the radar. They are, however, willing to get close to the authorities after their businesses have been raided, when they need help to lessen the impact of the incident.

Conclusion

Even though counterfeiting is illegal in China, it is a massive nationwide underground sector of the economy involving tens of millions of entrepreneurs and workers (Dimitrov 2009; Lin 2011; Mertha 2005). It is also deeply embedded in the legitimate local and international economies and supply chains (Mathews, Lin, and Yang 2017). Moreover, it is protected and abetted by local authorities through their provision, management, and regulation of physical markets for the distribution of counterfeit merchandise (Chow 2000, 2003). Under such circumstances, law enforcement authorities at the local level are more likely to be sympathetic with the counterfeiters than with the "victims"—the international fashion houses. However, under pressure from Western governments and multinational firms, Beijing may occasionally order local governments to crack down on counterfeiting. However, these actions rarely have any significant impact on the industry (Chow 2010). According to Sonny (H10), owner of a leather handbag business, these types of countermeasures are like "harvesting chives":

> Do you know how chives are harvested? You do not cut the chives from the very bottom, but from the middle, and the purpose is to let them grow before you harvest them again. Anti-counterfeiting in China is the same. The government will not completely uproot it [counterfeiting] because if they do, ordinary people will not be able to survive, and then there will be social unrest. That is why the government uses the same approach we use in harvesting chives when it comes to anti-counterfeiting. The main drive for the police and the AIC in fighting against counterfeiting is to collect fines, which provides a substantial amount of income for them.

Laoban (G2) concurred with Sonny: "Counterfeiting in China is a big underground economy. The government often turns a blind eye, mainly because there is a strong demand for counterfeit goods. It is also one way to stimulate the local economy and maintain social stability."

One research subject pointed out that local protectionism is strong because local authorities are concerned not only with the counterfeiting industry per se but also with the entire supply chain that supports and sustains the manufacturing and distribution of counterfeit goods. According to Chen Jian (H5), a handbag distributor:

> It is not possible for Beijing to suddenly wipe out the entire counterfeiting industry. Not because they cannot do so—if they wanted to, it would be an easy task for them. The question is, then what? The fact is that the counterfeit trade is linked to a supply chain. Manufacturing in China, especially in Guangzhou and the Pearl River Delta area, is more than just setting up a factory to produce goods, because there is also the question of how to source raw materials. Let

us say you are a handbag maker in Guangzhou. It is not convenient when you need zippers for your handbags to have to go far, far away to get them. The reason Guangzhou's manufacturing sector is well developed is because, regardless of what you produce, you can find all the manufacturing materials right here. This is not the case for other manufacturing hubs in China. In sum, when looking for a place to set up your factory, wages are not the only factor you have to consider, especially if you are operating a small factory or a workshop. These small businesses do not have the financial resources to stockpile raw materials; they often buy the materials right before production. That is why they have to be located in a place where they can quickly gain access to manufacturing materials.

9

FUTURE

In this concluding chapter, I examine a time my research subjects considered to be the "golden era of counterfeiting." They recalled with nostalgia how easy it was for them to sell whatever goods they had in their possession and how profitable their businesses were during that period. After that, I examine the future of counterfeiting by dividing my research subjects into three groups: the pessimists, the optimists, and the realists. The first group thinks the counterfeiting industry in China is dying and that sooner or later it will be history. The second group believes the counterfeit trade may never return to the good old days but that it is not going to disappear and will remain strong for many reasons. The third group anticipates the counterfeit trade will linger on, barely surviving.

The Golden Era of Counterfeiting

Most of my research subjects claimed that the golden era of the counterfeiting of luxury goods is over. Lau Fang (G21), a clothing merchant, said: "It was easy to make good money between 2004 to 2008. During those years, only a small amount of merchandise was in stock at the season's end. Whatever you produced, you sold." Xiao Zhen (H13), a leather handbag manufacturer, recalled the good old days when he said: "Between 2000 and 2008, doing business was easy because you sold out everything you manufactured, and you received good prices for your goods. There were also many overseas orders." Jane (G1) appeared excited when she recalled how good her business was once upon a time: "If you were in the counterfeiting business during those years, you certainly made money because you did not have to worry about not finding someone to buy your goods." She backed up her point with this story: "Many years ago, when one of my containers (filled with a variety of counterfeit goods) arrived in Taiwan from China, the retailers in Taiwan were exhilarated. Some called me in advance and begged me not to open the container until they arrived. When we got together, they got into a bidding war for my stuff. When we (women) buy fake handbags, we want to possess a copy of a designer brand and find it thrilling. The whole process (of opening the container, examining the goods, and fighting for them) brought so much fun to everybody at the event. We laughed with joy the entire time."

Zhao Zong (G14), a charismatic and outspoken owner of a fashion firm, recalled how perfect his business was in the early 2000s:

> Our business peaked in 2002, when buyers had to beg us for our goods. During that time, payment for goods was very different from what it is nowadays; buyers would show up with bundles of cash. I remember how some buyers would walk in, dump $12,000 on my table, and leave, saying I must deliver the goods to them. When I asked them to take the money with them, they would turn around and dash out of my office, determined to leave their money with me. Starting in 2010, this type of scenario stopped occurring. Nowadays, we have to press our customers to buy from us because the market is getting smaller and smaller and there are many more fashion designers or organizers like us.

Xiao Qin (H16), a leather handbag entrepreneur who has a dangkou and a xiezilou at the Baiyun Leather City, shook his head when he and I passed by the Baiyun market in his brand-new Land Rover. He said foot traffic around the market nowadays was only one-tenth of what it was in the past. During its heyday, a person had to brush shoulders with others to get in and out of the building. He explained how easy it was for him to make money in the past and how much he struggled nowadays to keep his business afloat:

> When the business environment is good, you make money no matter how you run your business. When the business environment is terrible, you lose money regardless of how you manage your business. In the past, I was busy eating, drinking, and partying all day long and was rarely involved in the day-to-day operations of my business. Even so, business was good, and money was pouring in. I made a name for myself in Guangzhou, and many people said my Chloé handbags

were marvelous. Now, the business environment is awful, and even though I come to work every day and work like hell, I still cannot make money.

Laoban (G2) thought the year 2008 was a turning point for the counterfeiting industry. He explained why:

During the 2008 financial crisis, the government dumped a large amount of capital into the market, about $586 billion. As a result, the market was overwhelmed with abundant capital, and the cost to do business increased rapidly and significantly. In addition, e-commerce began to rise, and became a challenge to many traditional entrepreneurs. Moreover, after 2008, the government's attitude toward the counterfeiting business began to change due to criticism from foreign governments, especially the U.S. government. For operators in the counterfeiting business, this was like putting ice on top of snow [adding fuel to fire], and the business atmosphere was not the same anymore. 2008 was a watershed year in the trajectory of counterfeiting in China.

If the golden era has passed, why are so many people still engaged in counterfeiting? My research subjects said the main reason is that many counterfeiters are stuck in this trade. The Chaoshanese leather handbag merchant Sonny (H10) explained: "This business is not easy to conduct anymore, and yet many people are involved in it. You know why? It is simple: they are familiar with this business; if they change course and switch to another type of business, they must start over again and learn a different type of business. They will lose money in the process. They think it is better for them to stay put and continue doing what they have been doing for a long time." Laoban introduced me to a businessman who ventured into real estate after making $3 million to $4.5 million in the clothing business. According to Laoban, this man lost almost all his savings in real estate. As mentioned in Chapter 5, the same is true with Xiao Ma (H4), once a well-established leather supplier, who tried hard to enter the restaurant business. Over four years, he operated four restaurants. They all failed, and he lost more than a million dollars. It is not easy for anyone to switch from one type of business to another, especially for counterfeiters, who are typically not highly educated.

The Future of Counterfeiting in China

What is the future of counterfeiting in China? My research subjects can be categorized as pessimists, optimists, or realists.

Pessimists

Most research participants consider the future of China's counterfeiting industry bleak, that it has passed its glory days and is in decline. They pointed out that, before the counterfeiting industry developed in China, there were many other countries where counterfeiting was rampant; but as these countries developed and prospered, the IPR violations began to decline and finally disappeared. They believed that China was following the same path. Xiao Yuen (G12), an apparel business owner from Yunnan Province, said: "The counterfeit business was transplanted to China from Japan, South Korea, Hong Kong, and Taiwan.[1] Many countries went through a counterfeiting stage when they were developing."

Laoban (G2), the Taiwanese who sold his fashion business in Guangzhou in 2015 and returned to Taiwan, was also pessimistic about the future. First, he thought that counterfeiting was temporary for any country: "When a country moves from underdeveloped to developed, it will go through a transitional stage, and that means counterfeiting. The purchase of fakes is an option for lower-class people; when people are rich, they buy genuine items." He said: "I think the counterfeiting industry will continue to decline, and very soon it will be history. People who want to be business owners are still entering this industry, but most of them are losing money. Nowadays, only landlords (who own the market buildings) make money."

Others thought that the demise of counterfeiting was inevitable because of the new policy of "emptying the cage, changing the bird" (tenglonghuanniao) in the PRD launched by Wang Yang when he was party secretary of Guangdong Province between 2007 and 2012. It means moving labor-intensive industries from the PRD to areas farther afield so that newer more high-tech industries could be developed in Guangzhou (J. Cheng 2018; Nylander 2020).

Xiao Ma (H4), born in Chaoshan, Guangdong Province, but raised in Hong Kong, provided a clear picture of a declining industry by using his business as an example: "My business began to drop steeply this year. It happened all of a sudden, and it was a disaster. In the past, we sold whatever we brought in. No matter how much stuff we brought into our warehouses, we were not afraid that we would not sell it. Our approach then was as long as we had the opportunity to buy goods, we were ready to stockpile them. Now, it is a different story. We do not dare to purchase goods at will, because we worry that we might not be able to sell them. The rent for my store was reduced from $8,000 to $1,100 a month, and the landlord allowed me to pay monthly. In the past, I had to pay three years' rent in advance. Besides, back then, when I signed the lease, I had to pay a lump sum of tens of thousands of dollars as a transfer fee. Now, stores everywhere are available for rent, but no one wants them."

The people I talked to offered many reasons for being fatalistic about the future of counterfeiting. Laoban offered a simple reason: "If you do not have your own brand, you do not have a root." He continued with a more nuanced explanation: "The golden era is gone. Now, operators have to deal with an uncertain environment in which the U.S.-China trade war, fluctuating currency exchange rates, changing geopolitics, and China's new economic policies all have a major impact."

Xiao Yuen (G12), another pessimist, came up with three reasons why he thought the counterfeiting industry would never regain its past glory: "This business began to take off in 2000, and it continued to grow until 2008. By 2010, it began to go downhill, and in the past few years, it has become tough to make money. There are three reasons for the decline. First, young people are not interested in buying fakes; only those born in the 1980s and 1990s are. Second, people in the coastal areas, especially those from the south, do not purchase fakes. The main market is in the northeastern provinces. Third, Beijing is strengthening China's anti-counterfeiting measures. Now, if counterfeiters are arrested, they will have to go through the entire legal process, regardless of the outcome. Some of them will have to serve time, which was not the case in the past. A friend of mine was arrested and received a three-year sentence; he is still inside." In a later interview, Xiao Yuen mentioned another reason for the decline, less demand abroad for counterfeits: "In the past, after May 1 we sold all our remaining garments to Taiwan at a significant discount. There were many night markets in Taiwan, which would quickly dispense of the leftover garments. This is not so anymore. In addition, there has been a decline in foreign orders, which has had a major impact on the counterfeiting industry. Export orders played a critical role in helping this business to take off in the first place."

Like Xiao Yuen, Ah Ting (G22), a clothing distributor, believed counterfeiting luxury goods in China is not going to last because nowadays the young people there pay little attention to foreign brands, not to mention counterfeit foreign-brand goods. In his words: "Post-00 youths [anyone born after the year 2000] do not wear name brands, do not buy fakes, nor care about whether their clothes have the elements of foreign brands. They only want clothes that are comfortable to wear and appealing to their own eyes. They also want their garments to be simple, without eye-catching logos."

Xiao Chi, a fashionable young woman with many friends in the counterfeiting business, summed up the dire situation of the trade as follows:

Many people are leaving this business because of police crackdowns. They are worried about getting into trouble with the law; so instead of living in fear, they quit so that they can enjoy the money they have already made. Some are still doing it [working in the counterfeiting business], and for them, it has become tougher and tougher to make money because the market for counterfeits is shrinking and competition is fierce. Many young people are not interested in counterfeit goods, and those moving up the economic ladder are switching to genuine products. They might not be able to afford expensive brands, but they can buy less expensive brands. For example, if I do not have the money to buy an authentic Louis Vuitton [handbag], I can buy a Coach [handbag] instead, but not a fake Louis Vuitton.

Optimists

Some of my research participants believed that the counterfeiting trade is not going to fade away anytime soon, regardless of what Beijing wants or does. They thought the strong demand for counterfeits was the key. According to Peter (G7), the owner of an apparel business: "We know there is a demand for fake goods, and when there is demand, there is supply. No matter how hard our government authorities try to suppress it, they will not eliminate it. As long as luxury brands continue to keep their prices sky-high, there will be a crack for counterfeiters to penetrate. If Louis Vuitton were to decrease the prices for its handbags significantly, there would not be space for Louis Vuitton copies to survive."

Ms. Yang, a stylish young woman born in Guangzhou and a graduate student at Columbia University, explained why so many people are crazy about buying fake luxury goods:

Converse and MJ [Michael Jordan] Air shoes are very popular among counterfeiters to copy. Genuine Converse shoes are not expensive; they only cost about $85 to $100 a pair. However, fake Converse shoes cost only $30 a pair; many people are willing to buy fake Converse shoes because they save more than $50 a pair, and the fake Converse shoes are very comfortable. In addition, many brands have products with limited editions, and once they are sold out, you cannot purchase them anymore. Under such circumstances, your only choice is to buy copies. That is why limited-edition goods are often duplicated.

Clothing business owner Zhao Zong (G14) believed that the counterfeiting industry is not going away anytime soon because of the demand for fakes and the reasons behind such demand:

Why are people still making fakes? It is simple; there is a market for them. Rich people can afford to buy genuine luxury goods, but many poor people cannot, and they, also, want to wear name-brand goods, even if those goods are fakes. At any rate, nobody would know whether what they wear is real or fake. I bought this jacket in Hong Kong in 1998. [He picked up a lightweight black jacket from a sofa in his office. It was a simple collarless jacket with two chest pockets.] I paid more than $1,000 for it. You might say it is expensive, but it is a Gucci jacket. I can make this jacket for a little more than $15, definitely not more than $30. It will be exactly the same as the original, except that the zipper and the buttons will not be as good as those on the genuine item because it is very hard to find the same zipper and buttons. There will be many people willing to buy the copy for considerably less than $1,000.

A manager of a travel agency in Guangzhou suggested that the counterfeit trade would continue to exist because there is a strong demand for counterfeit goods not only in China but also around the world. Besides, luxury brands do not wish to eliminate counterfeiting because its existence promotes their products. In essence, counterfeiting is good for both the counterfeiters and the brand owners.

Realists

Some in the counterfeiting business are neither pessimistic nor optimistic about the future of their trade. They think that it will not disappear anytime soon because it is not easy for participants in this trade to do anything else to make good money. They believe that some are "addicted" to counterfeiting. According to Sonny (H10): "The counterfeit trade is very lucrative, so these people are addicted to this trade and cannot quit. This business is like a money-making machine. A friend who is in the fake handbag business once said: 'Besides dealing baifen [white powder or heroin], what else can you do to make more money than selling bogus handbags?'"

Many research subjects expressed frustration with their attempts to develop their own brands so that they could leave the counterfeiting business. Wendy (G4), a businesswoman who tried to quit copying Japanese clothing, said: "It is tough to operate a local brand business in China. Chinese consumers are deeply influenced by the idea that only overseas brands have good-quality products, even though the goods by local brands may be of better quality. It is disheartening for people like me who invested a lot of time and energy in designing and producing a garment, yet found there was no market for it."

Laoban (G2), who viewed himself as an excellent fashion designer, insisted that some counterfeit dresses are better than the originals. After copying global brands for a few years, he began developing his own brand, in 2008, when he sensed that the Chinese government was getting serious about cracking down on counterfeiting. However, his attempt at designing and producing garments under his own brand failed miserably and, after abstaining from it for two years, he returned to counterfeiting.

Xiao Wen (G6), a soft-spoken thirty-nine-year-old man from Hunan, worked as a designer for Laoban for a few years. After Laoban returned to Taiwan, Xiao Wen started his own business with his wife, who had also worked for Laoban. He explained how much weight foreign brands carry in the fashion world of China: "Some of the local luxury brands are producing splendid garments. Not only do they use high-quality fabrics, but also their design and patterns are exceptional. However, they cannot sell their clothing. If you take an ordinary T-shirt and affix the label of a foreign designer brand, even if you misspell the name, whether by accident or intentionally, it will be a hit. Chinese consumers like any products with the elements of a foreign designer brand."

Xiao Yuen (G12) was puzzled by the allure of international brands to counterfeiters like himself. He said: "You do not have any feeling (ganjue) when you are doing your own brand because no matter how good your product is, it will not go anywhere. Once you follow in the footsteps of international brands, you immediately feel it because your goods now have their [international] elements and they are going to sell." Zheng Hua (G19) looked perplexed when he uttered these words: "It is bizarre: there are many fashion products which will not get hot unless they imitate designer brands."

Some research participants were confident that the manufacturing and distribution of name-brand luxury goods would continue because they were sure that the Chinese government would not eliminate these operations. For them, the reason is simple: so many ordinary people in China rely on these activities for a living. Xiao Fei (F11), a shoe hardware producer in Houjie, said: "Due to pressure from international brands, the Chinese government over the past few years has begun to crack down on this business, but it is not possible to eradicate it. If the Chinese authorities do, many people will have nothing to eat, and it will lead to social upheaval. That is why there is no way Beijing will wipe it out." Danny (H3), the owner of a well-established leather handbags factory in Dongguan, agreed with Xiao Fei: "There is only so much the authorities can do to stop counterfeiting. There is certainly a limit to their efforts because it involves the interests of a wide variety of people. Everyone needs to make a living, right?"

Realists also believed that Beijing must consider that, in addition to ordinary people, the counterfeiting industry also benefits local authorities. Many people in China believe that local authorities protect the counterfeiting industry; otherwise, it could not have flourished as it has. One likely way for local authorities to benefit from counterfeiting is to develop government-owned properties into legitimate wholesale markets where counterfeit goods are also traded. Laoban said: "Government units that own commercial real estate properties are the biggest beneficiaries of economic development in China. Shop vendors are the ones who bear all the business risks, but property owners need not take on any risk. We do not know who these markets' landlords are, and they will not let you know. They are all-powerful and well-connected for sure."

GLOSSARY OF SELECTED CHINESE TERMS

Pinyin	Character	English Translation
Adi	阿迪	Adidas
Baifen	白粉	White powder or heroin
Baodi	保底	Guaranteed minimum wage
Baotuan qunuan	抱团取暖	Huddle together for warmth
Bianlian	变脸	Face changing
Bushangmaoyi	补赏 贸易	Compensation trade; a foreign firm provides a Chinese firm with materials, equipment, machines, and technology to engage in the production of a commodity in China, and the Chinese firms repays the foreign firm with a certain amount of finished goods
Cabianqiu	擦边球	Literally, this means hitting the ball on the edge; it refers to what is called edge-ball infringement or derivative copying, in which, instead of copying an original point-by-point, a producer duplicates the style of the original but not its trademark.
Chaoban	抄板	Copying
Chengzhongcun	城中村	Urban village, or village in the city
Daibu	逮捕	Arrest
Daigou	代购	Purchasing agent

Pinyin	Character	English Translation
Dangkou	档口	Outlet, store, or shop for both retail and wholesale, usually located in a market with many other dangkou, as well as xiezilou, although the two types of premises are usually located on separate floors
Dian	店	Store or shop (stand-alone, retail)
Fangmao	仿冒	Crude imitation
Fayangguangda	发扬光大	Literally, this means to sustain and expand something good, supplemental copying; for counterfeiters in Guangzhou, this means manufacturing merchandise that is neither designed nor produced by a name brand but applying a name brand's trademark and logo to the merchandise.
Gaofang	高仿	High-quality imitation
Genban	跟板	Copying
Gonganju	公安局	Public Security Bureau
Gongshangju	工商局	AIC
Gongsi	公司	Literally, this means "company," but for counterfeiters in Guangzhou, gongsi refers not to a business entity but to a premises where such activities as design and distribution are conducted. Gongsi are located in areas where there are other gongsi; they are not located in markets.
Guanxi	关系	Connections
Jiagong	加工	Production or contract manufacturing
Jianghu	江湖	Literally, rivers and lakes. It denotes the rootlessness of members of this subculture.
Jiaotou	角头	Street corner or local groups in Taiwan
Jiedaoban	街道办	Street/block committee
Jubao	举报	Reporting to the authorities
Juliu	拘留	Detain
Lakezai	拉客仔	Solicitors or peddlers
Maohuo	毛货	Unpolished rough goods
Mingpai	名牌	Name brand
Modi	摩的	Illegal motorcycle taxi
Nanxun	南巡	Southern inspection tour (referring to a trip made by Deng Xiaoping in 1992)
Pianmen	偏门	Literally, side door. It means improper or illegal.
Quanmin jiebing	全民皆兵	Everyone is a soldier.
Quanmin jieshang	全民皆商	Everyone is a merchant.

Pinyin	Character	English Translation
Sanda liangjian	三打两建	Three strikes and two establishments (crackdown on commercial fraud and monopolies, counterfeiting, and bribery and establish social trust and a market control system)
Sanlaiyibu	三来一补	Three-plus-one trading mix; three types of contract manufacturing plus one type of supplemental trade between Chinese manufacturers and foreign companies, also known as the Guangdong Model or Dongguang Model
Shanzhai	山寨	Literally, mountain fortress, meaning knockoff, copy, fake, or counterfeit; used to refer to a product that is similar to merchandise produced by a well-established brand, but is not an exact replica and has its own label and logo
Shichanghuo	市场货	Market goods (ordinary goods)
Shuihuzhuan	水浒传	*Outlaws of the Marsh*, a Ming dynasty novel about the lives of 108 men and women forced into brigandry by injustice
Taobaocun	淘宝村	Taobao Villages (Taobao is the name of a Chinese e-commerce website)
Tenglonghuanniao	腾笼换鸟	Emptying the cage, changing the bird; the transformation of an area from relying on labor-intensive industry to high-tech industry
Weishang	微商	WeChat vendor
Xiahai	下海	Plunge into the sea of business
Xiezilou	写字楼	Literally, office building; but for counterfeiters in Guangzhou, xiezilou refers not to a building, but to an office in which wholesale business is conducted. Xiezilou are usually located in a market with many other xiezilou and dangkou, although the two types of premises are usually located on separate floors.
Yibiyi	一比一	One-to-one or point-by-point, used to refer to counterfeit products that are nearly exact replicas of the original, including trademark, logo, style, materials, metal fittings, and packaging

Pinyin	Character	English Translation
Yuandanhuo	原单货	Literally, original order goods, referring to branded products produced by workers from a contract manufacturer using authentic materials and accessories without the authorization of the brand owner
Yuantou	源头	Main source, meaning the designer/organizer or the manufacturer of a product
Zhanxilu	站西路	Station West Road
Zhuanbao	转包	Subcontracting

NOTES

CHAPTER 1

1. OECD is a Paris-based intergovernmental organization founded in 1961 to stimulate economic progress and world trade. EUIPO is a decentralized agency of the European Union responsible for the registration of EU-wide unitary trademarks and industrial design rights.

2. I gave all my research subjects Chinese or English pseudonyms to protect their identities. My pseudonyms can be categorized into six types: (1) the word Xiao (little) plus the person's family name. For example, a younger person with the surname Wang will be called Xiao Wang, meaning "Little Wang"; (2) the word Lao (old) plus the person's family name. An older person with the last name Sun will be called Lao Sun, meaning "Old Sun"; (3) the word Ah (no meaning) plus the person's first name. A woman with a first name Hua (flower) will be called Ah Hua; (4) a nickname, such as Laoban (boss); and (5) the word Zong (an abbreviation of the word zongzai, or chairman of the board) plus the person's family name. A business owner with a surname Li will be called Li Zong (Chairman Li); (6) an English pseudonym for a research subject if he or she has an English name. The names of the roads, the villages, the markets, and the cities in this book are all real names, except for the Panda Village.

3. I indicate the case number of the research subject whenever I quote him or her. Readers interested in the demographic background of a particular research subject can find the information in Tables 5.1, 5.2, and 5.3 by referring to his or her case number. The case numbers are categorized into three groups: G for subjects in the garment industry, H for those in the leather handbag industry, and F for those in the footwear industry. If there is no case number for a person I am quoting, the person is not involved in counterfeiting or was not formally interviewed as a research participant. Key informants were not assigned a case number.

4. Wenzhounese play a vital role in the counterfeiting business. Counterfeit garments produced in Wenzhou are reportedly more sophisticated than those made in Guangzhou, especially high-end men's clothing and women's dresses. The global supply chain and the distribution network in Wenzhou are also much better than in Guangzhou because Wenzhounese have a strong presence overseas, especially in certain European countries such as Italy. It is only natural for Wenzhounese to be ahead of others when it comes to counterfeiting because Wenzhounese in Europe can send recently released fashions and accessories back to China. The key to success in the counterfeiting business is to gain access to the latest fashion items from abroad and then copy them immediately.

CHAPTER 2

1. Both pin and huo mean "goods" or "products," and they are used interchangeably.
2. Henceforth, most of the figures cited in American dollars have been converted from Chinese yuan, or renminbi (RMB), and Hong Kong dollars. Because of the fluctuations in exchange rates (from 8.64 yuan to a dollar in 1994 to 6.15 yuan in 2013 to 6.91 yuan in 2019), the U.S. dollar amounts presented are ballpark estimates. The conversion accounts for why the amounts cited are seemingly often very specific, e.g., $43, $72, or $173.

CHAPTER 3

1. Kenny also showed me a dark blue Balenciaga men's hoodie that he bought for more than $1,000. Gigi presented a look-alike black Louis Vuitton women's fur coat. She said the original cost about $17,000, but she is selling the copy for $1,700. Her cost was about $1,300. Gigi also had a Chanel classic double-breasted long coat for women, which she is selling for about $290.
2. Xiao Ma owned three types of leather supply businesses. His main business was handbag leather, and he operated it with his wife. He hired Ah Bao (F12) to run his shoe leather supply business and another person to be in charge of a firm that supplied leather and fabric to luggage manufacturers. All three businesses were operated independently.

CHAPTER 4

1. Parapolice or chengguan are urban management officers responsible for street-level enforcement in China. Street vendors there are vulnerable to harsh treatment by the parapolice (Xu and Jiang 2018).

CHAPTER 5

1. Skechers USA, Inc., is an American multinational footwear company. Headquartered in Manhattan Beach, California, it was founded in 1992 and is the third-largest footwear brand in the United States.
2. During my stay in Guangzhou, Armani men's T-shirts were selling for $265 at Le Perle Mall, a high-end shopping area located across the street from the five-star Garden Hotel.
3. Sun Wukong, also known as the Monkey King, is a character in the sixteenth-century Chinese novel *The Journey to the West* (A. Yu 2012). He is an immortal who possesses many supernatural abilities. Sun earns a headband as punishment for killing six thieves shortly after he was released from a five-hundred-year-long imprisonment. The head-

band is a heaven-sent magic treasure designed to rein in the immortal's unruly and rebellious nature.

4. Parents in China play an important role in their children's marriages (Watson and Ebrey 1991). Wealth is an important criteria for parents looking for a spouse for their daughter (Raiber and Vinchon 2024). As a result, rich families with unmarried sons are often approached by neighbors or matchmakers with marriage proposals.

5. Hair salons in China have a bad reputation because some are fronts for commercial sex (K. Chin and Finckenauer 2012; M. Liu 2011).

CHAPTER 6

1. Unlike the distribution "offices" (xiezilou) mentioned earlier and in Chapter 3, these foreign buyers' offices are regular offices acting as intermediaries between foreign buyers and local producers (see Mathews 2015).

2. Triad societies in Hong Kong are alleged to be one of the largest, most dangerous, and best organized crime groups in the world. They evolved from patriotic secret societies formed three centuries ago to fight against the oppressive and corrupt Qing dynasty. The word "triad" means the unity of three essential elements of existence—heaven, earth, and men. There are tens of thousands of triad members in Hong Kong, belonging to three major groups: the 14K, the Sun Yee On, and the Wo Shing Wo (Chu 2000; Lo 2010).

3. The emergence of criminal organizations in Taiwan can be traced back to the 1930s, following China's recovery of Taiwan from Japan. In addition to the traditional trades (e.g., operating or protecting illegal gambling dens, brothels, collecting debts, and extorting money from store owners), it is believed that organized gang and jiaotou (street corner group) members have infiltrated legitimate business enterprises in Taiwan. Organized gang and jiaotou members in Taiwan have also penetrated the political arena of Taiwan (K. Chin 2003).

4. The word "tong" simply means "hall" or "gathering place." In the United States, the tongs, like the family and district associations, provided many needed services, such as job referrals and housing assistance, to Chinese immigrants who could not otherwise obtain them. The tongs also acted as power brokers mediating individual and group conflicts within the community. Most tong members are gainfully employed or have their own businesses. Historically, tongs have been active in operating or providing protection for opium use and dealing, gambling, and brothels (McIllwain 2003). U.S. authorities generally consider tongs to be organized crime groups that are heavily involved in many illegal activities and are the force behind the street gangs. There are many street gangs in the Chinatowns of North America; American authorities also consider these street gangs as organized crime groups because of their reputation for violence, their heavy involvement in money-generating local and transnational crimes, and their close affiliation with the tongs (K. Chin 2014).

5. Since the period of the Han dynasty (206 B.C.–A.D. 220), many secret societies have developed in China. The two most prominent and active groups were the Hung and the Qing societies. With tens of thousands of members worldwide, neither organization was a coordinated entity but rather composed of many fragmented and conflicting chapters and branches. The core norms and values of these two societies are loyalty, righteousness, nationalism, secrecy, and brotherhood. These societies are not criminal gangs per se, but the leadership structures of some of the chapters or branches could be penetrated by gangsters and become a host for criminal elements and their activities.

6. The novel describes how three generals, during the Warring States period of Ancient China, became "brothers" through an elaborate ceremony. After swearing to be "brothers," the three generals went on to conquer most of the country. The book had a profound impact on the structure and values of all the jianghu groups (Luo 2014).

7. The novel *Outlaws of the Marsh* (also translated as *Water Margin*) recounts the adventures of 108 vagabonds who formed an enclave on a remote mountain call Liangshan. They were loyal to one another and committed to fight corrupt officials and other bad elements who were viewed as the enemies of the poor (Shi 2024).

CHAPTER 7

1. The English translation of the notice is as follows:

Shijing is serious about stopping counterfeiting and will deal with all counterfeiting activities severely.

It will crack down on the production and distribution of counterfeit goods to safeguard market order.

Reporting the production and distribution of counterfeit goods will be rewarded.

Hotlines for reporting counterfeiting activities:

Shijing Anti-Counterfeiting Office: 6409309

24-hour hotline: 13760638637

Characteristics and patterns of the production of fake and shoddy merchandise: [followed by a list]

Procedures for reporting and claiming the rewards: [followed by a list]

CHAPTER 8

1. SAIC and AIC refer to the same institution, except that SAIC is at the national and provincial level and AIC is at the city and town level. SAIC and AIC are used interchangeably in this study.

CHAPTER 9

1. In the early 1980s, *Newsweek* called Taiwan the counterfeiting capital of the world (Alford 1995).

References

Adler, Patricia. 1985. *Wheeling and Dealing: An Ethnography of an Upper-Level Drug Dealing and Smuggling Community*. New York: Columbia University Press.

Al, Stefan, ed. 2014. *Villages in the City: A Guide to South China's Informal Settlements*. Hong Kong: Hong Kong University Press.

Albanese, Jay. 2012. "Deciphering the Linkages between Organized Crime and Transnational Crime." *Journal of International Affairs* 66 (1): 1–16.

Alford, William. 1995. *To Steal a Book Is an Elegant Offense: Intellectual Property Law in Chinese Civilization*. Stanford, CA: Stanford University Press.

Alibaba. 2016. *2015 Alibaba IPR Protection Annual Report* [2015 阿里巴巴知识产权保护年报]. Hangzhou: Alibaba.

———. 2018. *2017 Alibaba IPR Protection Annual Report* [2017 阿里巴巴知识产权保护年报]. Hangzhou: Alibaba.

Allum, Felia, and Stan Gilmour, eds. 2021. *The Routledge Handbook of Transnational Organized Crime*, 2nd ed. New York: Routledge.

Anderson, Susan Heller. 1981. "The Big Couture Rip-Off." *New York Times Magazine*, March 1. Available at https://www.nytimes.com/1981/03/01/magazine/the-big-couture-rip-off.html.

Ang, Yuen Yuen. 2016. *How China Escaped the Poverty Trap*. Ithaca, NY: Cornell University Press.

———. 2020. *China's Gilded Age: The Paradox of Economic Boom and Vast Corruption*. New York: Cambridge University Press.

Antonopoulos, Georgios, Alexandra Hall, Joanna Large, Anqi Shen, Michael Crang, and Michael Andrews. 2018. *Fake Goods, Real Money: The Counterfeiting Business and Its Financial Management*. Chicago: Policy.

Arias, Enrique Desmond. 2006. *Drugs & Democracy on Rio De Janeiro: Trafficking, Social Networks, & Public Security*. Chapel Hill: University of North Carolina Press.

Arruñada, Benito, and Xosé H. Vázquez. 2006. "When Your Contract Manufacturer Becomes Your Competitor." *Harvard Business Review* 84 (9): 135–145.

Beare, Margaret, ed. 2003. *Critical Reflections on Transnational Organized Crime, Money Laundering, and Corruption.* Toronto: University of Toronto Press.

Beebe, Barton. 2015. "Shanzhai, Sumptuary Law, and Intellectual Property Law in Contemporary China." In *The Luxury Economy and Intellectual Property: Critical Reflections,* edited by Haochen Sun, Barton Beebe, and Madhavi Sunder, 203–223. New York: Oxford University Press.

Bercht, A. L. 2013. "Glurbanization of the Chinese Megacity Guangzhou—Image-Building and City Development through Entrepreneurial Governance." *Geographic Helvetica* 68:129–138.

Bian, Xuemei, and Cleopatra Veloutsou. 2007. "Consumers' Attitudes regarding Non-deceptive Counterfeit Brands in the UK and China." *Journal of Brand Management* 14 (3): 211–222.

Boden, Graham. 2012. "China's Accession to the WTO: Economic Benefits." *Park Place Economist* 20 (1): 13–17.

Bosker, Bianca. 2013. *Original Copies: Architectural Mimicry in Contemporary China.* Honolulu: University of Hawaii Press.

Branigan, Tania. 2023. *Red Memory: The Afterlives of China's Cultural Revolution.* New York: W. W. Norton.

Brauer, Tricia. 2012. "You Say '普拉达' I Say 'Counterfeit': The Perils of Civil Litigation as a Trademark Protection Strategy in China." *John Marshall Review of Intellectual Property Law* 12:262–285.

Bresler, Fenton. 1981. *The Chinese Mafia.* New York: Stein and Day.

Bullock, Karen, Ronald Clarke, and Nick Tilley, eds. 2010. *Situational Prevention of Organised Crime.* Cullompton, UK: Willan.

Bunck, Julie, and Michael Fowler. 2012. *Bribes, Bullets, and Intimidation: Drug Trafficking and the Law in Central America.* University Park: Pennsylvania State University Press.

Burns, John. 1986. "Taiwan Curbs Its Counterfeiters." *New York Times,* March 30, https://www.nytimes.com/1986/03/30/business/taiwan-curbs-its-counterfeiters.html.

Campbell, Howard. 2009. *Drug War Zone: Frontline Dispatches from the Streets of El Paso and Juarez.* Austin: University of Texas Press.

Carey, Elaine. 2014. *Women Drug Traffickers: Mules, Bosses, and Organized Crime.* Albuquerque: University of New Mexico Press.

Carpenter, Jason, and Karen Lear. 2011. "Consumer Attitudes toward Counterfeit Fashion Products: Does Gender Matter?" *Journal of Textile and Apparel, Technology and Management* 7 (1): 1–16.

Chang, Leslie. 2009. *Factory Girls: From Village to City in a Changing China.* New York: Spiegel and Grau.

Chaudhry, Peggy, and Alan Zimmerman. 2009. *The Economics of Counterfeit Trade: Governments, Consumers, Pirates and Intellectual Property Rights.* New York: Springer.

Cheng, Chu-yuan. 1997. "Chaozhou People and Chaozhou Culture." *American Journal of Chinese Studies* 4 (1): 101–120.

Cheng, Joseph Yu-Shek. 2018. *The Development of Guangdong: China's Economic Powerhouse.* Singapore: World Science.

Chermak, Steven. 2015. "Understanding Counterfeiting Networks, Their Connections, and How to Disrupt Them." In *Brand Protection 2020: Perspectives on the Issues Shaping the Global Risk and Response to Product Counterfeiting,* edited by Jeremy Wilson,

21–22. A-CAPP Paper Series. Center for Anti-Counterfeiting and Product Protection. East Lansing: Michigan State University.

Chin, Chung. 1994. "Taiwan's DFI in Mainland China: Impact on the Domestic and Host Economies." In *The Economic Transformation of South China: Reform and Development in the Post-Mao Era*, edited by Thomas Lyons and Victor Nee, 215–242. Ithaca, NY: Cornell University Press.

Chin, Ko-lin. 1990. *Chinese Subculture and Criminality: Non-traditional Crime Groups in America*. Westport, CT: Greenwood.

———. 1996. *Chinatown Gangs: Extortion, Enterprise, and Ethnicity*. New York: Oxford University Press.

———. 1999. *Smuggled Chinese: Clandestine Immigration to the United States*. Philadelphia: Temple University Press.

———. 2003. *Heijin: Organized Crime, Business, and Politics in Taiwan*. Armonk, NY: M. E. Sharpe.

———. 2007. "Into the Thick of It: Methodological Issues in Studying the Drug Trade in the Golden Triangle." *Asian Journal of Criminology* 2 (2): 85–109.

———. 2009. *The Golden Triangle: Inside Southeast Asia's Drug Trade*. Ithaca, NY: Cornell University Press.

———. 2014. "Chinese Organized Crime." In *The Oxford Handbook of Organized Crime*, edited by Letizia Paoli, 219–233. New York: Oxford University Press.

Chin, Ko-lin, and James O. Finckenauer. 2011. "Chickenheads, Agents, Mommies, and Jockeys: The Social Organization of Transnational Commercial Sex." *Crime, Law and Social Change* 56 (5): 463–484.

———. 2012. *Selling Sex Overseas: Chinese Women and the Realities of Prostitution and Global Sex Trafficking*. New York: New York University Press.

Chin, Ko-lin, and Roy Godson. 2006. "Organized Crime and the Political-Criminal Nexus in China." *Trends in Organized Crime* 9 (3): 5–44.

Chin, Ko-lin, and Sheldon Zhang. 2015. *The Chinese Heroin Trade: Cross-Border Drug Trafficking in Southeast Asia and Beyond*. New York: New York University Press.

Chong, Jana Nicole Checa. 2008. "Sentencing Luxury: The Valuation Debate in Sentencing Traffickers of Counterfeit Luxury Goods." *Fordham Law Review* 77 (3): 1147–1181.

Chow, Danny. 2000. "Counterfeiting in the People's Republic of China." *Washington University Law Quarterly* 78 (1): 1–57.

———. 2003. "Organized Crime, Local Protectionism, and the Trade in Counterfeit Goods in China." *China Economic Review* 14:473–484.

———. 2010. "Anti-counterfeiting Strategies of Multi-national Companies in China: How a Flawed Approach Is Making Counterfeiting Worse." *Georgetown Journal of International Law* 41:749–779.

———. 2011. "Counterfeiting as an Externality Imposed by Multinational Companies on Developing Countries." *Virginia Journal of International Law* 51 (4): 785–823.

———. 2022. "Barriers to Criminal Enforcement against Counterfeiting in China." *Vanderbilt Journal of Entertainment and Technology Law* 4:633–673.

Chu, Yiu-kong. 2000. *Triads as Business*. New York: Routledge.

———. 2011. "Hong Kong Triads." In *The Routledge Handbook of International Criminology*, edited by Cindy Smith, Sheldon Zhang, and Rosemary Barberet, 226–236. New York: Routledge.

Chubb, Andrew. 2015. "China's *Shanzhai* Culture: 'Grabism' and the Politics of Hybridity." *Journal of Contemporary China* 24 (92): 260–279.

Coble, Parks. 2023. *The Collapse of Nationalist China: How Chiang Kai-shek Lost China's Civil War*. New York: Cambridge University Press.

Cocks, Sam. 2006. "The Hoods Who Move the Goods: An Examination of the Booming International Trade in Counterfeit Luxury Goods and an Assessment of the American Efforts to Curtail Its Proliferation." *Fordham Intellectual Property, Media and Entertainment Law Journal* 17 (2): 501–553.

Commission on the Theft of American Intellectual Property. 2013. *The IP Commission Report*. Washington, DC: National Bureau of Asian Research.

———. 2017. *Update to the IP Commission Report—The Theft of American Intellectual Property: Reassessments of the Challenge and United States Policy*. Washington, DC: National Bureau of Asian Research.

Cui, Lili. 2019. *Taobao Villages of China*. Montreal: Royal Collins.

Dean, Grace. 2021. "Xiaomi Has Overtaken Apple as the World's Second-Biggest Smartphone Seller: Here's How the Major Players Rank." *Business Insider*, July 16.

Decker, Scott, and Margaret Townsend Chapman. 2008. *Drug Smugglers on Drug Smuggling: Lessons from the Inside*. Philadelphia: Temple University Press.

Desroches, Frederick. 2007. "Research on Upper Level Drug Trafficking: A Review." *Journal of Drug Issues* 37 (4): 827–844.

Dickie, John. 2004. *Cosa Nostra: A History of the Sicilian Mafia*. New York: St. Martin's Griffin.

Dikotter, Frank. 2016. *The Cultural Revolution: A People's History, 1962–1976*. New York: Bloomsbury.

———. 2022. *China after Mao: The Rise of a Superpower*. New York: Bloomsbury.

Dimitrov, Martin. 2009. *Piracy and the State: The Politics of Intellectual Property Rights in China*. New York: Cambridge University Press.

Duran-Martinez, Angelica. 2018. *The Politics of Drug Violence: Criminals, Cops, and Politicians in Mexico and Colombia and Mexico*. New York: Oxford University Press.

English, T. J. 1995. *Born to Kill: America's Most Notorious Vietnamese Gang, and the Changing Face of Organized Crime*. New York: William Morrow.

Enright, Michael, Edith Scott, and Ka-mun Chang. 2005. *Regional Powerhouse: The Greater Pearl River Delta and the Rise of China*. New York: Wiley.

Fan, Feifei. 2018. "Heat Turned Up in Fight against Fakes: Market Regulator Targets Online Discounter Pinduoduo." *China Daily*, August 22, 1.

Farr, Kathryn. 2005. *Sex Trafficking: The Global Market in Women and Children*. New York: Worth Publishers.

Federal Research Division. 2020. *U.S. Intellectual Property and Counterfeit Goods—Landscape Review of Existing/Emerging Research*. Washington, DC: Library of Congress.

Fijnaut, Cyrille, and Letizia Paoli, eds. 2004. *Organised Crime in Europe: Concepts, Patterns and Control Policies in the European Union and Beyond*. Dordrecht, The Netherlands: Springer.

Finckenauer, James O. 2005. "Problems of Definition: What Is Organized Crime?" *Trends in Organized Crime* 8 (3): 63–83.

Finckenauer, James O., and Ko-lin Chin. 2006. "Asian Transnational Organized Crime and Its Impact on the United States." *Trends in Organized Crime* 10, no. 2 (Winter): 18–107.

Finckenauer, James O., and Elin Waring. 1998. *The Russian Mafia in America: Immigration, Culture, and Crime*. Boston: Northeastern University Press.

Forgione, Joseph. 2016–2017. "Counterfeiting, Couture, and the Decline of Consumer Trust in Online Marketplace Platforms." *New York Law School Law Review* 61:195–207.

Freemantle, Brian. 1986. *The Steal: Counterfeiting and Industrial Espionage*. London: Michael Joseph.

Friedberg, Aaron. 2022. *Getting China Wrong*. Cambridge: Polity.

Gaetano, Arianne. 2016. *Out to Work: Migration, Gender, and the Changing Lives of Rural Women in Contemporary China*. Honolulu: University of Hawaii Press.

Galbraith, Robert. 2006. "Made in Italy: Counterfeits That Were Once Mere Import." *New York Times*, October 3, https://www.nytimes.com/2006/10/03/style/03iht-RFAKE.30 15963.html?searchResultPosition=1.

Galloni, Alexandra. 2006. "Bagging Fakers and Sellers." *Wall Street Journal*, January 31, B1.

Gambetta, Diego. 1996. *The Sicilian Mafia: The Business of Private Protection*. Cambridge, MA: Harvard University Press.

Gerth, Karl. 2020. *Unending Capitalism: How Consumerism Negated China's Communist Revolution*. New York: Cambridge University Press.

Gewirtz, Julian. 2022. *Never Turn Back: China and the Forbidden History of the 1980s*. Cambridge, MA: Harvard University Press.

Gittings, John. 2005. *The Changing Face of China: From Mao to Market*. New York: Oxford University Press.

Gong, Ting, and Wenyan Tu. 2022. "Fighting Corruption in China: Trajectory, Dynamics, and Impact." *China Review* 22 (2): 1–19.

Gosline, Renee Richardson. 2010. "Counterfeit Labels: Good for Luxury Brands?" *Forbes*, February 12.

Greene, Jay. 2019. "How Amazon's Quest for More, Cheaper Products Has Resulted in a Flea Market of Fakes." *Washington Post*, November 14.

Griffith, Keith. 2023. "Senior Trump Defense Official Accuses China of 'Thievery' of F-22 Secrets to Create Their Own J-20 Stealth Fighter That Has Been 'Subsidized' by US Taxpayer . . . But Only Combat Would Prove Which Is More Lethal." *Daily Mail*, March 9.

Guangzhou Baima Special Edition, May 1–5, 2018.

Gundur, R. V. 2022. *Trying to Make It: The Enterprises, Gangs, and People of the American Drug Trade*. Ithaca, NY: Cornell University Press.

Hall, Casey. 2018. "A Turning Point for China's Stance on Counterfeit Luxury Goods." *BOF* [Business of Fashion], December 11.

Hamilton, Gary, and Cheng-Shu Kao. 2018. *Making Money: How Taiwanese Industrialists Embraced the Global Economy*. Stanford, CA: Stanford University Press.

Harney, Alexandra. 2009. *The China Price: The True Cost of Chinese Competitive Advantage*. New York: Penguin Books.

Hieke, Sophie. 2010. "Effects of Counterfeits on the Image of Luxury Brands: An Empirical Study from the Customer Perspective." *Journal of Brand Management* 18 (2): 159–173.

Hill, Peter. 2006. *The Japanese Mafia: Yakuza, Law, and the State*. New York: Oxford University Press.

Hu, Yongqi. 2018. "Fake Products in the Crosshairs as Buyers Get More Protection." *China Daily*, August 7, 7.

Huang, Xiaojing [黄小晶], Li Hanqiang [李汉强], and Feng Qiuhang [冯秋航], eds. 2018. *Brief Records of Contemporary Guangzhou Major Events* [广州当代大事纪略]. Guangzhou: Guangzhou Chubanshe.

Huang, Yasheng. 2008. *Capitalism with Chinese Characteristics: Entrepreneurship and the State*. New York: Cambridge University Press.

Huang, Yeqing, and Huihui Gong. 2022. "Educational Expectations of Left-Behind Children in China: Determinants and Gender Differences." *Applied Research in Quality of Life* 17:2501–2523.

Hughes, Donna. 2000. "The 'Natasha' Trade: The Transnational Shadow Market of Trafficking in Women." *Journal of International Affairs* 53:625–651.

IACC (International Anti-counterfeiting Coalition). 2013. "Special 301 Recommendations." Submission of the International Anti-counterfeiting Coalition to the United States Trade Representative, February 8, 2013.

IPEC (U.S. Intellectual Property Enforcement Coordinator). 2019. *Annual Intellectual Property Report to Congress.*

Irwin, Darrell, and Cecil Willis. 2013. "Success or Sorrow: The Paradoxical View of Crime Control Campaigns in China." *International Journal of Comparative and Applied Criminal Justice* 38 (1): 63–81.

Jiang, Ling, and Veronique Cova. 2012. "Love for Luxury, Preferences for Counterfeits—A Qualitative Study in Counterfeit Luxury Consumption in China." *International Journal of Marketing Studies* 4 (6): 1–9.

Jiang, Ling, and Juan Shan. 2016. "Counterfeits or *Shanzhai*? The Role of Face and Brand Consciousness in Luxury Copycat Consumption." *Psychological Reports* 119 (1): 181–199.

———. 2018. "Genuine Brands or High Quality Counterfeits: An Investigation of Luxury Consumption in China." *Canadian Journal of Administrative Sciences* 35 (2): 183–197.

Jin, Keyu. 2023. *The New China Playbook: Beyond Socialism and Capitalism.* New York: Viking.

Johnson, Graham. 1994. "Open for Business, Open to the World: Consequences of Global Incorporation in Guangdong and the Pearl River Delta." In *The Economic Transformation of South China: Reform and Development in the Post-Mao Era*, edited by Thomas Lyons and Victor Nee, 55–88. Ithaca, NY: Cornell University Press.

Keane, Michael. 2012. "Renegades on the Frontier of Innovation: The Shanzhai Grassroots Communities of Shenzhen in China's Creative Economy." *Eurasian Geography and Economics* 53 (2): 216–230.

Keefe, Patrick Radden. 2009. *The Snakehead: An Epic Tale of the Chinatown Underworld and the American Dream.* New York: Doubleday.

Keo, Chenda, Thierry Bouhours, Roderic Broadhurst, and Brigitte Bouhours. 2014. "Human Trafficking and Moral Panic in Cambodia." *Annals of the American Academy of Political and Social Science* 653:202–224.

Kerns, Robert. 2016. "The Counterfeit Food Crisis in China: A Systemic Problem and Possible Solutions." University of North Carolina Journal of International Law, 41 N.C. J. Int'l. & Com. Reg. 571, WVU Law Research Paper No. 2016-4.

Kyle, David, and John Dale. 2011. "Smuggling the State Back In: Agents of Human Smuggling Reconsidered." In *Global Human Smuggling: Comparative Perspectives*, 2nd ed., edited by David Kyle and Rey Koslowski, 33–59. Baltimore, MD: John Hopkins University Press.

Kyle, David, and Rey Koslowski, eds. 2011. *Global Human Smuggling: Comparative Perspectives*, 2nd ed. Baltimore, MD: John Hopkins University Press.

Lee, Maggy, ed. 2007. *Human Trafficking.* Cullompton, UK: Willan.

Lejeune, Johannes. 2014. "Weak Enforcement of Intellectual Property Rights in China: Integrating Political, Cultural and Structural Explanations." *Journal of Contemporary China* 23 (88): 698–714.

Li, Minghuan. 2012. "'Playing Edge Ball': Transnational Migration Brokerage in China." In *Transnational Flows and Permissive Polities: Ethnographies of Human Mobilities in Asia*, edited by Barak Kalir and Malini Sur, 207–228. Amsterdam: Amsterdam University Press.

Li, Shaomin. 2022. *The Rise of China, Inc.: How the Chinese Communist Party Transformed China into a Giant Corporation.* New York: Cambridge University Press.

Liao, Sara. 2020. *Fashioning China: Precarious Creativity and Women Designers in Shanzhai Culture*. London: Pluto.

Lin, Jessica Yi-Chieh. 2011. *Fake Stuff: China and the Rise of Counterfeit Goods*. New York: Routledge.

Ling, Bonny. 2018. "Prostitution and Female Trafficking in China: Between Phenomena and Discourse." *China Perspectives* 1–2:65–74.

Lintner, Bertil, and Michael Black. 2009. *Merchants of Madness: The Methamphetamine Explosion in the Golden Triangle*. Chiang Mai, Thailand: Silkworm Books.

Liu, Min. 2011. *Migration, Prostitution, and Human Trafficking: The Voice of Chinese Women*. New Brunswick, NJ: Transaction.

Liu, Zhanguo, and T. Wing Lo. 2020. *Understanding Crime in Villages-in-the-City in China: A Social and Behavioral Approach*. New York: Routledge.

Liu, Zhen. 2016. "China's Second Aircraft Carrier to Copy a Dated Soviet-Era Design as Naval Hardware Demands Increase." *South China Morning Post*, January 1.

Lo, T. Wing. 2010. "Beyond Social Capital: Triad Organized Crime in Hong Kong and China." *British Journal of Criminology* 50 (5): 851–872.

Longmire, Slyvia. 2011. *Cartel: The Coming Invasion of Mexico's Drug Wars*. New York: Palgrave MacMillan.

Lu, Zhongguang [卢忠光]. 2018. *The Secret Code of Guangshang* [莞商密码]. Guangzhou: Huacheng Chubanshe.

Luo, Guangzhong. 2014. *Three Kingdoms: A Historical Novel*. Translated by Moss Roberts. Berkeley: University of California Press.

Lupo, Salvatore. 2011. *History of the Mafia*. New York: Columbia University Press.

Ma, Si. 2018. "Online Sales Boost White Goods Offtake." *China Daily*, August 10, 2018, 17.

Macfarquhar, Roderick, and Michael Schoenhals. 2006. *Mao's Last Revolution*. Cambridge, MA: Harvard University Press.

Magnus, George. 2018. *Red Flags: Why Xi's China Is in Jeopardy*. New Haven, CT: Yale University Press.

Mahdavi, Pardis. 2011. *Gridlock: Labor, Migration, and Human Trafficking in Dubai*. Stanford, CA: Stanford University Press.

Maher, Lisa, and Susan Hudson. 2007. "Women in the Drug Economy: A Metasynthesis of the Qualitative Literature." *Journal of Drug Issues* 37 (4): 805–826.

Malarek, Victor. 2003. *The Natashas: Inside the New Global Sex Trade*. New York: Arcade Publishing.

Marquis, Christopher, and Kunyuan Qiao. 2022. *Mao and Markets: The Communist Roots of Chinese Enterprise*. New Haven, CT: Yale University Press.

Martin, Brian. 1996. *The Shanghai Green Gang: Politics and Organized Crime, 1919–1937*. Berkeley: University of California Press.

Mathews, Gordon. 2015. "Africans in Guangzhou." *Journal of Current Chinese Affairs* 44 (4): 7–15.

Mathews, Gordon, with Linessa Dan Lin and Yang Yang. 2017. *The World in Guangzhou: African and Other Foreigners in South China's Global Marketplace*. Chicago: University of Chicago Press.

McIllwain, Jeffrey. 2003. *Organizing Crime in Chinatown: Race and Racketeering in New York, 1890–1910*. Jefferson, NC: McFarland.

Merry, Sally Engle. 2016. *The Seductions of Quantification: Measuring Human Rights, Gender Violence, and Sex Trafficking*. Chicago: University of Chicago Press.

Mertha, Andrew. 2005. *The Politics of Piracy: Intellectual Property in Contemporary China*. Ithaca, NY: Cornell University Press.

Midler, Paul. 2011. *Poorly Made in China: An Insider's Account of the China Production Game*. Hoboken, NJ: John Wiley and Sons.

Moore, Michael. 2010. "Hilton Hotel Closed by Chinese Police over Prostitution Charges." *The Telegraph*, June 21, 2010.

Morawska, Eva. 2007. "Trafficking into and from Eastern Europe." In *Human Trafficking*, edited by Maggy Lee, 92–115. Collumpton, UK: Willan.

Muhlhahn, Klaus. 2019. *Making China Modern: From the Great Qing to Xi Jinping*. Cambridge, MA: Harvard University Press.

Muscolino, Micah. 2013. "Underground at Sea: Fishing and Smuggling across the Taiwan Strait, 1970s–1990s." In *Mobile Horizons: Dynamics across the Taiwan Strait*, edited by Wen-hsin Yeh, 99–123. Center for Chinese Studies, Institute of East Asian Studies. Berkeley: University of California.

Naim, Moises. 2005. *Illicit: How Smugglers, Traffickers, and Copycats Are Hijacking the Global Economy*. New York: Anchor Books.

Naylor, R. T. 2003. "Follow-the-Money-Methods in Crime Control Policy." In *Critical Reflections on Transnational Organized Crime, Money Laundering, and Corruption*, edited by Margaret Beare, 256–290. Toronto: University of Toronto Press.

Nee, Victor. 1994. "Institutional Change and Regional Growth: An Introduction." In *The Economic Transformation of South China: Reform and Development in the Post-Mao Era*, edited by Thomas Lyons and Victor Nee, 1–16. Ithaca, NY: Cornell University Press.

Ngai, Pun. 2005. *Made in China: Women Factory Workers in a Global Workplace*. Durham, NC: Duke University Press.

Nylander, Johan. 2020. *The Epic Split: Why 'Made in China' Is Going Out of Style*. Hong Kong: One Hour Asia.

OECD/EUIPO. 2017. *Mapping the Real Routes of Trade in Fake Goods*. Paris: OECD.

———. 2019. *Trends in Trade in Counterfeit and Pirated Goods*. Paris: European Union Intellectual Property Office.

———. 2021. *Global Trade in Fakes: A Worrying Threat*. Paris: European Union Intellectual Property Office.

Oi, Jean. 1989. *State and Peasant in Contemporary China: The Political Economy of Village Government*. Berkeley: University of California Press.

Orscheln, Colleen Jordan. 2015. "Bad News Birkins: Counterfeit in Luxury Brands." *John Marshall Review of Intellectual Property* 14:249–267.

Paluch, Gabrielle. 2023. *The Opium Queen: The Untold Story of the Rebel Who Ruled the Golden Triangle*. Lanham, MD: Rowan and Littlefield.

Pang, Laikwan. 2012. *Creativity and Its Discontents: China's Creative Industries and Intellectual Property Rights Offenses*. Durham, NC: Duke University Press.

Paoli, Letizia. 2003. *Mafia Brotherhoods: Organized Crime, Italian Style*. New York: Oxford University Press.

———, ed. 2014. *The Oxford Handbook of Organized Crime*. New York: Oxford University Press.

Paoli, Letizia, Victoria Greenfield, and Peter Reuter. 2009. *The World Heroin Market: Can Supply Be Cut?* New York: Oxford University Press.

Parrenas, Rhacel Salazar. 2011. *Illicit Flirtations: Labor, Migration, and Sex Trafficking in Tokyo*. Stanford, CA: Stanford University Press.

Pei, Minxin. 2016. *China's Crony Capitalism: The Dynamics of Regime Decay*. Cambridge, MA: Harvard University Press.

Phillips, Tim. 2005. *Knockoff: The Deadly Trade in Counterfeit Goods*. London: Kogan Page.

Picarelli, John. 2007. "Historical Approaches to the Trade in Human Beings." In *Human Trafficking*, edited by Maggy Lee, 26–48. Cullompton, UK: Willan.

Pierson, David. 2017. "Counterfeit Yeezys and the Booming Sneaker Black Market." *Los Angeles Times*, September 5, 2017.

Posner, Gerald. 1988. *Warlords of Crimes*. New York: McGraw-Hill.

Pratt, Stephen, and Christine Zeng. 2020. "The Economic Value and Determinants of Tourists' Counterfeit Purchases: The Case of Hong Kong." *Tourism Economics* 26 (1): 155–178.

Radon, Anita. 2012. "Counterfeit Luxury Goods Online: An Investigation of Consumer Perceptions." *International Journal of Marketing Studies* 4 (2): 74–79.

Raiber, Eva, and Timothee Vinchon. 2024. "Love Is in the Park: Parents' Marital Preferences in China." *Dialogue Economiques*, March 13, 2024.

Raustiala, Kal, and Christopher Jon Sprigman. 2012. *The Knockoff Economy: How Imitation Sparks Innovation*. New York: Oxford University Press.

———. 2015. "Let Them Eat Fake Cake: The Rational Weakness of China's Anti-counterfeiting Policy." In *The Luxury Economy and Intellectual Property: Critical Reflections*, edited by Haochen Sun, Barton Beebe, and Madhavi Sunder, 263–288. New York: Oxford University Press.

Reuter, Peter. 1983. *Disorganized Crime: Illegal Markets and the Mafia*. Cambridge, MA: MIT Press.

Richard, Amy O'Neill. 2000. *International Trafficking in Women to the United States: A Contemporary Manifestation of Slavery and Organized Crime*. Washington, DC: Center for the Study of Intelligence.

Rigger, Shelley. 2021. *The Tiger Leading the Dragon: How Taiwan Propelled China's Economic Rise*. Lanham, MD: Rowman and Littlefield.

Rozelle, Scott, and Natalie Hell. 2020. *Invisible China: How the Urban-Rural Divide Threatens China's Rise*. Chicago: University of Chicago Press.

Sanchez, Gabriella. 2015. "Human Smuggling Facilitators in the US Southwest." In *The Routledge Handbook on Crime and International Migration*, edited by Sharon Pickering and Julie Ham, 275–286. New York: Routledge.

Saviano, Roberto. 2008. *Gomorrah: A Personal Journey into the Violent International Empire of Naples' Organized Crime System*. New York: Picador.

Schmidle, Nicholas. 2010. "Inside the Knockoff-Tennis-Shoe Factory." *New York Times Magazine*, August 19, 2010. Available at https://www.nytimes.com/2010/08/22/magazine/22fake-t.html.

Shao, Grace. 2019. "From Gucci to Louis Vuitton, New York's Fake Luxury Goods Highlight a Rising Counterfeit Market." *South China Morning Post*, April 26, 2019.

Shelley, Louise. 2010. *Human Trafficking: A Global Perspective*. New York: Cambridge University Press.

Shen, Anqi. 2018. "'Being Affluent, One Drinks Wine': Wine Counterfeiting in Mainland China." *International Journal for Crime, Justice and Social Democracy* 7 (4): 16–32.

Shen, Anqi, Sue Turner, and Georgios Antonopoulos. 2022. "Driven to Death: A Chinese Case Study on the Counterfeiting of Automotive Components." *Asian Journal of Criminology* 17 (3): 311–329.

Shen, Jianfa, and Gordon Kee. 2017. *Development and Planning in Seven Major Coastal Cities in Southern and Eastern China*. New York: Springer.

Shi, Naian. 2024. *The Water Margin: Outlaws of the Marsh*. Translated by J. H. Jackson. North Clarendon, VT: Tuttle Publishing.

Shirk, Susan. 2022. *Overreach: How China Derailed Its Peaceful Rise*. New York: Oxford University Press.

Shum, Desmond. 2021. *Red Roulette: An Insider's Story of Wealth, Power, Corruption, and Vengeance in Today's China*. New York: Scribner.

Siegel, Dina, and Henk van de Bunt, eds. 2012. *Traditional Organized Crime in the Modern World: Responses to Socioeconomic Changes*. New York: Springer.

Smith, Cindy, Sheldon Zhang, and Rosemary Barberet, eds. 2011. *The Routledge Handbook of International Criminology*. New York: Routledge.

Southern Metropolis Daily [南方都市报]. 2018a. "Editorial. The Way to Get Out of the Predicament Is to Face the Problem of Counterfeiting" [直面假货争议才能走出困局], July 31, 2018, A02.

———. 2018b. "Humen: 'Sanlaiyibu' Ignited the Fire of Chinese Manufacturing" [虎门: "三来一补" 点烂中国制造星星之火], August 13, 2018, 8–9.

Spence, Jonathan. 1991. *The Search for Modern China*. New York: W. W. Norton.

Spener, David. 2011. "Global Apartheid, Coyotaje, and the Discourse of Clandestine Migration: Distinctions between Personal, Structural, and Cultural Violence." In *Global Human Smuggling: Comparative Perspectives*, edited by David Kyle and Rey Koslowski, 157–185. Baltimore, MD: John Hopkins University Press.

Spink, John, Douglas Moyer, Hyeonho Park, and Justin Heinonen. 2013. "Defining the Types of Counterfeiters, Counterfeiting, and Offender Organizations." *Crime Science* 2 (8): 1–10.

Staake, Thorsten, and Elgar Fleisch. 2008. *Countering Counterfeit Trade: Illicit Market Insights, Best-Practice Strategies, and Management Toolbox*. Berlin: Springer.

Staley, Willi. 2013. "The Bag Men of Chinatown." *New York Times*, February 8, 2013.

Sun, Andy. 1998. "From Pirate King to Jungle King: Transformation of Taiwan's Intellectual Property Protection." *Fordham Intellectual Property, Media and Entertainment Law Journal* 9 (1): 67–171.

Sun, Qunyang, Larry Qiu, and Jie Li. 2006. "The Pearl River Delta: A World Workshop." In *China as the World Factory*, edited by Kevin Honglin Zhang, 27–52. New York: Routledge.

Tabassum, Rahela, and Shehbaz Ahmed. 2020. "Xiaomi Invades the Smartphone Market in India." *Decision* 47:215–228.

Thomas, Dana. 2007. *Deluxe: How Luxury Lost Its Luster*. New York: Penguin Books.

Ting, Chang. 2004. *China Always Says "No" to Narcotics*. Beijing: Foreign Language Press.

Ting, Mao-Seng, Yen-Nee Goh, and Salmi Mohd Isa. 2016. "Determining Consumer Purchase Intentions toward Counterfeit Luxury Goods in Malaysia." *Asia Pacific Management Review* 21 (4): 219–230.

Transnational Alliance to Combat Illicit Trade (TRACIT). 2020. *Mapping the Impact of Illicit Trade on Sustainable Development Growth*. New York: TRACIT.

Tsai, Kellee. 2007. *Capitalism without Democracy: The Private Sector in Contemporary China*. Ithaca, NY: Cornell University Press.

Tuckman, Jo. 2012. *Mexico: Democracy Interrupted*. New Haven, CT: Yale University Press.

UNICEF (United Nation Children's Fund). 2019. *Country Office Annual Report China 2019*. New York.

UNODC (United Nations Office on Drugs and Crime). 2010. *The Globalization of Crime: A Transnational Organized Crime Threat Assessment*. Vienna.

———. 2013. *Transnational Organized Crime in East Asia and the Pacific: A Threat Assessment*. Vienna.

———. 2014. *The Illicit Trafficking of Counterfeit Goods and Transnational Organized Crime*. Vienna.

———. 2019. *Transnational Organized Crime in Southeast Asia: Evolution, Growth, and Impact*. Vienna.

U.S. Attorney's Office Eastern District of New York. 2021. "Four Defendants Arrested in Multimillion-Dollar Counterfeit Goods Trafficking Scheme." Press Release, August 12, 2021.

U.S. DHS (U.S. Department of Homeland Security). 2020. *Combating Trafficking in Counterfeit and Pirated Goods: Report to the President of the United States*. January 24, 2020.

U.S. DOJ (U.S. Department of Justice). 2008. *Overview of the Law Enforcement Strategy to Combat International Organized Crime*. April 2008.

USTR (U.S. Trade Representative). 2009–2022. *Out-of-Cycle Review of Notorious Markets*. Washington, DC.

Vanderklippe, Nathan. 2018. "Canada Goose Battles Knock-Offs as Brand Makes a Splash in Chinese Market." *Globe and Mail*, December 2, 2018.

van Kemenade, Willem. 1997. *China, Hong Kong, Taiwan, Inc.: The Dynamics of a New Empire*. New York: Alfred A. Knopf.

Varela, Miguel, Paula Lopes, and Rita Mendes. 2021. "Luxury Brand Consumption and Counterfeiting: A Case Study of the Portuguese Market." *Innovative Marketing* 7 (3): 45–55.

Varese, Federico. 2011. *Mafias on the Move: How Organized Crime Conquers New Territories*. Princeton, NJ: Princeton University Press.

Vogel, Ezra. 1989. *One Step Ahead in China: Guangdong under Reform*. Cambridge, MA: Harvard University Press.

———. 2013. *Deng Xiaoping and the Transformation of China*. Cambridge, MA: Harvard University Press.

von Lampe, Klaus. 2016. *Organized Crime: Analyzing Illegal Activities, Criminal Structures, and Extra-Legal Governance*. Thousand Oaks, CA: Sage.

von Lampe, Klaus, Marin Kurti, Anqi Shen, and Georgios Antonopoulos. 2012. "The Changing Role of China in the Global Illegal Cigarette Trade." *International Criminal Justice Review* 22 (1): 43–67.

Wall, David, and Joanna Large. 2010. "Jailhouse Frocks: Locating the Public Interest in Policing Counterfeit Luxury Goods." *British Journal of Criminology* 50:1094–1116.

Wang, Katherine. 2018. China's New State Administration for Market Regulation: What to Know and What to Expect. Ropes and Gray, April 3, 2018. Available at https://www.ropesgray.com/en/insights/alerts/2018/04/chinas-new-state-market-regulatory-administration-what-to-know-and-what-to-expect.

Wang, Peng. 2017. *The Chinese Mafia: Organized Crime, Corruption, and Extra-Legal Protection*. New York: Oxford University Press.

Wang, Tao. 2023. *Making Sense of China's Economy*. New York: Routledge.

Watson, Rubie, and Patricia Ebrey, eds. 1991. *Marriage and Inequality in Chinese Society*. Berkeley: University of California Press.

Wikipedia. (2023, September 3). "Bian Lian." In *Wikipedia, The Free Encyclopedia*. Accessed November 27, 2023. Available at https://en.wikipedia.org/w/index.php?title=Bian_lian&oldid=1173587533.

Wilson, Jeremy, ed. 2015. *Brand Protection 2020: Perspectives on the Issues Shaping the Global Risk and Response to Product Counterfeiting*. A-CAPP Paper Series. Center for Anti-counterfeiting and Product Protection. East Lansing: Michigan State University.

Wong, Chun Han. 2023. *Party of One: The Rise of Xi Jinping and China's Superpower Future*. New York: Avid Reader.

Woodiwiss, Michael, and David Bewley-Taylor. 2005. *The Global Fix: The Construction of a Global Enforcement Regime*. Amsterdam: Transnational Institute.

WTO (World Trade Organization). 2024. Glossary—Counterfeit. Available at https://www.wto.org/english/thewto_e/glossary_e/glossary_e.htm.

Wu, Jieh-min. 1997. "Strange Bedfellows: Dynamics of Government-Business Relations between Chinese Local Authorities and Taiwanese Investors." *Journal of Contemporary China* 6 (15): 319–346.

———. [吴介民]. 2019. *The Rent-Seeking Developmental State in China: The Taishang, Guangdong Model and Global Capitalism* [寻租中国:台商广东模式与全球资本主义]. Taipei: National Taiwan University Press.

Xia, Ming. 2006. "Assessing and Explaining the Resurgence of China's Criminal Underworld." *Global Crime* 7 (2): 151–175.

Xu, Jianhua, and Anli Jiang. 2018. "Police Civilianization and the Production of Underclass Violence: The Case of Para-police *Chengguan* and Street Vendors in Guangzhou, China." *British Journal of Criminology* 59:64–84.

Yang, Fan. 2016. *Faked in China: Nation Branding, Counterfeit Culture, and Globalization*. Bloomington: Indiana University Press.

Yao, Vincent Wenxiong. 2006. "An Economic Analysis of Counterfeit Goods: The Case of China." *Journal of the Washington Institute of China Studies* 1 (1): 116–124.

Young, Laura Wen-yu. 2016. "Understanding *Michael Jordan v. Qiaodan*: Historical Anomaly or Systemic Failure to Protect Chinese Consumers?" *Trademark Reporter* 106 (5): 883–914.

Yu, Anthony C., trans. and ed. 2012. *The Journey to the West*. Chicago: University of Chicago Press.

Yu, Hua. 2011. *China in Ten Words*. New York: Anchor Books.

Zaichkowsky, J. L. 2006. *The Psychology behind Trademark Infringement and Counterfeiting*. Mahwah, NJ: Lawrence Erlbaum.

Zaitch, Damian. 2002. *Trafficking Cocaine: Colombian Drug Entreneurs in the Netherlands*. The Hague, The Netherlands: Kluwer Law International.

Zhang, Kevin Honglin, ed. 2006. *China as the World Factory*. New York: Routledge.

Zhang, Sheldon. 2007. *Smuggling and Trafficking in Human Beings: All Roads Lead to America*. Westport, CT: Praeger.

———. 2008. *Chinese Human Smuggling Organizations: Families, Social Networks, and Cultural Imperatives*. Stanford, CA: Stanford University Press.

Zhang, Sheldon, and Ko-lin Chin. 2002. "Enter the Dragon: Inside Chinese Human Smuggling Organizations." *Criminology* 40 (4): 737–768.

———. 2003. "The Declining Significance of Triad Societies in Transnational Illegal Activities." *British Journal of Criminology* 43 (3): 463–482.

———. 2018. "China's New Long March to Control Illicit Substance Use: From a Punitive Regime towards Harm Reduction." *Journal of Drug Policy Analysis* 11 (1). Available at https://doi.org/10.1515/jdpa-2015-0023.

Zhang, Sheldon, Ko-lin Chin, and Jody Miller. 2007. "Women's Participation in Chinese Transnational Human Smuggling: A Gendered Market Perspective." *Criminology* 45 (3): 699–733.

Zheng, Tiantian. 2009. *Red Lights: The Lives of Sex Workers in Postsocialist China*. Minneapolis: University of Minnesota Press.

Zheng, Yiran. 2018. "Experts: Mobile Internet in Urgent Need of Upgrade." *China Daily*, August 10, 2018, 17.

Zhou, Cissy. 2021. "China's Domestic Brands Boom, Fueled by Nationalism, with Li-Ning, Anta Standing Out from the Crowd." *South China Morning Post*, July 28, 2021.

Zhou, Min, Tao Xu, and Shabnam Shenasi. 2015. *Entrepreneurship and Interracial Dynamics: A Case Study of Self-Employed Africans and Chinese in Guangzhou, China*. Los Angeles: UCLA Program on International Migration.

Zhou, Qunfeng [周群峰]. 2016. "Anti-corruption Season in Guangdong's Officialdom" [广东反腐季]. Beijing: Xinwen Zhoukan, April 11, 2016, 16–24.

Zhu, Xiaojun [朱晓军], and Liping Yang [杨丽萍]. 2017. *Courier Services in China* [帝国的跑道: 互联网下的快递中国]. Taipei: Duli Zuojia Chubanshe.

Zuccaro, Esther. 2016. "Gucci v. Alibaba: A Balanced Approach to Secondary Liability for E-Commerce Platforms." *North Carolina Journal of Law and Technology* 17 (5): 144–184.

Index

Sample pattern cutter, 53, 142
Samsung, 187
Secret societies, 185, 265n2, 265n5
Shanzhai, 28, 43, 49; as a cultural
  phenomenon, 187–191. *See also* Pianmen
Shen, Anqi, 179, 243
Skechers, 74, 129, 132–133, 161, 264n1
Smokescreening, 175
Sony Ericsson, 187
Special Economic Zones, 29–30
Street/block committees, 239
Structure, 163, 170; designer, 165–167;
  saleswoman, 163–165; streamlining, 210;
  warehouse worker. *See also* Distribution,
  operating entities
Subcontracting, 172–173
Supercopies. *See* Point-to-point
  counterfeiting: quality
Supplemental copying, 28, 43, 50
Suppliers, 51–52; fabric, 70; leather, 70–72,
  143–146; metal fittings, 72–73, 205; shoe
  uppers, 73–74

Tencent. *See* Markets, online: WeChat
Thai, David, 184
Thomas, Dana, 5, 6, 94
Three-plus-one trading mix
  (sanlaiyibu), 24–25, 27; definition, 31;
  role of Hongkongers, 31–32; role of
  Taiwanese, 32–33. *See also* Contract
  manufacturing
Three strikes and two establishments
  (sanda liangjian), 222
Timberland, 133, 184, 190
Tongs, 179, 184–185, 265n4
TRACIT (Transnational Alliance to
  Combat Illicit Trade), 9
Trademarks, 4, 11, 134; affixing, 209, 229
Triads, 175, 177, 265n2
True Religion, 183
Tsai, Kellee, 215

UGG, 183–184
UNODC (United Nations Office on Drugs
  and Crime), 1, 177

Urban villages (chengzhongcun), 60–63,
  76–77, 97
USCBP (United States Customs and Border
  Protection), 2
USDHS (United States Department of
  Homeland Security), 6, 104, 177
USTR (United States Trade Representative),
  2, 80, 88, 143, 219

Varese, Federico, 176
Versace, 127, 167
Villages-in-the-city. *See* Urban villages
Violence, 12, 173–175
Vogel, Ezra, 28, 30, 124

Wall, David, 178
Wang Yang, 222–223, 252
Warehouse: multiple, 201; protecting, 209;
  workers, 167–170
Wellington, Daniel, 109
Wenzhou; area, 24, 121, 147; people, 81, 102,
  122–123, 264n4
Wilson, Jeremy, 10
Workshops, 60, 63–66
WTO (World Trade Organization), 4, 30,
  37, 222
Wu Jieh-min, 124–125

Yakuza, 175, 177
Yao, Vincent Wenxiong, 221
Yeezy, 65, 184
Yu Hua, 187–189

Xi Jinping, 30, 223, 246
Xintang, 67–68
Xioami, 49–50
Xi Zhongxun, 30

Y-3, 142

Zhang, Sheldon, 176, 232
Zhanjiangnese, 121–123, 168
Zhanxi Road, 78–85, 196, 214
Zhou, Min, 102
Zuccaro, Esther, 103–106

Ko-lin Chin is a Distinguished Professor in the School of Criminal Justice at Rutgers University–Newark. He is the coauthor of *The Chinese Heroin Trade: Cross-Border Drug Trafficking in Southeast Asia and Beyond* and *Selling Sex Overseas: Chinese Women and the Realities of Prostitution and Global Sex Trafficking*, and the author of *The Golden Triangle: Inside Southeast Asia's Drug Trade* and *Smuggled Chinese: Clandestine Immigration to the United States* (Temple).